Practice*Planners*®

The Couples Psychotherapy Treatment Planner, with DSM-5 Updates, Second Edition

Practice*Planners*® Series

Treatment Planners
The Complete Adult Psychotherapy Treatment Planner, Fifth Edition
The Child Psychotherapy Treatment Planner, Fifth Edition
The Adolescent Psychotherapy Treatment Planner, Fifth Edition
The Addiction Treatment Planner, Fifth Edition
The Continuum of Care Treatment Planner
The Couples Psychotherapy Treatment Planner, with DSM-5 Updates, Second Edition
The Employee Assistance Treatment Planner
The Pastoral Counseling Treatment Planner
The Older Adult Psychotherapy Treatment Planner, with DSM-5 Updates, Second Edition
The Behavioral Medicine Treatment Planner
The Group Therapy Treatment Planner
The Gay and Lesbian Psychotherapy Treatment Planner
The Family Therapy Treatment Planner, with DSM-5 Updates, Second Edition
The Severe and Persistent Mental Illness Treatment Planner, with DSM-5 Updates, Second Edition
The Mental Retardation and Developmental Disability Treatment Planner
The Social Work and Human Services Treatment Planner
The Crisis Counseling and Traumatic Events Treatment Planner, with DSM-5 Updates, Second Edition
The Personality Disorders Treatment Planner
The Rehabilitation Psychology Treatment Planner
The Special Education Treatment Planner
The Juvenile Justice and Residential Care Treatment Planner
The School Counseling and School Social Work Treatment Planner, with DSM-5 Updates, Second Edition
The Sexual Abuse Victim and Sexual Offender Treatment Planner
The Probation and Parole Treatment Planner
The Psychopharmacology Treatment Planner
The Speech-Language Pathology Treatment Planner
The Suicide and Homicide Treatment Planner
The College Student Counseling Treatment Planner
The Parenting Skills Treatment Planner
The Early Childhood Intervention Treatment Planner
The Co-occurring Disorders Treatment Planner
The Complete Women's Psychotherapy Treatment Planner
The Veterans and Active Duty Military Psychotherapy Treatment Planner, with DSM-5 Updates

Progress Notes Planners
The Child Psychotherapy Progress Notes Planner, Fifth Edition
The Adolescent Psychotherapy Progress Notes Planner, Fifth Edition
The Adult Psychotherapy Progress Notes Planner, Fifth Edition
The Addiction Progress Notes Planner, Fifth Edition
The Severe and Persistent Mental Illness Progress Notes Planner, Second Edition
The Couples Psychotherapy Progress Notes Planner, Second Edition
The Family Therapy Progress Notes Planner, Second Edition
The Veterans and Active Duty Military Psychotherapy Progress Notes Planner

Homework Planners
Couples Therapy Homework Planner, Second Edition
Family Therapy Homework Planner, Second Edition
Grief Counseling Homework Planner
Group Therapy Homework Planner
Divorce Counseling Homework Planner
School Counseling and School Social Work Homework Planner, Second Edition
Child Therapy Activity and Homework Planner
Addiction Treatment Homework Planner, Fifth Edition
Adolescent Psychotherapy Homework Planner, Fifth Edition
Adult Psychotherapy Homework Planner, Fifth Edition
Child Psychotherapy Homework Planner, Fifth Edition
Parenting Skills Homework Planner
Veterans and Active Duty Military Psychotherapy Homework Planner

Client Education Handout Planners
Adult Client Education Handout Planner
Child and Adolescent Client Education Handout Planner
Couples and Family Client Education Handout Planner

Complete Planners
The Complete Depression Treatment and Homework Planner
The Complete Anxiety Treatment and Homework Planner

PracticePlanners®

Arthur E. Jongsma, Jr., Series Editor

The Couples Psychotherapy Treatment Planner, with DSM-5 Updates, Second Edition

K. Daniel O'Leary

Richard E. Heyman

Arthur E. Jongsma, Jr.

WILEY

Library of Congress Cataloging-in-Publication Data:
O'Leary, K. Daniel, 1940–
    The couples psychotherapy treatment planner / K. Daniel O'Leary, Richard E. Heyman, Arthur E.
Jongsma.—2nd ed.
        p. cm.—(Practice planners)
ISBN 978-1-119-06312-4 (pbk.: acid-free paper)
ISBN 978-1-119-06424-4 (eMobi)
ISBN 978-1-119-06417-6 (ePub)
ISBN 978-1-119-06438-1 (ePDF)

1. Couples therapy—Planning—Handbooks, manuals, etc.   I. Heyman, Richard E. II. Jongsma, Arthur
E., 1943- III. Title.
  RC488.5.O395 2010
  616.89'1562--dc22   2010037266

Printed in the United States of America

SKY10019884_071620

To my wife, Judy, who has made us much better as a couple for 47 years than I could ever be as a single person.

—AEJ

To Maria, with whom 24 years of marriage has been like one long date, and to Bob Weiss, for teaching me most everything I'll ever need to know about couples interventions.

—REH

To Susan, who has been a strong support, sounding board, and professional colleague since graduate school.

—KDO

CONTENTS

▽Indicates that selected Objective/Interventions are consistent with those found in evidence-based treatments.

PRACTICE*PLANNERS*® SERIES PREFACE

Accountability is an important dimension of the practice of psychotherapy. Treatment programs, public agencies, clinics, and practitioners must justify and document their treatment plans to outside review entities in order to be reimbursed for services. The books in the Practice*Planners*® series are designed to help practitioners fulfill these documentation requirements efficiently and professionally.

The Practice*Planners*® series includes a wide array of treatment planning books including not only the original *Complete Adult Psychotherapy Treatment Planner*, *Child Psychotherapy Treatment Planner*, and *Adolescent Psychotherapy Treatment Planner*, all now in their fifth editions, but also *Treatment Planners* targeted to specialty areas of practice, including:

- Addictions
- Co-occurring disorders
- Behavioral medicine
- College students
- Couples therapy
- Crisis counseling
- Early childhood education
- Employee assistance
- Family therapy
- Gays and lesbians
- Group therapy
- Juvenile justice and residential care
- Mental retardation and developmental disability
- Neuropsychology
- Older adults
- Parenting skills
- Pastoral counseling
- Personality disorders
- Probation and parole
- Psychopharmacology
- Rehabilitation psychology
- School counseling and school social work
- Severe and persistent mental illness
- Sexual abuse victims and offenders

- Social work and human services
- Special education
- Speech-language pathology
- Suicide and homicide risk assessment
- Veterans and active military duty
- Women's issues

In addition, there are three branches of companion books that can be used in conjunction with the *Treatment Planners*, or on their own:

- **Progress Notes Planners** provide a menu of progress statements that elaborate on the client's symptom presentation and the provider's therapeutic intervention. Each *Progress Notes Planner* statement is directly integrated with the behavioral definitions and therapeutic interventions from its companion *Treatment Planner*.

- **Homework Planners** include homework assignments designed around each presenting problem (such as anxiety, depression, substance use, anger control problems, eating disorders, or panic disorder) that is the focus of a chapter in its corresponding *Treatment Planner*.

- **Client Education Handout Planners** provide brochures and handouts to help educate and inform clients on presenting problems and mental health issues, as well as life skills techniques. The handouts are included on CD-ROMs for easy printing from your computer and are ideal for use in waiting rooms, at presentations, as newsletters, or as information for clients struggling with mental illness issues. The topics covered by these handouts correspond to the presenting problems in the *Treatment Planners*.

The series also includes adjunctive books, such as *The Psychotherapy Documentation Primer* and *The Clinical Documentation Sourcebook*, containing forms and resources to aid the clinician in mental health practice management.

The goal of our series is to provide practitioners with the resources they need in order to provide high-quality care in the era of accountability. To put it simply: We seek to help you spend more time on patients, and less time on paperwork.

ARTHUR E. JONGSMA, JR.
Grand Rapids, Michigan

ACKNOWLEDGMENTS

We want to acknowledge the hundreds of couples whom we have treated and who provided us with their insights and perspectives on relationships. There are many ways that individuals work with one another and they often do so in highly idiosyncratic ways. The ability of individuals to work with their partners under quite difficult circumstances due to external and internal pressures is remarkable and honorable. We thank individuals and couples who have shown us how to cope with problems and how to change their attitudes and behaviors so that they can function in a fashion that is more acceptable and satisfying to both.

Our first *Couples Therapy Treatment Planner* was written over a decade ago and some new problems that couples face have emerged across this period such as problems related to use of the Internet for sexual purposes, problems associated with our aging population, and couple issues related to an economic recession. To address some of these trends we have added chapters on problems related to retirement, the transition to parenthood, and the use of Internet sex. The chapters on couple problems related to intimate partner violence and to financial matters have been updated to bring the chapters into a more current perspective.

In all our chapters, we have relied on both the empirical literature and the observations, reactions, and insights of the couples who have faced and coped with the various problems covered in this book, and we thank them for their assistance and perspectives. In many cases, the changes were so positive that the individuals in the relationship felt more caring and love for one another. In some cases the changes were not enough for individuals to decide to stay together, but in such cases the decision not to stay together often allowed the individuals to feel significantly better about themselves.

Throughout many of the chapters we are indebted to the self-regulation work of Kim Halford (e.g., Halford, 2004) and to the "situational analysis" approach to cognitive behavioral therapy pioneered by Jim McCullough (2003). These two approaches are complementary and encourage self-regulation by clients. Perhaps most importantly, they are pragmatic—joining with clients to examine and change thoughts and behaviors to increase the probability of achieving important outcomes rather than on denigrating clients as thinking "irrationally." We also acknowledge the intellectual input of researchers in the couples arena whose work has informed our assessment and treatment. They include Steven Beach, Ileana Arias, Mark Whisman, Donald Baucom, Doug Snyder, Alan Gurman, and Murray Straus. We are also indebted to our colleagues, Dina Vivian and Jose Luis Grana with whom we have repeatedly discussed the treatment of individual cases over the years.

K. DANIEL O'LEARY and RICHARD E. HEYMAN

It is with great respect that I acknowledge the depth of knowledge and expertise that Rick Heyman and Dan O'Leary brought to this project. They are both very busy psychologists but they managed to give quality time to the content in this book. It was my privilege to work with them over the last year to update this second edition of the *Couples Psychotherapy Treatment Planner*. They are familiar with the research literature on counseling with couples over a variety of presenting problems and they brought that expertise to bear as they informed the Objectives and Interventions in this book with this evidence-based data. I salute them and thank them for their collaborative manner and gracious spirit throughout the project.

I also want to thank the editorial and production staff at John Wiley & Sons. They are professionals of the highest order and I am indebted to them for many years of fine work on the Practice*Planner* series. Kudos to you all!

A final thanks is due to Sue Rhoda, our manuscript manager, who brings organization out of chaos and style out of a jumble of good content. Thank you again, Sue.

ARTHUR E. JONGSMA, JR.

The Couples Psychotherapy Treatment Planner,
Second Edition

INTRODUCTION

ABOUT PRACTICE*PLANNERS*® TREATMENT PLANNERS

Pressure from third-party payers, accrediting agencies, and other outside parties has increased the need for clinicians to quickly produce effective, high-quality treatment plans. *Treatment Planners* provide all the elements necessary to quickly and easily develop formal treatment plans that satisfy the needs of most third-party payers and state and federal review agencies.

Each *Treatment Planner:*

- Saves you hours of time-consuming paperwork.
- Offers the freedom to develop customized treatment plans.
- Includes over 1,000 clear statements describing the behavioral manifestations of each relational problem, and includes long-term goals, short-term objectives, and clinically tested treatment options.
- Has an easy-to-use reference format that helps locate treatment plan components by behavioral problem or *DSM-5* diagnosis.

As with the rest of the books in the Practice*Planners*® series, our aim is to clarify, simplify, and accelerate the treatment planning process, so you spend less time on paperwork, and more time with your clients.

ABOUT *THE COUPLES THERAPY TREATMENT PLANNER*

This second edition of the popular *Couples Therapy Treatment Planner* comes as a result of the positive response that we received over the past decade with the success of the first planner. The first edition, which ran for almost 10 years, was a bestseller. As a revision, we have included three new chapters (Internet Sexual Use, Retirement, Transition to Parenthood Strains) and separated the intimate partner violence (IPV) chapter into two, one covering bidirectional IPV and one covering "intimate terrorism" IPV. All chapters, totaling 32 in all, were updated to include research and clinical developments over the last decade and to indicate evidence-based treatment interventions throughout.

The cornerstone of early behavioral marital interventions was clearly on decreasing negative interchanges and increasing positive interchanges between partners (Jacobson & Margolin, 1979; O'Leary & Turkewitz, 1978) because discordant couples differ from happy couples in positive and negative interactions (Broderick & O'Leary, 1986; Johnson & O'Leary, 1996; Wills, Weiss, & Patterson, 1974). Studies based largely on these foci showed that significant increases in marital satisfaction could be obtained, but it also became evident that, while there were significant improvements, there were many couples who needed more specific assistance in dealing with various and often long-standing problems. In fact, this *Couples Therapy Treatment Planner* is organized around various problems that often coexist with relationship problems, and each chapter provides up-to-date references related to the numerous and varied problems that often occur simultaneously with relationship problems.

Many of the chapters in this *Treatment Planner* incorporate elements of a cognitive behavioral self-regulation model (e.g., Bandura, 1986, 1995; Karoly, 1993), which has emerged in recent years as a unifying component and active ingredient in a wide variety of empirically supported programs. Halford (2001; Halford, Moore, Wilson, Dyer, & Farrugia, 2004; Wilson & Halford, 2008) has made the most use of this model with couples and we are indebted to his approach. In a self-change or self-regulatory model, clients (a) self-select elements relevant to them that they determine will assist them in achieving their goals; (b) develop and enact plans to make changes; and (c) self-assess their progress and make corrections to improve future success. This model has demonstrated effectiveness for targets as diverse as alcohol problems (e.g., Lundahl et al., 2010), chronic depression (e.g., Keller et al., 2000), relationship enhancement (e.g., Halford et al., 2004), and child behavior problems in the context of both prevention and intensive intervention services (e.g., de Graaf et al., 2008a).

Many of the chapters also incorporate McCullough's (2003) distillation of cognitive-behavioral therapy (CBT) using "situational analysis." We have included a sample situational analysis form in Appendix D. Instead of focusing on purportedly "irrational thoughts," the situational analysis has clients focus on what actually happened (e.g., beginning, middle, and end of a discrete incident), what the actual outcome was, and what the desired outcome was. Clients then examine their thoughts and behavior through the pragmatic lens of whether they helped or hurt the client getting the desired outcome. We have found this focused form of CBT to be incredibly useful in couples treatment. Therapists wishing to use this approach would be well served by reading McCullough's (2003) book, *Treatment for Chronic Depression: Cognitive Behavioral Analysis System of Psychotherapy (CBASP)*. Though focused on chronic depression, further instruction on situational analysis can be found there.

This book also goes hand-in-hand with the the *Family Therapy Treatment Planner,* Second Edition (Dattilio, Jongsma, & Davis) since very often family conflicts emanate from problems in the couples' relationship. In such cases, the therapist should refer to the *Family Therapy Treatment Planner,* Second Edition for more specific suggestions regarding treating the couple's relationship.

INCORPORATING EVIDENCE-BASED TREATMENT INTO THE *TREATMENT PLANNER*

Evidence-based or empirically supported treatment (that is, treatment that has shown efficacy in research trials) is rapidly becoming of critical importance to the mental health community as the demands for quality and accountability increase. Indeed, identified empirically supported treatments, such as those of the APA Division 12 (Society of Clinical Psychology) and the Substance Abuse and Mental Health Services Administration's (SAMHSA) National Registry of Evidence-based Programs and Practices (NREPP), are being referenced by a number of local, state, and federal funding agencies, some of which are beginning to restrict reimbursement to these treatments, as are some managed care and insurance companies.

In this second edition of *The Couples Therapy Treatment Planner*, we have made an effort to include, in almost all of the chapters, evidence-based interventions by highlighting Short-term Objectives (STOs) and Therapeutic Interventions (TIs) that are consistent with psychological treatments or therapeutic programs that have demonstrated some level of efficacy through empirical study. Such STOs and TIs are noted with an icon as an indication that an Objective/Intervention is consistent with those found in evidence-based treatments (EBT).

References to the empirical work supporting these interventions have been included in Appendix B. For information related to the identification of evidence-based practices (EBPs), including the benefits and limitations of the effort, we suggest the APA Presidential Task Force on Evidence-Based Practice (2006); Bruce and Sanderson (2005); Chambless et al. (1996, 1998); Chambless and Ollendick (2001); Castonguay and Beutler (2006); Drake, Merrens, and Lynde (2005); Hofmann and Tompson (2002); Nathan and Gorman (2007); and Stout and Hayes (2005). Sprenkle, Davis, and Lebow (2009) provide a review of this literature as it pertains to marriage and family therapy.

In this *Planner*, we have included STOs and TIs consistent with identified EBTs for couple problems and mental disorders commonly seen by practitioners in public agency and private practice settings. It is important to note that the empirical support for the EBT material found in each chapter has *not* necessarily been established for treating that problem within a couples context, but rather, is particular to the problem identified in the chapter title. For example, the STOs and TIs consistent with cognitive behavioral therapy for anxiety, which can be found in the chapter entitled "Anxiety," are based on this treatment approach, which has been well established as an empirically supported individual treatment for anxiety, yet can be easily modified for treatment in a couples setting. Furthermore, it is important to remember that an EBT such as Behavioral Couples Therapy (e.g., Epstein & Baucom, 2002), Integrative Behavioral Couple Therapy (Jacobson & Christensen, 1996), and Emotionally Focused Marital Therapy (e.g., Johnson, 2004) can be applied to a wide variety of problems. Therefore, although many chapters present common problems faced by couples (e.g., parenting conflicts) on which no studies have specifically focused, an EBT, such as behaviorally based parenting techniques or problem-solving skills, can be used to help the couple through that particular challenge.

Beyond references to the empirical studies supporting these interventions, we have provided references to therapist- and client-oriented books and treatment manuals that describe the use of identified EBTs or treatments consistent with their objectives and interventions. Of course, recognizing that there are STOs and TIs that practicing clinicians have found useful but that have not yet received empirical scrutiny, we have included those that reflect common best practice among experienced clinicians. The goal is to provide a range of treatment plan options, some studied empirically, others reflecting common clinical practice, so the user can construct what they believe to be the best plan for a particular client. Most of the STOs and TIs associated with the EBTs are described at a level of detail that permits flexibility and adaptability in their specific application. As with all *Planners* in this series, each chapter includes the option to add STOs and TIs at the therapist's discretion.

Criteria for Inclusion of Evidence-Based Therapies

The EBTs from which STOs and TIs were taken have different levels of empirical evidence supporting them. For example, some have been well established as efficacious for the problems that they target (e.g., exposure-based therapies for anxiety disorders). Others have less support, but nonetheless have demonstrated efficacy. We have included EBPs, the empirical support for which has either been well established or demonstrated at more than a preliminary level as defined by those authors who have undertaken the task of identifying them, such as the APA Division 12 (Society of Clinical Psychology); Drake and colleagues (2003, 2005); Chambless and colleagues (1996, 1998); Gurman (2008); and Nathan and Gorman (2007).

At a minimum, efficacy needs to be demonstrated through a clinical trial or large clinical replication series with features reflecting good experimental design (e.g., random assignment, blind assignments, reliable and valid measurement, clear inclusion and exclusion criteria, state-of-the-art diagnostic methods, and adequate sample size or replications). Well-established EBTs typically have more than one of these types of studies demonstrating their efficacy, as well as other desirable features such as demonstration of efficacy by independent research groups and specification of client characteristics for which the treatment was effective.

Lastly, all interventions, empirically supported or not, must be adapted to the particular client in light of his/her personal circumstances, cultural identity, strengths, and vulnerabilities. The STOs and TIs included in this *Planner* are written in a manner to suggest and allow this adaptability.

Summary of Required and Preferred EBT Inclusion Criteria

Required

- Demonstration of efficacy through at least one randomized controlled trial with good experimental design, or
- Demonstration of efficacy through a large, well-designed clinical replication series.

Preferred

- Efficacy has been shown by more than one study.
- Efficacy has been demonstrated by independent research groups.
- Client characteristics for which the treatment was effective were specified.
- A clear description of the treatment was available.

HOW TO USE THIS *TREATMENT PLANNER*

Use this *Treatment Planner* to write treatment plans according to the following progression of six steps:

1. **Problem Selection.** Although the client may discuss a variety of issues during the assessment, the clinician must determine the most significant problems on which to focus the treatment process. Usually a primary problem will surface, and secondary problems may also be evident. Some other problems may have to be set aside as not urgent enough to require treatment at this time. An effective treatment plan can only deal with a

few selected problems or treatment will lose its direction. Choose the problem within this *Planner* that most accurately represents your client's presenting issues.

2. **Problem Definition.** Each client presents with unique nuances as to how a problem behaviorally reveals itself in his or her life. Therefore, each problem that is selected for treatment focus requires a specific definition about how it is evidenced in the particular client. The symptom pattern should be associated with diagnostic criteria and codes such as those found in the *DSM-5* or the *International Classification of Diseases*. This *Planner* offers such behaviorally specific definition statements to choose from or to serve as a model for your own personally crafted statements.

3. **Goal Development.** The next step in developing your treatment plan is to set broad goals for the resolution of the target problem. These statements need not be crafted in measurable terms but can be global, long-term goals that indicate a desired positive outcome to the treatment procedures. This *Planner* provides several possible goal statements for each problem, but one statement is all that is required in a treatment plan.

4. **Objective Construction.** In contrast to long-term goals, objectives must be stated in behaviorally measurable language so that it is clear to review agencies, health maintenance organizations, and managed care organizations when the client has achieved the established objectives. The objectives presented in this *Planner* are designed to meet this demand for accountability. Numerous alternatives are presented to allow construction of a variety of treatment plan possibilities for the same presenting problem.

5. **Intervention Creation.** Interventions are the actions of the clinician designed to help the client complete the objectives. There should be at least one intervention for every objective. If the client does not accomplish the objective after the initial intervention, new interventions should be added to the plan. Interventions should be selected on the basis of the client's needs and the treatment provider's full therapeutic repertoire. This *Planner* contains interventions from a broad range of therapeutic approaches, and we encourage the provider to write other interventions reflecting his or her own training and experience.

    Some suggested interventions listed in the *Planner* refer to specific books that can be assigned to the client for adjunctive bibliotherapy. Appendix A contains a full bibliographic reference list of these materials. For further information about self-help books, mental health professionals may wish to consult *The Authoritative Guide to Self-Help Resources in Mental Health, Revised Edition* (2003) by Norcross et al. (available from Guilford Press, New York).

6. **Diagnosis Determination.** The determination of an appropriate diagnosis is based on an evaluation of the client's complete clinical presentation. The clinician must compare the behavioral, cognitive, emotional, and interpersonal symptoms that the client presents with the criteria for diagnosis of a mental illness condition as described in *DSM-5*. Despite

arguments made against diagnosing clients in this manner, diagnosis is a reality that exists in the world of mental health care, and it is a necessity for third-party reimbursement. It is the clinician's thorough knowledge of *DSM-5* criteria and a complete understanding of the client assessment data that contribute to the most reliable, valid diagnosis.

Congratulations! After completing these six steps, you should have a comprehensive and individualized treatment plan ready for immediate implementation and presentation to the client. A sample treatment plan for anger management is provided at the end of this introduction.

A FINAL NOTE ON TAILORING THE TREATMENT PLAN TO THE CLIENT

One important aspect of effective treatment planning is that each plan should be tailored to the individual's client's problems and needs. Treatment plans should not be mass-produced, even if clients have similar problems. The individual's strengths and weaknesses, unique stressors, social network, family circumstances, and symptom patterns must be considered in developing a treatment strategy. Drawing upon our own years of clinical experience, we have put together a variety of treatment choices. These statements can be combined in thousands of permutations to develop detailed treatment plans. Relying on their own good judgment, clinicians can easily select the statements that are appropriate for the individuals whom they are treating. In addition, we encourage readers to add their own definitions, goals, objectives, and interventions to the existing samples. As with all of the books in the *Treatment Planners* series, it is our hope that this book will help promote effective, creative treatment planning—a process that will ultimately benefit the client, clinicians, and the mental health community.

REFERENCES

APA Presidential Task Force on Evidence-Based Practice. (2006). Evidence-based practice in psychology. *American Psychologist, 61,* 271–285.

Bandura, A. (1986). *Social foundations of thought and action: A social cognitive theory.* Englewood Cliffs, NJ: Prentice-Hall.

Broderick, J., & O'Leary, K. D. (1986). Contributions of affect, attitudes and behavior to marital satisfaction. *Journal of Consulting and Clinical Psychology, 54,* 514–517.

Bruce, T. J., & Sanderson, W. C. (2005). Evidence-based psychosocial practices: Past, present, and future. In C. Stout & R. Hayes (Eds.), *The handbook of evidence-based practice in behavioral healthcare: Applications and new directions.* Hoboken, NJ: John Wiley & Sons.

Caldwell, B. E., Woolley, S. R., & Caldwell, C. J. (2007). Preliminary estimates of cost-effectiveness for marital therapy. *Journal of Marital and Family Therapy, 33*(3), 392–405.

Castonguay, L. G., & Beutler, L. E. (2006). *Principles of therapeutic change that work.* New York, NY: Oxford University Press.

Chambless, D. L., Baker, M. J., Baucom, D., Beutler, L. E., Calhoun, K. S., Crits-Christoph, P., … Woody, S. R. (1998). Update on empirically validated therapies: II. *The Clinical Psychologist, 51*(1), 3–16.

Chambless, D. L., & Ollendick, T. H. (2001). Empirically supported psychological interventions: Controversies and evidence. *Annual Review of Psychology, 52,* 685–716.

Chambless, D. L., Sanderson, W. C., Shoham, V., Johnson, S. B., Pope, K. S., Crits-Christoph, P., … McCurry, S. (1996). An update on empirically validated therapies. *The Clinical Psychologist, 49*(2), 5–18.

Dattilio, F. M. (2010). *Cognitive-behavioral therapy with couples and families: A comprehensive guide for clinicians.* New York, NY: Guilford Press.

Dattilio, F., Jongsma, A., and Davis, S. (2010). *The family therapy treatment planner.* Hoboken, NJ: John Wiley & Sons.

de Graaf, I., Speetiens, P., Smit, F., de Wolff, M., & Tavecchio, L. (2008a). Effectiveness of the Triple P Positive Parenting Program on behavioral problems in children. *Behavior Modification, 32,* 714–735.

de Graaf, I., Speetiens, P., Smit, F., de Wolff, M., & Tavecchio, L. (2008b). Effectiveness of the Triple P-Positive Parenting Program on parenting: A meta-analysis. *Family Relations, 57,* 553–566. DOI: 10.1111/j.1741-3729.2008.00522.x

Drake, R. E., & Goldman, H. (2003). *Evidence-based practices in mental health care.* Washington, DC: American Psychiatric Association.

Drake, R. E., Merrens, M. R., & Lynde, D. W. (2005). *Evidence-based mental health practice: A textbook.* New York, NY: W.W. Norton & Company.

Epstein, N., & Baucom, D. H. (2002). *Enhanced cognitive-behavioral therapy for couples: A contextual approach.* Washington, DC: American Psychological Association.

Gurman, A. S. (2008). *Clinical handbook of couple therapy.* New York, NY: Guilford Press.

Halford, W. K. (2001). *Brief therapy for couples: Helping partners help themselves.* New York NY, Guilford Press.

Halford, W. K., Moore, E. M., Wilson, K. L., Dyer, C., & Farrugia, C. (2004). Benefits of a flexible delivery relationship education: An evaluation of the Couple CARE program. *Family Relations, 53,* 469–476.

Hofmann, S. G., & Tompson, M. G. (2002). *Treating chronic and severe mental disorders: A handbook of empirically supported interventions.* New York, NY: Guilford Press.

Jacobson, N. S., & Christensen, A. (1996). *Acceptance and change in couple therapy: A therapist's guide to transforming relationships.* New York, NY: Norton.

Jacobson, N. S., & Margolin, G. (1979). *Marital therapy: Strategies based on social learning and behavioral exchange principles.* New York, NY: Brunner/Mazel.

Jacobson, N. S., Christensen, A., Prince, S. E., Cordova, J., & Eldridge, K. (2000). Integrative Behavioral Couple Therapy: An acceptance-based, promising new treatment for couple discord. *Journal of Consulting and Clinical Psychology, 68,* 351–355.

Johnson, S. M. (2004). *The practice of emotionally focused marital therapy: Creating connection* (2nd ed.). New York, NY: Brunner/Routledge.

Johnson, P. L., & O'Leary, K. D. (1996). Behavioral components of marital satisfaction: An individualized assessment approach. *Journal of Consulting and Clinical Psychology, 64,* 417–423.

Karoly, P. (1993). Mechanisms of self regulation: A systems view. *Annual Review of Psychology, 44,* 23–52.

Keller, M., McCullough, J. P., Klein, D. N., Arnow, B., Gelenberg, A. J., Markowitz, J. C., & Zajeckar, J. (2000). A comparison of Nefazodone, the Cognitive Behavioural-Analysis System of Psychotherapy, and their combination for the treatment of chronic depression. *New England Journal of Medicine, 342,* 1462–1470.

Lundahl, B. W., Kunz, C., Brownell, C., Tollefson, D., & Burke, B. L. (2010). A meta-analysis of motivational interviewing: Twenty-five years of empirical studies. *Research on Social Work Practice, 20,* 137–160. DOI: 10.1177/1049731509347850

Nathan, P. E., & Gorman, J. M. (Eds.). (2007). *A guide to treatments that work (Vol. III)*. New York, NY: Oxford University Press.

O'Leary, K. D., & Turkewitz, H. (1978). Marital therapy from a behavioral perspective. In T. J. Paolino, Jr. & B. S. McCrady (Eds.), *Marriage and marital therapy: Psychoanalytic, behavioral and systems theory perspectives* (pp. 240–297). New York, NY: Brunner/Mazel.

O'Leary, K. D., Heyman, R. E., & Jongsma, A. E. (1998). *The couples psychotherapy treatment planner*. New York, NY: John Wiley & Sons.

Piercy, F. P., Sprenkle, D. H., Wetchler, J. L., & Associates. (1996). *The family therapy sourcebook*, 2nd ed. New York, NY: Guilford Press.

Shadish, W. R., & Baldwin, S. A. (2002). Meta-analysis of MFT interventions. In D. H. Sprenkle (Ed.), *Effectiveness research in marriage and family therapy* (pp. 339–370). Virginia: American Association of Marriage and Family Therapy.

Sprenkle, D. H., Davis, S. D., & Lebow, J. (2009). *Common factors in couple and family therapy: The overlooked foundation of effective practice*. New York, NY: Guilford Press.

Stout, C., & Hayes, R. (1995). *The handbook of evidence-based practice in behavioral healthcare: Applications and new directions*. New York, NY: John Wiley & Sons.

Wills, T. A., Weiss, R. L., & Patterson, G. R. (1974). A behavioral analysis of the determinants of marital satisfaction. *Journal of Consulting and Clinical Psychology, 42,* 802–811.

Wilson, K. L., & Halford, W. K. (2008). Processes of change in self-directed couple relationship education. *Family Relations, 57,* 625–635.

SAMPLE TREATMENT PLAN

COMMUNICATION

BEHAVIORAL DEFINITIONS

1. Frequent arguments or arguing in ways that cause significant upset.
2. Difficulty resolving problems.
3. Frequent misunderstandings during discussions.

LONG-TERM GOALS

1. Partners discuss and resolve problems effectively without verbal fighting.
2. Each partner listens to and understands the other partner's perspective.

SHORT-TERM OBJECTIVES	THERAPEUTIC INTERVENTIONS
▽ 1. Identify specific communication deficits.	1. Have the couple attempt to solve a major problem while the therapist quietly watches and takes notes about communication skills and deficits. ▽
	2. Praise the couple for things they do well (such as making eye contact or attempting to define the problem) and provide direct feedback regarding things that need improvement (such as maintaining a civil tone of voice or overcoming tendency to interrupt). ▽
▽ 2. Partners implement the two overarching communication skills of: "Be Clear" and "Be Considerate."	1. Teach the partners the communication skill that emphasizes that interchanges should be (a) clear (i.e., be specific; share thoughts and feelings; pay attention; ask

clarifying questions; summarize
content and feelings); and
(b) considerate (i.e., include
positives, show consideration
when expressing negatives, let
partner know that one is
listening even if one disagrees;
reserve judgment). ▽

2. Ask the partners to discuss a
low-conflict area of desired
change and ask them to rate how
well they did being clear. ▽

3. Ask the partners to discuss a
low-conflict area of desired
change and ask them to rate how
well they did being
considerate. ▽

▽ 3. Practice defining problems in
specific, non-blaming terms.

1. Have the partners take turns
pinpointing problems (that is,
making requests for change that
are specific, observable, and ask
for increases rather than
decreases in the other partner's
behavior). ▽

2. Have the partners use the
"speaker-listener" technique, with
the listener trying to convey
understanding after the speaker
makes an "I" statements in the
following form: "When _____
happens, I feel _____. I would
like _____." ▽

▽ 4. Demonstrate an understanding
of communication that is
focused on problem-solving and
on venting.

1. Teach partners that
communication tends to serve
one of two purposes
—venting (i.e., sharing feelings)
or problem-solving; have
partners identify how they feel
when one person is pursuing
venting and the other problem-
solving. ▽

2. Role-play the couple discussing a
current problem while having the

listener ask the speaker which he/she wants out of the discussion—venting or problem-solving. ▽

▽ 5. Identify cues for arguments and practice argument-control strategies.

1. Help the partners identify cues that an argument is impending (e.g., behaviors, thoughts, feelings, bodily sensations) and have them contract with each other actions they will take time to cool off (e.g., pause the conversation, calm themselves down separately, and think about ways in which they are contributing to the problem) before talking further. ▽

2. Help the partners identify times that are conducive to discussing and/or solving problems (such as after the children are in bed) and times that are not conducive (such as when dinner is being prepared). ▽

▽ 6. Use problem-solving skills to resolve a problem.

1. Choose a moderate area of conflict that has been pinpointed and have the partners practice brainstorming, whereby each partner generates at least two solutions to a problem before trying to solve that problem. ▽

2. Teach partners to evaluate the pros and cons of the brainstormed solutions and have them practice this in session on areas of conflict. ▽

3. Teach partners how to select specific, operationalized plan for attaining a solution based on the pros and cons of that solution; ask the partners to implement the selected action plan before the next session. ▽

4. Ask partners to give an evaluation of how they did on the action plan before the next session. The rating scale is 0 = Didn't think about it or do it; 1 = thought about it; 2 = gave it a weak try; 3 = tried, partially succeeded; and 4 = did a great job. Ask them to jot down short answers to the following: What did we actually do? What positives resulted? What negatives resulted? What do we need to do from here?▽

▽ 7. Attend to and compliment other partner for helpful or caring behaviors.

1. Assign both partners to track on paper and bring to the next session the "Catch your partner pleasing you" exercise, noting (a) at least one positive behavior the partner did each day; and (b) at least one positive behavior they did themselves that day.▽

DIAGNOSTIC SUGGESTIONS

ICD-9-CM	_ICD-10-CM_	_DSM-5_ Disorder, Condition, or Problem
309	F43.21	Adjustment Disorders with Depressed Mood
_____	_____	_____
_____	_____	_____

ALCOHOL ABUSE

BEHAVIORAL DEFINITIONS

1. Frequent use of alcohol by one or both partners, in large enough quantities to meet a diagnosis of alcohol abuse or alcohol dependence (e.g., interference in major role obligations, recurrent use in spite of danger to self, or health, legal, vocational, and/or social problems). The AUDIT, a 10-item screening instrument for alcohol problems, is an easy-to-use instrument that can help identify problematic alcohol use (Saunders, Aaslan, Barbor et al., 2006).
2. Many arguments between partners over the issue of the alcohol abuser's continuing pattern of drinking.
3. Consistent failure of the partner with alcohol abuse to keep repeated promises to quit or significantly reduce frequency and quantity of drinking.
4. Periodic episodes of violence or threats of physical harm, especially when the partner with alcohol abuse is intoxicated.
5. Significant deterioration of the relationship due to the effects of alcohol abuse (e.g., there is little or no communication, shared recreation, mutually satisfying sexual intercourse, or attempts to meet each other's emotional needs).
6. The partner without alcohol abuse consistently enables the partner with alcohol abuse by making excuses for the other's drinking, doing anything to please him/her, and denying the seriousness of the problem, while allowing self to be disparaged or abused repeatedly without offering assertive, constructive resistance.
7. Financial pressures (e.g., indebtedness, behind on rent, no savings) due to alcohol abuse, squandering of money, loss of jobs, and/or low-wage employment.

---

*Special Caution: Conjoint treatment generally is not advisable for individuals with alcohol dependence that requires detoxification. In such cases, inpatient alcoholism rehabilitation or a detoxification program is first in order (see O'Farrell, 1993).

8. Social isolation (e.g., the partner with alcohol abuse drinks too frequently and/or visits only with fellow alcohol users, and the other partner becomes passively withdrawn).

—. _____

_____

—. _____

_____

—. _____

_____

LONG-TERM GOALS

1. Partner with alcohol abuse accepts the need for abstinence and actively participates in a recovery program.
2. Partner with alcohol abuse consistently and significantly reduces frequency and amount of alcohol consumption, such that no negative effects remain.
3. Quality of the relationship improves through a focus on support for sobriety, improved communication, and more frequent enjoyable social and sexual interactions.
4. Partner without alcohol abuse supports other partner's recovery and become more assertive, independent, and free from denial.
5. Partners establish a relationship of mutual trust and respect that is free of violence and has a pattern of seeking to meet each other's needs.
6. Partners address the impact that alcohol use has had on the relationship and engage in problem-solving to address ways the relationship will need to change when alcohol use is reduced or eliminated.

—. _____

_____

—. _____

_____

—. _____

_____

SHORT-TERM OBJECTIVES

THERAPEUTIC INTERVENTIONS

▽ 1. Describe the negative effects of alcohol abuse on self-esteem, family, work, social relationships, health, recreation, and finances. (1)

1. Have both partners describe the negative effects of alcohol abuse on the relationship and family in individual sessions before conjoint treatment begins to avoid the effects of intimidation and mutual supported denial (or assign "Substance Abuse Negative Impact Versus Sobriety's Positive Impact" in the *Adult Psychotherapy Homework Planner,* 2nd ed. by Jongsma). ▽

▽ 2. Partner with alcohol abuse signs a controlled-drinking contract as a means of assessing his/her ability to limit alcohol consumption to moderate levels. (2)

2. Have the partner with alcohol abuse sign a controlled-drinking contract that stipulates the frequency of drinking allowed per week (e.g., twice) and the maximum number of drinks per instance (e.g., three in two hours); if this contract is broken three times, a nondrinking contract will be signed. ▽

▽ 3. Partner with alcohol abuse reads material on controlled drinking. (3)

3. Assign the partner with alcohol abuse to read information on controlled drinking (e.g., NIAAA pamphlet *How to Cut Down on Your Drinking* and/or *How to Control Your Drinking* by Miller & Munoz). ▽

▽ 4. Both partners attend sessions alcohol-free. (4)

4. Require that both partners attend sessions alcohol-free; enforce the rule firmly and consistently by terminating a session if it becomes apparent that alcohol has been recently consumed and is still in the bloodstream. ▽

▽ 5. Both partners sign a nonviolence contract, and a safety plan is developed for the partner without alcohol abuse. (5, 6)

5. Have both partners sign a non-violence contract that prohibits the use of physically assaultive contact, weapons, or threats of

same (Fals-Stewart, Klosterman, & Clinton-Sherrod); emphasize to the couple that there is excellent evidence that the couple approach leads to better aggression reduction than individual approaches. ▽

6. If individual treatment is in order to address anger issues before conjoint treatment, provide supportive counseling to the partner without alcohol abuse to address his/her anxiety and self-blame; devise a safety plan to deal with partner's violence (O'Leary & Cohen). ▽

▽ 6. Partners agree to attend conjoint individual sessions. (7)

7. Discuss the appropriateness of couple and/or individual treatment; if violence is severe and has caused injury and/or significant fear, recommend individual treatment for the physically abusive partner before conjoint treatment is implemented. ▽

▽ 7. Identify the perceived or sought-after benefits of alcohol intoxication. (8)

8. Probe the benefits (e.g., reduced social anxiety, altered mood, lessened family demands) the partner with alcohol abuse is seeking in becoming intoxicated. ▽

▽ 8. Identify nondrinking behavioral alternatives that can produce the results sought after in alcohol abuse. (9)

9. Assist the drinking partner in identifying constructive behavioral alternatives to produce the results sought in becoming intoxicated, such as meditation, sleep induction techniques, exercise, relaxation procedures, spending time talking with friends. ▽

▽ 9. Partner with alcohol abuse practices anxiety- or stress-reduction techniques that can be substituted for alcohol abuse. (10)

10. Teach the partner with alcohol abuse the use of anxiety- or stress-reduction techniques (e.g., deep muscle relaxation, aerobic

exercise, verbalization of concerns, positive guided imagery, recreational diversions, hot bath).▽

▽ 10. Partner with alcohol abuse practices anger-management strategies that can be substituted for alcohol abuse and violence. (11, 12)

11. Teach the partner with alcohol abuse anger-management techniques (e.g., time-out, thought-stopping, positive thought substitution, count down serial 7s from 100); or assign "Alternatives to Destructive Anger" in the *Adult Psychotherapy Homework Planner*, 2nd ed. by Jongsma.▽

12. Teach the partners assertiveness as a healthy alternative to aggression.▽

11. Understand and identify the social and biological causes for alcoholism that apply to their situation. (13)

13. Educate the partners regarding the social and biological factors that contribute to alcoholism; assign reading, including *Alcoholism: Getting the Facts* (NIAAA, 1996).

▽ 12. Partner with alcohol abuse who cannot control drinking signs a nondrinking contract. (14)

14. Have the partner with alcohol abuse who cannot control drinking sign a nondrinking contract that stipulates complete abstinence, cooperation with counseling, and attendance at AA meetings at least twice per week (daily, if necessary).▽

13. Partner with alcohol abuse agrees to a more intense level of treatment. (15, 16)

15. Require that if the partner with alcohol abuse violates the nondrinking contract, conjoint treatment will end unless he/she describes explicit steps (e.g., daily AA meetings, detox treatment, inpatient or IOP treatment) that he/she will take in the next week to become abstinent.

16. If drinking continues despite psychological intervention,

provide physician referrals for Antabuse treatment and/or referrals for more intense alcoholism treatment (e.g., residential, inpatient, or IOP treatment).

▽ 14. List and implement actions each partner can do to please the other partner as a means of giving of self. (17)

17. Assign each partner to do favors (even small ones) that will be appreciated by the other partner (e.g., help with or do a chore, run an errand, purchase a small present); or assign "How Can We Meet Each Other's Needs and Desires" in the *Adult Psychotherapy Homework Planner*, 2nd ed. by Jongsma. ▽

▽ 15. Agree on a list of recreational activities to be enjoyed together and how they will be planned and implemented. (18)

18. Encourage the partners to engage in shared recreational activities (e.g., a family outing, visiting friends together), stipulating who is responsible for which steps in implementing the activity. ▽

▽ 16. Each partner lists ways that he/she interferes with healthy, open, communication between partners. (19, 20)

19. Have each partner describe the ways that he/she interferes with the communication process in the relationship (e.g., raises voice, walks away, refuses to respond, changes subject, calls partner names, uses profanity, becomes threatening). ▽

20. Assist the partners in self-exploration about their own communication styles and how they may have learned such styles from their family-of-origin experiences. ▽

▽ 17. Demonstrate listening and empathy skills in a communication exercise. (21)

21. Choose a relationship conflict topic (e.g., child discipline, finances, assigning home chores) and have the couple discuss it in session; assess and provide feedback on the partners'

listening and communication styles to improve healthy, accurate, effective communication. ▽

▽ 18. Each partner identifies at least one instance since the last session when he/she was listened to and understood by the other partner. (22)

22. Review and reinforce specific positive communication experiences between the partners that have occurred since the last session. ▽

▽ 19. Describe a problem in the relationship in a nonblaming, nonhostile manner. (23)

23. Encourage partners to describe a problem between them in a non-blaming, nonhostile manner; give feedback and guidance using modeling and role-playing. ▽

▽ 20. Practice problem-solving techniques within the session. (24)

24. Model and role-play problem-solving discussions using the following steps: (a) define the problem (with the help of the therapist); (b) generate many solutions, even if some are not practical, encouraging creativity; (c) evaluate the pros and cons of the proposed solutions; (d) select and implement a solution; (e) evaluate the outcome and adjust actions if necessary (or assign "Applying Problem-Solving to Interpersonal Conflict" in the *Adult Psychotherapy Homework Planner,* 2nd ed. by Jongsma). ▽

▽ 21. Identify at least one instance since the last session when partners made cooperative use of problem-solving techniques learned in session. (25)

25. Review and reinforce partners' reported instances of successfully implementing problem-solving techniques at home since the last session. ▽

▽ 22. Partner with alcohol abuse apologizes (makes amends) to each family member for the distress he/she has caused. (26)

26. Encourage the partner with alcohol abuse to make amends by apologizing to each family member for specific behaviors that have caused distress. ▽

▽ 23. Identify triggers to episodes of drinking, and agree to alternative, nondrinking responses to cope with situations. (27, 28)

24. The nondrinking partner acknowledges his/her role as an enabler of the continuation of the alcohol abuse. (29)

▽ 25. The partner without alcohol abuse asserts self and refuses to take responsibility for the behavior or feelings of the partner with alcohol abuse. (30)

▽ 26. The partner without alcohol abuse confronts the other partner's irresponsible, abusive, or disrespectful behavior. (31)

27. Assist the partners in identifying situations that trigger relapses of drinking episodes. ▽

28. Assist the partner with alcohol abuse in developing positive alternative coping behaviors (e.g., calling a sponsor, attending an AA meeting, practicing stress-reduction skills, turning problem over to a higher power) as reactions to trigger situations (or assign "Relapse Triggers" in the *Adult Psychotherapy Homework Planner,* 2nd ed. by Jongsma). ▽

29. Confront the partner without alcohol abuse regarding behaviors that support the continuation of abusive drinking by the other partner (e.g., lying to cover up for the drinker's irresponsibility, minimizing the seriousness of the drinking problem, taking on most of the family responsibilities, tolerating the verbal, emotional, and/or physical abuse).

30. Model and role-play examples of the partner without alcohol abuse refusing to accept responsibility for the behavior and/or feelings of the other partner; reinforce the partner without alcohol abuse for practicing this assertiveness in situations at home. ▽

31. Encourage and reinforce instances of the partner without alcohol abuse confronting the partner with alcohol abuse for treating him/her with disrespect or blatant abuse. ▽

27. Partners discuss income and financial obligations and then formulate a budget to meet expenses. (32)

28. Partners develop a plan together for initiating contact for activities with other couples that do not involve alcohol consumption. (33)

32. Assign the partners to discuss finances and prepare a mutually agreed-upon budget that begins to deal with the financial stress caused by the drinking problem.

33. Encourage and assist the partners in planning for nonalcohol-consuming social activities with other couples (e.g., church, hobby, and recreational groups or work associates).

__. _____   __. _____
    _____   _____
__. _____   __. _____
    _____   _____
__. _____   __. _____
    _____   _____

DIAGNOSTIC SUGGESTIONS

ICD-9-CM	*ICD-10-CM*	*DSM-5* Disorder, Condition, or Problem
303.90	F10.20	Alcohol Use Disorder, Moderate or Severe
305.00	F10.10	Alcohol Use Disorder, Mild
300.4	F34.1	Persistent Depressive Disorder
301.6	F60.7	Dependent Personality Disorder
301.82	F60.6	Avoidant Personality Disorder
V61.10	Z63.0	Relationship Distress with Spouse or Intimate Partner
_____	_____	_____
_____	_____	_____

ANGER[1]

BEHAVIORAL DEFINITIONS

1. Uncontrolled expressions of anger that are perceived by the other partner as hurtful or threatening.
2. Swift and harshly judgmental, critical, demeaning statements made to or about the partner.
3. Use of passive-aggressive patterns of behavior (e.g., refusal to communicate, uncooperative in dealing with household tasks, etc.) to express anger toward the partner.
4. One partner continues to feel threatened even when the other believes that expressions of anger have modulated.
5. Violating the rights of the other partner through attempts to enforce legitimate wishes via coercive means.
6. Yelling, cursing, and throwing or breaking of objects during conflicts.

__. _____
_____

__. _____
_____

__. _____
_____

---

[1]Extreme, out-of-control expressions of anger in a conjoint session can be especially detrimental to therapeutic progress. The therapist should assess the level of anger in individual sessions prior to any conjoint sessions. If outbursts in conjoint sessions become disruptive, individual sessions should be resumed until progress in anger control becomes evident. In most cases, the therapist should alert couples to the possibility of mixing individual and conjoint sessions as clinically indicated. Such alerts should be given before any problems occur, so that moving back to individual sessions does not appear to be punitive.

LONG-TERM GOALS

1. Express anger in a respectful, controlled manner.
2. Reduce the intensity and frequency of anger expressions.
3. Learn to recognize the positive and negative consequences of current styles of expressing and managing anger.
4. Learn to recognize the gradations of anger and when to intervene with the other partner for maximum effectiveness.
5. Understand the different functions of anger, and learn to satisfy function-related needs in a more constructive manner.
6. Learn to recognize and verbally express hurt feelings instead of expressing them through angry outbursts.

—. _____
   _____
   _____
—. _____
   _____
   _____
—. _____
   _____

SHORT-TERM OBJECTIVES

▽ 1. Verbalize an understanding of anger as an adaptive physiological response to fight a perceived threat. (1, 2, 3)

THERAPEUTIC INTERVENTIONS

1. Educate the partners that the purpose of anger control is not to eliminate anger, because anger is an important, natural signal that something important is at stake. ▽

2. Educate the partners that anger motivates the body's general response to fight a perceived threat and that the form these responses take can either help or hurt one's self and the relationship. ▽

3. Educate the partners that the goals of anger control are first to recognize the importance of a provocative situation, and then to manage anger in a way that

▽ 2. Identify the short- and long-term pros and cons of their current style of expressing anger. (4, 5)

▽ 3. Identify the successful and unsuccessful anger-management strategies of the past and their consequences. (6, 7)

▽ 4. Identify the "mutual trap" whereby one or both partners' anger-management strategy is misinterpreted and leads to continued anger escalation. (8)

▽ 5. Each partner constructs and implements a self-change plan regarding an anger-evoking situation. (9, 10, 11)

strengthens rather than weakens the relationship. ▽

4. Have each partner write down and then read aloud what he/she currently does when angry and what the pros (gains) and cons (negative consequences) are in the short term. ▽

5. Have each partner write down and then read aloud what he/she currently does when angry and what the pros (gains) and cons (negative consequences) are in the long term. ▽

6. Ask how each partner has tried to manage or de-escalate his/her anger in ways that have worked well in the past. ▽

7. Ask how each partner has tried to manage or de-escalate his/her anger in ways that have been counterproductive. ▽

8. Assist the partners in identifying the "mutual trap" underlying their de-escalation strategy (e.g., leaving the room during a conflict) that has been perceived as a provocation (e.g., "he is ignoring and disrespecting me") to the other. ▽

9. Teach the partners the five steps of a Self-Change Plan: (1) Describe the behavior to be changed; (2) Examine the pros and cons of the current behavior; (3) Set a goal, describing as precisely as possible what is to happen; (4) Create an Action Plan, pinpointing a specific plan for enacting the goal; and (5) Evaluate enacting of the plan. Have the partners practice this in

session on an area that has evoked anger that each would like to change.▽

10. Have both partners agree to use self-change plans to improve their own anger responses instead of managing the other's behavior.▽

11. Ask the partners to make a global evaluation of how they did on implementing the action plan before the next session. The rating scale is 0 = didn't think about it or do it; 1 = thought about it; 2 = gave it a weak try; 3 = tried, partially succeeded; and 4 = did a great job. Ask them to jot down short answers to the following: What did we actually do? What positives resulted? What negatives resulted? What do we need to do from here?▽

▽ 6. Both partners contract to manage their anger and use therapy constructively. (12)

12. Ask both partners to contract to use therapy sessions for constructive purposes and to abide by the therapist's directions if the process becomes destructive. ▽

▽ 7. Contract to discuss angry feelings respectfully by balancing concern for the other partner's feelings with the need to express self. (13)

13. Teach both partners the speaker skill of "editing" or "measured truthfulness" (i.e., each balances the need to comment about the other against a concern for the other's feelings); have them practice this skill on areas of conflict, and contract to use at home. ▽

▽ 8. Verbalize recognition of the gradations of anger cues in the three channels of anger (i.e., affective, cognitive, and behavioral). (14)

14. Assist the partners in identifying the behavioral, cognitive, and affective cues of being at low levels of anger (0–30 on a 0–100 scale), moderate levels of anger (31–50 on a 0–100 scale), the danger zone of anger (51–70 on a

0–100 scale), and the extreme zone of anger, where emotional and/or physical aggression becomes more likely (71–100 on a 0–100 scale). ▽

▽ 9. Identify the degree of anger (on a scale of 0–100) that in the past has led to destructive expressions of anger and lack of control. (15, 16, 17)

15. Inquire from the couple at what levels (on a 0-100 scale) anger has been constructive and destructive in the past. ▽

16. Inquire from the couple at what level (on a 0-100 scale) of anger effective control over behavior begins to erode. ▽

17. Assist the couple in identifying at what level of anger (on a 0-100 scale) the anger-management skills should be exercised. ▽

▽ 10. Implement the use of the "Pause, Calm, and Think" (i.e., time-out) technique to modulate anger. (18, 19)

18. Teach the partners the "Pause, Calm, and Think" technique: *Pause* the conversation (i.e., letting the other partner know that you want to pause the discussion); *Calm* down (e.g., focusing on diaphragmatic breathing, counting to 10, focusing on calming self down); *Think* (e.g., taking responsibility for ways in which you are making the conflict worse; planning ways to respond in a mindful, nonescalating manner instead of an automatic, escalating manner; examining thinking by asking self "How TRUE is this thought?" Is it about JUST THIS SITUATION? Will it HELP me get what I want?). ▽

19. Practice using "Pause, Calm, and Think" within the session with situations from a real-life experience of the couple and then assign at-home implementation. ▽

▽ 11. Verbalize an understanding of the three main functions for anger expression. (20)

▽ 12. Identify anger episodes where the goal was to get something. (21)

▽ 13. Identify anger episodes where the goal was to assert independence. (22)

▽ 14. Identify anger episodes where the goal was protection or a reaction to a perceived injury. (23)

▽ 15. Track anger-eliciting situations at home and identify the goal of the anger (e.g., to get something, to assert independence, or to protect self). (24, 25)

20. Teach the partners that people act in angry ways to get a particular outcome and describe the three main reasons for acting angry toward a partner: (1) to get something, (2) to assert independence, and (3) to protect self. ▽

21. Have the partners verbally identify episodes in which the function of their anger was intended to get something (i.e., angry behavior that (a) resulted in getting one's way or getting partner's attention or (b) resulted from frustration over not getting one's way). ▽

22. Ask the partners to verbally identify episodes in which their anger was intended to assert independence (i.e., anger that results from perceptions that the other partner is trying to exert control over one's life or actions). ▽

23. Have the partners verbally identify episodes in which their anger was intended for protection (i.e., anger that results from perceptions that one is hurt, threatened, or vulnerable). ▽

24. Assign to each partner anger-tracking homework that identifies the situations that trigger anger as well as the thoughts and behaviors that occur during anger-eliciting situations (see "Anger Journal" in the *Adult Psychotherapy Homework Planner,* 2nd ed. by Jongsma). ▽

25. Ask the partners to review their anger-tracking homework and

identify those situations where they were trying to get something, those where they were asserting independence, those where they felt the need to protect themselves, and those that had some other function. ▽

⧩ 16. Organize a list of thoughts, behaviors, actual outcomes, and desired outcomes via situational analysis of anger experiences. (26, 27)

26. Using individual sessions as needed, have a partner choose from his/her homework specific anger-eliciting situations and tell what his/her interpretations/ cognitions were, what his/her behavior was, and what the actual outcome of the situation was (see "Anger Journal" in the *Adult Psychotherapy Homework Planner*, 2nd ed. by Jongsma). ▽

27. As the concluding step in the situational analysis, have the partner describe what his/her desired outcome was in the specified situation. ▽

⧩ 17. Verbalize thoughts that were unhelpful, global, or inaccurate, and then state more beneficial self-talk. (28, 29)

28. Help the partners determine whether each thought in the situational analysis was (a) accurate, (b) anchored to the specific situation, and (c) helpful in getting the desired outcome. ▽

29. If any thoughts are not accurate, anchored, and helpful in getting the desired outcome, have the partner reword the thoughts so they meet criteria (for example, "She's always on my back about spending time with the kids" can become "She's exhausted and is looking for a break."). ▽

⧩ 18. Report seeking outcomes over which he/she has control (versus those outcomes over which he/she has no control) in anger-eliciting situations. (30)

30. Help the partner determine whether the desired outcome was achievable (i.e., under his/her control). If not, have the partner reword the desired outcome so

that it becomes achievable (for example, "I want him to listen to me when I'm upset" can become "I want to ask him to schedule a time for us to talk about problems that we're having.").▽

19. Identify self-corrective skills by stating lessons learned from situational analysis exercises. (31)

31. Have the partner summarize the situation by deriving a lesson to be learned from the situational analysis.▽

20. Verbalize the differences between unassertive, assertive, and aggressive responses. (32)

32. Distinguish differences between being unassertive (i.e., not standing up for one's wishes or rights), assertive (i.e., appropriately asserting one's wishes or rights without infringing on the rights of others), and aggressive (i.e., asserting one's wishes or rights without regard to the rights of others).▽

21. Practice assertive behaviors until successful. (33)

33. For the "get-something" desired outcomes, have the speaker practice assertive (not aggressive) communication skills such as "I" statements (see the chapter on Communication in this *Planner*); ask the speaker to create a Self-Change Plan to enact assertive skills between sessions.▽

22. Practice paraphrasing the other partner's appropriate expressions of anger. (34, 35)

34. For the "get-something" desired outcomes, have the listener paraphrase the speaker's message, focusing on the speaker's implicit or explicit desired outcome and not the angry affect.▽

35. For the "assert independence" desired outcomes, have the listener paraphrase the speaker's message, focusing on the speaker's perceptions and not the listener's desire to defend his/her actions.▽

▽ 23. Practice assertive skills to establish independence from the other partner's coercive control. (36, 37)

▽ 24. Recognize and verbalize "softer" emotions (sadness, disappointment, hurt, fear, vulnerability) that precede anger. (38)

▽ 25. Verbalize a perceived need and request care instead of becoming defensively aggressive. (39, 40, 41)

▽ 26. Reflect and empathize with the other partner's vulnerabilities and hurts. (42)

36. For the "assert independence" desired outcomes, have the speaker practice assertive (not aggressive) communication skills that identify the specific behaviors that trigger his/her perceptions of being controlled. ▽

37. Ask each partner to create a Self-Change Plan related to acting independently/coping with partner acting independently and to enact the plans between sessions. ▽

38. For the "protection" desired outcomes, have the speaker identify emotions that precede anger (e.g., hurt, fear, or vulnerability). ▽

39. For "protection" desired outcomes, have the speaker practice making "I" statements that acknowledge his/her personal vulnerabilities. ▽

40. For "protection" desired outcomes, have the speaker practice making requests for support and caring from the other partner when hurt, fearful, or vulnerable. ▽

41. Ask the speaker to create a Self-Change Plan related to protection and to enact it between sessions. ▽

42. For the "protection" desired outcomes, have the listener reflect the underlying emotion felt by the speaker when hurt or vulnerable. ▽

—. _____   —. _____
   _____   _____

—. _____   —. _____
   _____   _____

—. _____   —. _____
   _____   _____

DIAGNOSTIC SUGGESTIONS

ICD-9-CM	_ICD-10-CM_	_DSM-5_ Disorder, Condition, or Problem
309.3	F43.24	Adjustment Disorder, With Disturbance of Conduct
305.00	F10.10	Alcohol Use Disorder, Mild
296.xx	F31.71	Bipolar I Disorder
312.34	F63.81	Intermittent Explosive Disorder
296.xx	F32.x	Major Depressive Disorder, Single Episode
296.xx	F33.x	Major Depressive Disorder, Recurrent Episode
V61.10	Z63.0	Relationship Distress with Spouse or Intimate Partner
V61.12	Z69.12	Encounter for Mental Health Services for Perpetrator of Spouse or Partner Violence, Physical
995.81	Z69.11	Encounter for Mental Health Services for Victim of Spouse or Partner Violence, Physical
301.7	F60.2	Antisocial Personality Disorder
301.83	F60.3	Borderline Personality Disorder
301.81	F60.81	Narcissistic Personality Disorder
_____	_____	_____
_____	_____	_____

ANXIETY

BEHAVIORAL DEFINITIONS

1. Repeated experiences of perceived threat and worry that impede normal fulfillment of important roles.
2. One or both partners experience disruptions severe enough to meet a diagnosis of an anxiety disorder (excessive and unwarranted worry, motor tension, autonomic hyperactivity, hypervigilance).
3. Arguments over the anxiety problem, or over the adaptations that it has forced both partners to make.
4. Social isolation, caused by the anxiety problem, that is distressing to one or both partners.
5. Lengthy, repetitive discussions of worry that do not reduce the anxiety, or are irritating to the other partner.

—. _____
_____

—. _____
_____

—. _____
_____

LONG-TERM GOALS

1. Learn to recognize anxiety problems and to overcome them using cognitive and behavioral coping strategies.
2. Support each other in overcoming the anxiety problem.
3. Participate together in exposure and response-prevention sessions to reduce the anxious partner's distress.
4. Replace anxiety-producing cognitions with healthy, realistic self-talk.

5. Actively schedule and participate in anxiety- and stress-reducing activities, both individually and together.
6. Learn to communicate with each other about positive coping, and to limit discussions about worries.

__. _____

   _____

__. _____

   _____

__. _____

   _____

SHORT-TERM OBJECTIVES

THERAPEUTIC INTERVENTIONS

▽ 1. Verbally identify the triggers for, and symptoms of, the current anxiety problem. (1, 2)

1. Ask the partner with the anxiety problem to describe the anxiety and avoidance symptoms that he/she is experiencing as well as triggers for the anxiety response. ▽

2. Ask the partner without the anxiety problem to provide his/her perspective on the other partner's anxiety and avoidance symptoms. (This input may bring to light other anxiety or avoidance symptoms that have not previously been mentioned.) ▽

▽ 2. Verbally track how the anxiety problem has changed over time. (3)

3. Have the partner with the anxiety problem describe the developmental course of the anxiety problem. ▽

3. List the ways that the anxiety problem has impacted each partner individually. (4, 5)

4. Have the partner with the anxiety problem describe the effect that his/her problem has had on self.

5. Ask the partner without the anxiety problem to describe

the effect the other partner's problem has had on him/her individually.

4. List the ways that the anxiety problem has impacted the couple's relationship. (6, 7)

6. Ask the partner with the anxiety problem to describe the effect that his/her problem has had on the couple's relationship.

7. Ask partner without the anxiety problem to describe the effect the other partner's problem has had on the couple's relationship.

5. Articulate past attempts at coping with the anxiety problem. (8)

8. Ask the partner with the anxiety problem to describe past attempts at coping with the anxiety problem (or assign "Past Successful Anxiety Coping" in the *Adult Psychotherapy Homework Planner*, 2nd ed. by Jongsma).

6. Describe how support for the partner with the anxiety problem by the partner without the anxiety problem has changed over time. (9)

9. Ask the partner without the anxiety problem to describe how his/her supportiveness of the other partner struggling with the anxiety problem has changed over time.

7. Describe the ways in which the anxiety problem produces a relationship conflict. (10)

10. Guide the couple in discussing the ways in which the anxiety problem has precipitated relationship conflicts.

8. Describe how the anxiety problem has changed the ways in which relationship roles are fulfilled. (11, 12)

11. Have both partners describe how the anxiety problem has affected their current role arrangement.

12. Guide the couple in discussing how the current role arrangement came about. Did they discuss their current responsibility allocations overtly, or did the current arrangement evolve implicitly?

9. Verbalize an understanding of anxiety as an adaptive physiological response to fight or

13. Educate the partners that anxiety activates the body's general response to fight or flee

flee from a perceived threat, and generate the advantages and disadvantages this has on each partner and on the relationship. (13, 14)

10. Verbalize an understanding of the principal that anxiety can be broken by testing the accuracy of the feelings of the threat. (15, 16)

11. Practice exposing self to the avoided stimulus situation in gradual steps of time and intensity, while monitoring actual versus imagined feelings of threat. (17)

perceived threats; identify what the predominant anxiety responses are for the partner with the anxiety problem.

14. Educate the partners that while anxiety can serve a useful protective function, overuse of this defense mechanism can exhaust both the individual and the relationship; ask partners to list the pros and cons of the predominant anxiety response on the anxious partner, on the other partner, and on the relationship.

15. Educate the partners that to break an anxiety habit, one must face feared situations to test whether the feared consequences are real or overestimated. Due to generalization, appropriate anxiety resulting from a specific, high-threat situation in the past often gets inappropriately applied to new, lower-threat situations.

16. Explain to the couple that to truly break an anxiety habit, successful exposure to feared situations must prevent the client with the anxiety problem from using maladaptive coping responses (e.g., escape). Exposure also must be long enough and frequent enough for the anxiety to subside (i.e., the behavioral principle of habituation).

17. Encourage the partner with the anxiety problem to face a specific anxiety-producing situation in gradually increasing steps of time and intensity without using escape. During exposure, have

the partner with the anxiety problem monitor actual versus imagined feelings of threat while the other partner gently encourages him/her. ▽

▽ 12. Verbalize recognition of the three channels of anxiety—affective/physiological, cognitive, and behavioral. (18)

▽ 13. Read instructional material about panic disorder. (19)

▽ 14. Read instructional material about generalized anxiety disorder. (20)

15. Contract for partner without anxiety problem to serve as a coping coach for the other partner. (21, 22)

▽ 16. Recognize and rate the gradations of the anxiety experienced. (23, 24, 25)

18. Educate the partners that anxiety operates through three channels—behavioral, cognitive, and affective/physiological. ▽

19. Assign both partners to read *Mastery of Your Anxiety and Panic—Workbook* (Barlow & Craske); use a follow-up session to process the material read. ▽

20. Assign both partners to read *Mastering Your Anxiety and Worry—Patient's Workbook* (Craske & Barlow et al.); use a follow-up session to process the material read. ▽

21. Determine whether the partner with anxiety problem would feel comfortable with the other partner serving as coach, assisting in anticipation of anxiety-producing situations, and prompting the use of coping strategies (if both clients are anxious, ask if each can serve as coach for the other).

22. With the partner without the anxiety problem serving as coach, have the couple anticipate potential problems and brainstorm ways to avoid them; have both partners contract to use the relationship as a source of help and strength in conquering the problem.

23. Educate the partners that anxiety is not an on/off phenomenon, but rather one of gradations. ▽

24. Teach the couple to use the Subjective Units of Discomfort Scale (SUDS), in which the partner with the anxiety problem rates perceived anxiety on a 0–100 scale. ▽

25. Have the partner with the anxiety problem describe for the other partner what his/her current SUDS score is, what elements of the situation are affecting the SUDS, and what internal cues he/she is using to determine the SUDS. ▽

17. Use SUDS ratings as a shorthand, low-key way to communicate with the other partner about anxiety in public. (26)

26. Have the partners contract to discreetly use SUDS scores to signal to each other the level of anxiety being experienced in various public situations.

▽ 18. Describe the difference, at increasing levels of anxiety, in anxiety cues in the affective, cognitive, and behavioral channels. (27, 28, 29, 30)

27. Ask the partner with the anxiety problem to describe to the other partner the behavioral, cognitive, and affective cues associated with experiencing low levels of anxiety (0–30 on a 0–100 scale). ▽

28. Ask the partner with the anxiety problem to describe to the other partner the behavioral, cognitive, and affective cues that signal anxiety associated with the moderate level (31–50 on a 0–100 scale). ▽

29. Ask the partner with the anxiety problem to describe to the other partner the behavioral, cognitive, and affective cues that signal anxiety associated with the high moderate zone (51–70 on a 0–100 scale). ▽

30. Ask the partner with the anxiety problem to describe to the other partner the behavioral, cognitive, and affective cues that signal

anxiety associated with the extreme zone (71–100 on a 0–100 scale). ▽

▽ 19. Practice using diaphragmatic, deep breathing to reduce anxiety. (31, 32)

31. Teach both partners diaphragmatic breathing, including the skills of (a) differentiating diaphragmatic breathing from chest breathing, (b) taking deep breaths, (c) inhaling slowly and deeply for 5 seconds while thinking the word "calm," and (d) exhaling for 10 seconds. The partner without the anxiety problem should learn diaphragmatic breathing both to learn tension management for own benefit and to be a supportive coach to the other partner. ▽

32. Assign both partners to individually practice dia-phragmatic breathing for three 10-minute sessions each day; assign them to record the time and date, their SUDS score prior to the practice session, and their score following the session. ▽

▽ 20. Identify and rank in order feared situations that occur in the natural environment. (33, 34)

33. Assign anxiety-tracking homework that uses a written journal to identify the situations that trigger the partner's anxiety as well as the thoughts and behaviors that occur during anxiety-eliciting situations. ▽

34. Identify feared situations, have the partner with the anxiety problem generate estimated SUDS scores for each situation, and generate a hierarchical list of feared situations (or assign "Gradually Reducing Your Phobic Fear" in the *Adult Psychotherapy Homework Planner*, 2nd ed. by Jongsma). ▽

▽ 21. Practice exposing self to feared situations in session and at home while avoiding the use of maladaptive coping responses (e.g., withdrawal). (35, 36)

▽ 22. Practice challenging anxiety-eliciting cognitions that overestimate threat. (37, 38, 39)

35. Conduct in session imagined exposure of the partner with the anxiety problem to a feared situation, beginning at the lower end of the hierarchy; model for the other partner how to ask for SUDS ratings every several minutes and how to be encouraging during the exposure. ▽

36. Assign the couple to conduct *in vivo* exposures at home, to record the SUDS scores, and to note any problems encountered. ▽

37. Define probability over-estimation (the belief that relatively rare, feared events happen more frequently than they actually do) for the couple (or assign "Analyze the Probability of a Feared Event" in the *Adult Psychotherapy Homework Planner*, 2nd ed. by Jongsma). ▽

38. Model dialogue that challenges probability overestimation. Have the partner with the anxiety problem estimate the probability of a feared event happening (e.g., son getting hurt in a car accident); focus on the evidence to support such estimations (e.g., "So, if the probability of Fred being in an accident were 50 percent, one out of every two trips would involve an accident. Does it happen that frequently?"). ▽

39. Have the partner without the anxiety problem calmly discuss probability overestimation with the other partner in a manner similar to that previously modeled by the therapist.

▽ 23. Practice challenging anxiety-eliciting cognitions that catastrophize. (40, 41, 42)

40. Define catastrophizing (magnifying insignificant consequences out of proportion) for the couple. ▽

41. Model self-talk or partner dialogue that challenges catastrophizing by the partner with the anxiety problem; ask him/her to imagine the worst-case scenario, and discuss how the couple would cope with such an event (or assign "Negative Thoughts Trigger Negative Events" in the *Adult Psychotherapy Homework Planner*, 2nd ed. by Jongsma). ▽

42. Ask the partner without the anxiety problem to discuss catastrophizing with the other partner in a calm manner similar to that modeled by the therapist. ▽

▽ 24. Schedule anxiety-reducing activities that can be done individually. (43)

43. Have both partners commit to and schedule regular individual stress-reducing activities, such as diaphragmatic breathing or deep-muscle relaxation techniques, exercise, music, or hobbies (or assign "Identify and Schedule Pleasant Activities" in the *Adult Psychotherapy Homework Planner*, 2nd ed. by Jongsma). ▽

25. Schedule anxiety reducing activities that can be done with partner. (44)

44. Ask each partner to identify actions that he/she could take to be a source of support and anxiety reduction to the other partner; have them commit to and schedule regular couple anxiety- and stress-reducing activities, such as foot rubs, back rubs, social engagements, walks, sex, or shared hobbies.

26. Engage in positive discussions about the future. (45)

▽ 27. Report on the success of limiting discussions about anxiety to set times of limited duration. (46)

45. Have the couple engage in confident discussions about the future, both in session and at home, focusing on planning and coping for future events.

46. Assign couple to schedule set times for brief "worry meetings" to discuss anxieties; airing of anxieties should be limited to these meetings.

__. _____

 _____

__. _____

 _____

__. _____

 _____

 _____

__. _____

 _____

__. _____

 _____

__. _____

DIAGNOSTIC SUGGESTIONS

ICD-9-CM	_ICD-10-CM_	_DSM-5_ Disorder, Condition, or Problem
300.02	F41.1	Generalized Anxiety Disorder
300.22	F40.00	Agoraphobia
300.01	F41.0	Panic Disorder
309.24	F43.22	Adjustment Disorder, With Anxiety
309.28	F43.23	Adjustment Disorder, With Mixed Anxiety and Depressed Mood
V61.10	Z63.0	Relationship Distress with Spouse or Intimate Partner
_____	_____	_____
_____	_____	_____

BLAME

BEHAVIORAL DEFINITIONS

1. One partner repeatedly blames the other for the relationship problems and the relationship dissatisfaction (e.g., "If you weren't so crazy our marriage would be fine," or "Our whole problem is you and your ideas," or "If you would stop being so critical I'd be happy").
2. Both partners express dissatisfaction with the relationship.
3. The blaming partner is very resistant to examining his/her role in the conflict.
4. The blaming partner projects responsibility for his/her behavior, thoughts, and feelings onto the other partner.
5. Virtually all discussions result in being caught up in blaming rather than honest, open self-examination.
6. The blamed partner lacks consistent assertiveness and tends to terminate communication in a show of helplessness and frustration.
7. The blamed partner verbalizes feelings of low self-esteem and of not being valued by the other partner.
8. The blamed partner feels rejected and avoids interactions with the partner.

__. _____
   _____
__. _____
   _____
__. _____
   _____

LONG-TERM GOALS

1. Eliminate or reduce the frequency of partner blame.
2. Reduce the anger that is often associated with blaming.
3. Reduce the frequency of critical comments often associated with blaming.
4. Help the blaming partner develop a less-unidirectional view of the causes of relationship problems.
5. Increase positive interactions between the partners.

__. _____
_____
__. _____
_____
__. _____
_____

SHORT-TERM OBJECTIVES

▽ 1. Describe problems in the relationship in a respectful, calm manner. (1, 2, 3)

THERAPEUTIC INTERVENTIONS

1. In individual sessions, have each partner describe the problems in the relationship; discourage blaming and reinforce respectful descriptions of problems that have their basis in both partners' behavior (Beach & O'Leary, 1990; Halford, 2001).▽

2. Assess whether chemical dependence, physical or sexual abuse, or an extramarital affair is the basis for most of the blaming in the relationship; if so, employ guidelines from the appropriate *Treatment Planner* chapters to focus conflict resolution on that issue.▽

3. In conjoint sessions, use modeling and reframing to encourage each partner to state problems in a respectful, noncondemning manner.▽

▽ 2. Each partner describes their own actions that contribute to the identified problems (i.e., projecting all blame onto the other partner). (4, 5, 6)

4. Encourage and reinforce each partner to take responsibility for how he/she contributes to the problems rather than projecting all blame onto the other partner (Halford, 2001). ▽

5. Have each partner sign a therapeutic agreement indicating that he/she is partly responsible for the satisfaction and/or dissatisfaction in the relationship. ▽

6. Have each of the partners separately present some problems, however minor, for which they feel they can admit partial responsibility and can agree to make constructive changes. ▽

▽ 3. Verbalize problems in the present tense instead of focusing on issues of the past. (7, 8)

7. Using modeling and praise, encourage and reinforce both partners' efforts at focusing on current problems rather than fixating on the distant past (Jacobson & Margolin, 1979; Rathus & Sanderson, 1999). ▽

8. Encourage the blaming partner to give up anger about a hurt from the distant past and to practice forgiveness that heals, rather than bitterness that divides. ▽

▽ 4. Verbalize concerns about the other partner's behavior by using "I" messages, rather than disparaging the other partner. (9)

9. Using role-playing and modeling, reinforce the use of "I" messages (i.e., stating first what thoughts and feelings were experienced, before stating the partner's behavior that seemed to trigger those thoughts and feelings). ▽

5. Report an increase in respectful communication at home (i.e., discussions are open and free from hostility). (10)

10. Using role-playing and modeling, encourage assertiveness versus passiveness or aggressiveness as an effective means of expressing thoughts and feelings.

▽ 6. Each partner identify two behaviors to engage in that will please the other partner. (11, 12)

7. Report an increase in positive, complimentary, appreciative comments made to the other partner. (13)

▽ 8. Assume responsibility for own behavior, thoughts, and feelings. (14)

9. Blaming partner lists positive behaviors desired by the other partner (rather than pointing out negative behaviors that trigger criticism). (15)

▽ 10. Blamed partner agrees to make efforts at engaging in positive behaviors that will please the other partner. (16)

11. Blaming partner lists times the blamed partner has been praised for pleasing changes in behavior. (17)

11. Have each partner stipulate and then engage in two behaviors that he/she feels would be appreciated by the other partner, in order to provide some clear examples of how each can take responsibility for increasing satisfaction in the relationship. ▽

12. Have each partner report on a positive interchange that reflects change and improvement in the relationship; reinforce each instance of positive interaction, highlighting what contributes to it being pleasant. ▽

13. Assign each partner to express appreciation for two things each day that are pleasing to him/her about the other partner's behavior. ▽

14. Teach the partners that each is responsible for his/her own behavior, thoughts, and feelings, as each have a myriad of choices as a reaction to the other's behavior (O'Leary, Heyman, & Neidig, 1999). ▽

15. Assign the blaming partner to list positive behaviors that the blamed partner could engage in to please the blaming partner (i.e., focus on the positive that is desired rather than the negative that is criticized).

16. Solicit from the blamed partner an agreement to make a reasonable, sincere effort to please the other partner. ▽

17. Have the blaming partner review occasions when he/she has complimented behavior in the other partner; encourage and

reinforce the blaming partner for shifting to a position of praise from one of criticism.

▽ 12. List the "basic rules" of the relationship that cause hurt, anger, and blaming when they are violated. (18, 19)

18. Assist each partner in articulating the "basic rules" of the couple's relationship (for example, that the husband should help to put the children to bed, and the wife should assist in yard work). ▽

19. Clarify how "rules of the relationship" are being broken and how these rule violations evoke negative feelings. ▽

▽ 13. Agree to a renegotiated set of "basic rules" that will increase satisfaction with the relationship if adhered to. (20)

20. Assist both partners in renegotiating rules and roles that are agreeable to each, as a means of reducing blaming behavior. ▽

▽ 14. List external stressors that put pressure on the relationship and lead to blaming. (21)

21. Have each partner list the external stressors that are putting pressure on the couple's relationship. ▽

▽ 15. Engage in problem-solving discussions with the other partner and then verbalize agreement on how to constructively cope with external stressors (rather than reacting with anger and blaming). (22)

22. Aid partners in using problem-solving techniques as a means of coping with external pressures as a team, rather than shifting all the responsibility to one partner. ▽

—. _____

_____

—. _____

_____

—. _____

_____

—. _____

_____

—. _____

_____

—. _____

_____

DIAGNOSTIC SUGGESTIONS

ICD-9-CM	_ICD-10-CM_	_DSM-5_ Disorder, Condition, or Problem
305.00	F10.10	Alcohol Use Disorder, Mild
303.90	F10.20	Alcohol Use Disorder, Moderate or Severe
296.xx	F32.x	Major Depressive Disorder, Single Episode
296.xx	F33.x	Major Depressive Disorder, Recurrent Episode
312.34	F63.81	Intermittent Explosive Disorder
V61.10	Z63.0	Relationship Distress with Spouse or Intimate Partner
301.0	F60.0	Paranoid Personality Disorder
301.7	F60.2	Antisocial Personality Disorder
301.83	F60.3	Borderline Personality Disorder
301.81	F60.81	Narcissistic Personality Disorder
——	——	————————————
——	——	————————————

BLENDED FAMILY PROBLEMS

BEHAVIORAL DEFINITIONS

1. Frequent arguments between parent and stepparent over child discipline differences.
2. Frequent arguments between the partners over favoritism or financial support and gifts for biological versus nonbiological children.
3. Financial pressures and resentment about the financial aspects of divorce settlements.
4. Parental jealousy and sibling rivalry stemming from differences in the social and emotional development of the children from two different marriages.
5. Concerns about leaving opposite-sex teenage stepsiblings alone together (i.e., concerns about sexual activity or sex abuse).
6. Suspicions by the female partner that the male partner is sexually attracted to her daughter.
7. Suspicions by the male partner that the female partner is sexually attracted to his son.
8. The partners describe conflicts about visitation and transportation to and from noncustodial ex-partner's home (e.g., ex-partner's lateness in picking up a child, ex-partner's failure to show up for visitation, ex-partner who enters home to get a child).

---

*Families in the 21st century often will be outside what has been called the traditional or nuclear family. There is no clear agreement on words used to describe families characterized by one adult with at least one child from a previous union who establishes a household with someone who has no legal ties with that child. In this *Treatment Planner*, we choose to use the words "blended family" and "combined family" to characterize such families. Combined families include individuals related by blood (parents and children) and individuals related by marriage (stepparents and stepchildren). Government statistics are not available on the percentage of current blended families, but the demographer Paul Glick estimated that by 2000 about half of all children would be in blended families. Thus, planning for the issues that naturally occur in blended/combined families is certainly prudent. This *Treatment Planner* is designed to aid a therapist in helping members of combined families.

9. Distrust and jealousy regarding other partner's suspected emotional and/or sexual connection to ex-partner.
10. Internalizing and/or externalizing child-behavior problems.

—. _____
   _____
—. _____
   _____
—. _____
   _____

LONG-TERM GOALS

1. All members of the combined family treat each other with mutual respect, equality, and fairness.
2. The partners trust each other's loyalty, love, and commitment, and work cooperatively on child-rearing.
3. Communication with ex-partners regarding children occurs frequently and without major disagreements.
4. The partners resolve jealousy, hurt, and anger toward their ex-partners.
5. Each partner develops understanding about the dilemmas and conflicts that the other experiences with his/her ex-partner.
6. The nonbiological parent learns to establish a respectful, appropriate relationship with the other partner's child or children.
7. Disciplinary actions by a nonbiological parent occur only after a relationship has been established between that parent and the child.

—. _____
   _____
—. _____
   _____
—. _____
   _____

SHORT-TERM OBJECTIVES

▽ 1. Describe conflicts with the ex-partners. (1)

2. Describe the guilt about the ex-partner and about the dilemmas their children face because of a separation or divorce. (2, 3)

▽ 3. Review any implicit or explicit divorce or separation financial agreements and discuss their implications. (4, 5)

▽ 4. Make explicit any implicit financial, child-care, or visitation and transportation agreements that have evolved with the ex-partners. (6)

▽ 5. Agree about budgeting for expenses not covered in agreements. (7)

THERAPEUTIC INTERVENTIONS

1. Ask the partners to describe their feelings about, and conflicts with, their ex-partner. ▽

2. Have the partners relate the ways in which they experience conflict about dealing with their ex-partner.

3. Encourage the partners to openly discuss their guilty feelings about the "failure" of the former relationships, and how these feelings affect their present relationship with their ex-partners and children.

4. Discuss the respective divorce and separation agreements, and have the partners discuss the short- and long-term implications of these agreements. ▽

5. Guide the partners in discussing how they will cope with problems that may result from respective legal and/or financial agreements (e.g., a husband having to pay a large percentage of his salary to his ex-wife, leaving relatively little money for the combined family, educational expenses of the children). ▽

6. Ask the partners to make explicit the implicit agreements that have evolved between them and the ex-partners (e.g., who is to pick up the children for visitation). ▽

7. Have the partners discuss who will pay expenses not covered in the divorce agreement (e.g., music and athletic lessons, team uniforms, camp). ▽

▽ 6. Learn and implement problem-solving and conflict-resolution skills. (8, 9, 10)

8. Assist the partners in identifying conflicts that can be addressed using communication, conflict-resolution, and/or problem-solving skills (see "Behavioral Marital Therapy" by Holzworth-Munroe and Jacobson in *Handbook of Family Therapy* by Gurman and Knickerson [Eds.]). ▽

9. Use behavioral techniques (education, modeling, role-playing, corrective feedback, and positive reinforcement) to teach the partners problem-solving and conflict-resolution skills including defining the problem constructively and specifically, brainstorming options, evaluating options, using compromise, choosing options and implementing a plan, and evaluating the results. ▽

10. Assign the partners a homework exercise to use and record newly learned problem-solving and conflict-resolution skills (or assign "Applying Problem-Solving to Interpersonal Conflict" in the *Adult Psychotherapy Homework Planner*, 2nd ed. by Jongsma); process results in session. ▽

7. Agree on the nature and timing of a response to an ex-partner for a broken divorce agreement. (11)

11. If an ex-partner has violated a divorce agreement regarding child support and/or maintenance, have the partners discuss how long they will allow the violation to continue before taking some action, such as having the financial matters handled directly by the court. Also make agreements regarding potential future violations.

▽ 8. Verbalize feelings about, and acceptance of, the visitation agreement that the biological parent has with his/her children. (12)

12. Remind the parents that in most states visitation is viewed as a privilege, not a legal responsibility; have them verbalize the difficulties and pain they may experience about an ex-partner's infrequent or nonexistent visits with the children. ▽

▽ 9. Agree to defer whenever practical to the biological parent on disciplinary matters relating to his/her children. (13)

13. Solicit agreement from nonbiological parent to support biological parent's discipline behaviors and to defer such responsibilities to biological parent whenever practical (especially with children more than 10 years old). ▽

▽ 10. Discuss financial and disciplinary matters in private, rather than in the presence of the children. (14)

14. Have the partners discuss disciplinary and financial matters that generate disagreement; assign similar discussions for private homework (i.e., not in the presence of the children). ▽

▽ 11. Initiate relationship-building activities with stepchildren, and refrain from assuming a disciplinary role before that relationship is well established. (15)

15. Have the partners initiate appropriate relationship-building activities with the nonbiological child (for example, bike riding, attending child's sport or musical activities, playing together, talking about child's interests, watching a child's video together). ▽

▽ 12. If relations among family members permit, plan an activity or outing that involves the children from each side of the family. (16)

16. Encourage the partners to plan activities that foster relationship building between the stepchildren (e.g., dinner, movie, shopping venture) that involves the children from each side of the family (or assign "Interaction as a Family" in the *Adolescent Psychotherapy Homework Planner II* by Jongsma, Peterson, & McInnis). ▽

▽ 13. Talk positively and respectfully about ex-partners, especially in front of the children. (17)

▽ 14. Accept the view that all members of a combined family need not love one another, but they do need to be cordial and respectful. (18, 19, 20, 21)

15. Encourage parents to speak positively of their ex-partners (when realistic) by describing some of those positive attributes to the children. (22)

17. Encourage the partners to avoid blaming their respective ex-partners (and their respective ex-partner's new love interest) for the "dissolution of our family." ▽

18. Encourage the partners to help each child demonstrate acceptance of his/her new stepmother, stepfather, and stepsiblings via cordial, respectful, and civil interactions (or assign "Stepparent and Sibling Questionnaire" in the *Adolescent Psychotherapy Homework Planner,* 2nd ed. by Jongsma, Peterson, & McInnis). ▽

19. Remind the partners that "instant love" of new family members is a myth; it is unrealistic to expect children to like (and certainly to love) the partner who is serving in the new-parent role. ▽

20. Help the partners accept the position that siblings from different biological families need not like or love one another, but should be mutually respectful and kind. ▽

21. If siblings from two different biological families do not get along well, have the partners plan separate outings with each set of children. ▽

22. Role-play and model with the partners some of the positive things they can say in front of the children about the positive qualities of the ex-partner.

▼ 16. Ask children about enjoyable activities they have had with the parent's ex-partner during visitation. (23)

▼ 17. Verbalize acceptance of the view that having to talk with ex-partners is necessary. (24)

18. Avoid arguments with ex-partner, especially in front of the children. (25)

23. Assign the partners to talk with their children about some of the nice things the children experienced during visitation, or vacation, with an ex-partner; review and discuss these attempts to talk positively about ex-partner. ▼

24. Help the partners agree about the need for open communication with ex-partners about matters pertaining to the children. ▼

25. Rehearse with the partners ways they can avoid arguments and hostile interactions during problem-solving meetings with their ex-partners. ▼

__. _____

_____

__. _____

_____

__. _____

_____

__. _____

_____

__. _____

_____

__. _____

_____

DIAGNOSTIC SUGGESTIONS

ICD-9-CM	_ICD-10-CM_	_DSM-5_ Disorder, Condition, or Problem
V61.20	Z62.820	Parent-Child Relational Problem
V61.10	Z63.0	Relationship Distress with Spouse or Intimate Partner
V61.8	Z62.891	Sibling Relational Problem
_____	_____	_____
_____	_____	_____

COMMUNICATION

BEHAVIORAL DEFINITIONS

1. Frequent arguments or arguing in ways that cause significant upset.
2. Difficulty resolving problems.
3. Frequent misunderstandings during discussions.
4. View disagreements as symbols of global problems (e.g., such core themes as love and respect) rather than specific problems.
5. Consistent failure to verbally acknowledge the positive actions of the other partner.

—. _____
   _____
—. _____
   _____
—. _____
   _____

LONG-TERM GOALS

1. Partners communicate about feelings without escalating hostility.
2. Partners discuss and resolve problems effectively without verbal fighting.
3. Each partner listens to and understands the other partner's perspective.
4. Arguments no longer feel like uncontrollable, inevitable events, as partners learn to recognize cues of verbal fighting, and control them before they start.
5. Each partner notices and verbalizes appreciation to the other for acts of kindness, thoughtfulness, and caring.

—. _____
   _____
—. _____
   _____
—. _____
   _____

SHORT-TERM OBJECTIVES

▽ 1. Identify specific communication deficits. (1, 2)

▽ 2. Identify the core themes of arguments. (3)

▽ 3. Identify process by which the partners become increasingly polarized. (4)

THERAPEUTIC INTERVENTIONS

1. Have the couple attempt to solve a major problem while the therapist quietly watches and takes notes about communication skills and deficits. ▽

2. Praise the couple for things they do well (such as making eye contact or attempting to define the problem) and provide direct feedback regarding things that need improvement (such as maintaining a civil tone of voice or overcoming the tendency to interrupt). ▽

3. Help partners identify the core themes (e.g., closeness/distance, respect, responsibility, power differentials) that underlie their most affectively charged arguments. ▽

4. Ask the partners to discuss the ways in which their behavior, in response to the core themes, has become increasingly polarized (e.g., the closeness seeker becomes clingier while the distancer becomes more withdrawn). ▽

▽ 4. Identify the "mutual trap" whereby one partner's response (e.g., withdrawal) evokes the other partner's response (e.g., demand for closeness) and vice versa. (5)

▽ 5. Partners implement the two overarching communication skills of: "Be Clear" and "Be Considerate." (6, 7, 8)

▽ 6. Practice defining problems in specific, nonblaming terms. (9, 10, 11)

5. Assist the partners in identifying the "mutual trap" underlying their communication problems, whereby one partner's solution to the core theme (e.g., demanding more time together) triggers the other's solution (e.g., withdrawal) and vice versa. ▽

6. Teach the partners the communication skill that emphasizes that interchanges should be (a) clear (i.e., be specific, share thoughts and feelings, pay attention, ask clarifying questions, summarize content and feelings); and (b) considerate (i.e., include positives, show consideration when expressing negatives, let partner know that one is listening even if one disagrees, reserve judgment). ▽

7. Ask the partners to discuss a low-conflict area of desired change and ask them to rate how well they did being clear. ▽

8. Ask the partners to discuss a low-conflict area of desired change and ask them to rate how well they did being considerate. ▽

9. Have the partners take turns pinpointing problems (that is, making requests for change that are specific, observable, and ask for increases rather than decreases in the other partner's behavior). ▽

10. Have the partners use the "speaker-listener" technique, with the listener trying to convey understanding after the speaker makes "I" statements in the

following form: "When _____ happens, I feel _____. I would like _____."▽

11. If either partner is mind reading the other, have him/her rephrase the statements so that he/she is speaking only for self and expressing his/her own perceptions. ▽

▽ 7. Practice listening in a manner that promotes empathy and understanding. (12, 13, 14)

12. While one partner is serving as the speaker, have the other paraphrase (i.e., summarize content) by repeating back in his/her own words, the speaker's overt point (e.g., "You would like me to balance the checkbook with you each month."). ▽

13. While one partner is serving as the speaker, have the other reflect (i.e., summarize feelings) by repeating back, in his/her own words, the speaker's underlying emotion (e.g., "You're frustrated about our inability to save money."). ▽

14. Have the listening partner practice validation skills (i.e., the listener conveys that he/she understands and can empathize with the speaker's feelings, even if not agreeing with them). ▽

▽ 8. Practice sharing thoughts and feelings in a manner that promotes intimacy. (15, 16)

15. Have partners share their feelings regarding issues about which they'd like to be closer; provide a list of "emotion" words, if necessary, to cue partners to the subtleties of words expressing feelings. ▽

16. Teach partners the speaker skill of "editing" or "measured truth-fulness" (i.e., balancing the need to comment about the partner against a concern for his/her

▼ 9. Demonstrate an understanding of communication that is focused on problem-solving and on venting. (17, 18)

▼ 10. Practice accepting and rejecting requests for positive activities. (19, 20)

▼ 11. Set aside 10 to 15 minutes several times per week for discussion of personal issues. (21)

▼ 12. Demonstrate de-escalating conflict. (22, 23, 24, 25)

feelings), and have them practice this on areas of conflict. ▼

17. Teach partners that communication tends to serve one of two purposes—venting (i.e., sharing feelings) or problem-solving; have partners identify how they feel when one person is pursuing venting and the other problem-solving. ▼

18. Role-play the couple discussing a current problem while having the listener ask the speaker what he/she wants out of the discussion—venting or problem-solving. ▼

19. Have one partner practice making suggestions for enjoyable activities together and the other practice accepting (by making eye contact, reinforcing the person for asking, and planning when to do the activity). ▼

20. Have one partner practice making suggestions for enjoyable activities together and the other practice counter-offering using the positive-negative-positive "sandwich" method (rewarding the partner for asking, identifying the specific element being modified, and making a counter-suggestion). ▼

21. Assign the partners to set aside 10 to 15 minutes two or three times a week for a "couple meeting" to discuss suggestions and/or complaints in a constructive, controlled, respectful manner. ▼

22. Teach the partners the listener skill of "editing" (i.e., responding

to provocation in a manner that is in one's long-term best interest, rather than for retaliation or debate) and have them practice this on areas of conflict (e.g., when one partner brings up the other partner's spending, the listener paraphrases rather than defensively listing ways the speaker has overspent). ▽

23. Teach the partners the listener skill of "metacommunication" (i.e., commenting on the process rather than the content of the speaker's statement) and have them practice this to overtly correct dysfunctional communication, rather than acting out of anger over negative communication behaviors (e.g., when the conversation deviates from the issue being solved, the listener mentions that they've gotten off track and refocuses the discussion on the key problem). ▽

24. Ask each partner to identify behaviors that he/she employs during discussions to (a) soothe him/herself or the other partner (e.g., deep breathing, reminding him/herself that the partner is not the enemy, apologizing to the partner), or (b) de-escalate the conflict (e.g., lower his/her voice, acknowledge good points the partner is making). ▽

25. Ask each partner to confirm whether he/she interprets the other's supposed soothing/ de-escalation behaviors as such; if so, ask for future increases in soothing/de-escalation but if not,

have partners discuss their opposing interpretations of the behavior. ▽

▽ 13. Identify cues for arguments and practice argument-control strategies. (26, 27, 28)

26. Help the partners identify cues that an argument is impending (e.g., behaviors, thoughts, feelings, bodily sensations) and have them contract with each other actions they will take to allow time to cool off (e.g., pause the conversation, calm themselves down separately, and think about ways in which they are contributing to the problem) before talking further. ▽

27. Assign the partners to track times and places that trigger arguments. ▽

28. Help the partners identify times that are conducive to discussing and/or solving problems (such as after the children are in bed) and times that are not conducive (such as when dinner is being prepared). ▽

▽ 14. List the cues that each partner will use to judge that the other is receptive to problem-solving at a specific time. (29)

29. Help the partners identify the cues that indicate that either is receptive to discussing and/or solving problems (for example, partner is awake, alert, and not too tired; no distractions are present; no alcohol has been consumed; and enough time is available for attaining closure). ▽

▽ 15. Verbalize how a problem may be opened for discussion. (30, 31)

30. Use role-playing and modeling to teach the partners how to effectively approach the other to discuss a problem. ▽

31. Have both partners agree on an agenda and time limit for problem-solving discussions. ▽

▽ 16. Define the exact nature of one problem before trying to resolve it. (32, 33)

32. Teach the partners to agree to their mutual satisfaction that a problem has been correctly pinpointed before actually trying to solve the problem; have them practice this in session on areas of conflict. ▽

33. Have both partners agree to discuss only one problem during problem-solving sessions. ▽

▽ 17. Use problem-solving skills to resolve a problem. (34, 35, 36, 37)

34. Choose a moderate area of conflict that has been pinpointed and have the partners practice brainstorming, whereby each partner generates at least two solutions to a problem before trying to solve that problem. ▽

35. Teach partners to evaluate the pros and cons of the brainstormed solutions and have them practice this in session on areas of conflict. ▽

36. Teach partners how to select a specific, operationalized plan for attaining a solution based on the pros and cons of that solution; ask the partners to implement the selected action plan before the next session. ▽

37. Ask partners to give an evaluation of how they did on the action plan before the next session. The rating scale is 0 = didn't think about it or do it; 1 = thought about it; 2 = gave it a weak try; 3 = tried, partially succeeded; and 4 = did a great job. Ask them to jot down short answers to the following: What did we actually do? What positives resulted? What negatives resulted? What do we need to do from here? ▽

▼ 18. Attend to and compliment other partner for helpful or caring behaviors. (38)

38. Assign both partners to track on paper and bring to the next session the "Catch Your Partner Pleasing You" exercise, noting (a) at least one positive behavior the partner did each day; and (b) at least one positive behavior they did themselves that day. ▼

__. _____

__. _____

__. _____

__. _____

__. _____

__. _____

DIAGNOSTIC SUGGESTIONS

ICD-9-CM	_ICD-10-CM_	_DSM-5_ Disorder, Condition, or Problem
309.0	F43.21	Adjustment Disorder, With Depressed Mood
300.4	F34.1	Persistent Depressive Disorder
296.xx	F32.x	Major Depressive Disorder, Single Episode
296.xx	F33.x	Major Depressive Disorder, Recurrent Episode
V61.12	Z69.12	Encounter for Mental Health Services for Perpetrator of Spouse or Partner Violence, Physical
V61.10	Z63.0	Relationship Distress with Spouse or Intimate Partner

_____ _____ _____

_____ _____ _____

DEPENDENCY

BEHAVIORAL DEFINITIONS

1. Derives self-worth almost solely from positive partner comments, leading to incessant solicitation of feedback.
2. Fears being abandoned by partner.
3. Has difficulty making decisions without confirmation by, or support of, his/her partner.
4. Avoids expressing disagreement with partner because of fear of disapproval or rejection.
5. Assumes a servant role with partner, doing almost anything to gain approval.
6. Has a history of going from one relationship to another with little time between relationships.
7. Initiates contact with partner in diverse settings (e.g., when partner is at work, driving, or at gym) because of need for reassurance and fear of being alone.
8. Jealous of time partner spends with work colleagues and suspected sexual partners.
9. Feels anxious if partner is not available for support or encouragement.

__. _____
   _____
__. _____
   _____
__. _____
   _____

_____

*There are no couples treatment outcome studies that address dependency in a relationship. However, the issue of dependency often arises in generic couples therapy and in couples therapy for depression (Cohen & O'Leary, 2010). It is important to address the issue of general dependency as a personality trait or style, and if it is deemed that there is both general and partner-specific dependency, then it is worthwhile to consult the dependency module in the *Adult Psychotherapy Treatment Planner*, 2nd ed. (Jongsma & Peterson, 2006).

LONG-TERM GOALS

1. Increase self-esteem and self-confidence, leading to efficient decision-making, greater tolerance for being alone, and a sense of secure independence.
2. Accepts legitimate absences of partner (such as being at work) without anxiety.
3. Contacts partner only when necessary if partner is at work or engaged in a recreational activity.
4. Makes routine decisions independently (i.e., without partner).
5. Accepts the need for partner to spend time with colleagues and friends.
6. Broadens sources of self-worth (i.e., not just the partner).

—. _____

_____

—. _____

_____

—. _____

_____

SHORT-TERM OBJECTIVES	THERAPEUTIC INTERVENTIONS
1. Dependent partner acknowledges excessively contacting partner. (1, 2)	1. Ask the dependent partner to list the situations that lead to anxiety such that he/she contacts the other partner unnecessarily when partner has a right to be alone or to conduct personal activities without intrusion; ask the dependent partner to complete the Spouse-Specific Dependency Scale (Rathus and O'Leary).
	2. Have the nondependent partner provide feedback about how the intrusiveness of the dependent partner affects him/her, and obtain feedback on how dependent the partner seems on other individuals such as family members, neighbors, and physician.

2. Dependent partner reads books on dependency in intimate relationships and then identifies how he/she is demonstrating dependent behaviors in his/her relationship with other partner. (3, 4, 5)

3. Assign the dependent partner to read books on dependency in intimate relationships (e.g., *Co-Dependent No More* and *Beyond Codependency* by Beattie).

4. Discuss material read in books on dependency in a conjoint session and have the dependent partner identify his/her dependent patterns as discovered in the content of the books read.

5. Ask the dependent partner to list the boundaries that he/she crossed in the last week with partner.

3. Identify behavioral goals that will be incompatible with continuing the dependency patterns that are causing conflict in the relationship. (6)

6. Assist the dependent partner in setting graduated behavioral goals (e.g., no contact with their partner for five hours, meet with friends alone, make request for rebate from company for item returned to firm) for increasing independence in the relationship (or assign "Taking Steps toward Independence" in the *Adult Psychotherapy Homework Planner*, 2nd ed. by Jongsma).

4. Dependent partner identifies those areas of the other partner's life that should not be intruded upon, and pledges to provide privacy. (7)

7. In a conjoint session, assist the partners in listing areas of the nondependent partner's life that the dependent partner will no longer intrude upon; solicit a pledge from the dependent partner to adhere to this agreement.

5. Dependent partner describes interactions with the other partner that demonstrate a change from dependency behaviors to independence. (8, 9)

8. Have the dependent partner describe to the other partner how he/she is becoming less dependent and demonstrating self-confidence as well as freedom from fear of rejection or disapproval (e.g., has been

comfortable being separated from the other partner, and/or asked the nondependent partner for a specific favor).

9. Have the nondependent partner provide feedback to the dependent partner about progress that he/she has made in observing boundaries and becoming less dependent; encourage the nondependent partner to positively reinforce this independent behavior in daily living.

6. Nondependent partner offers reassurance, compliments, and expressions of appreciation to other partner on a regular basis, without being prompted. (10)

10. Encourage the nondependent partner to tell the dependent partner noncontingently that he/she cares for him/her (i.e., give reassurance only when dependent partner is not asking for it).

7. Acknowledge that the pattern of insecurity, eagerness to please, and low self-esteem in relationships goes beyond the present relationship and has roots in the family of origin. (11, 12)

11. Explore and resolve the dependent partner's fear of rejection that originates in lack of acceptance from his/her family of origin; help him/her separate the early fear and anger from the current relationship.

12. Explore abandonment experiences in family of origin and with significant others in adulthood (i.e., past events that could be fueling the current fears of abandonment).

8. Both partners acknowledge ways that a healthy interdependence with the other partner can be demonstrated, as differentiated from total emotional dependence. (13)

13. Discuss in a conjoint session how both independence and dependence (i.e., healthy interdependence) can be positive for the relationship (e.g., encourages mutual respect for personal traits and abilities, allows each partner to give support to the other).

9. Dependent partner states the boundaries needed for self in nonintimate relationships. (14)

14. Have the dependent partner list what boundary behaviors he/she must instill into nonintimate relationships (such as keeping certain thoughts and feelings private, allowing others privacy and time alone, and making personal decisions without anxiety or seeking approval).

10. Dependent partner lists other relationships that have similar patterns of fear of abandonment, need for constant reassurance, and a persistent attempt to please. (15)

15. Have the dependent partner discuss whether boundary issues are restricted to the other partner or are generalized (i.e., occur with coworkers, other family members); point out the need for this dependency to be changed across all relationships.

11. Acknowledge and report instances of imposing self on people other than partner because of the strong need for reassurance and fear of being alone. (16)

16. Ask dependent partner to list any specific boundaries that he/she crossed during the last week with coworkers and/or family members; help the dependent partner understand how fear of rejection or disapproval influences relationships with others beyond nondependent partner; encourage confidence and assertiveness.

12. Verbalize the benefits of not imposing fears, needs, and private thoughts on others. (17)

17. Assist the dependent partner in listing the benefits of being more private in casual relationships (e.g., less alienation of self from others, more pride and respect for self, projects image of more competence and less neediness).

13. Both partners identify sources of emotional support outside of the other partner and list five reasons why social support outside the relationship is good for the relationship. (18, 19)

18. Assist the partners in listing potential sources of emotional support each or both of them could draw upon apart from leaning on each other (e.g., friends at work, extended family members, church acquaintances, interest groups, neighbors).

14. Dependent partner identifies how being an independent person is good both for one's self-esteem and for the relationship. (20)

15. Dependent partner reports instances of progress in independence in nonintimate relationships. (21)

16. Dependent partner reports increasingly greater amounts of time spent away from partner, doing daily routine duties without initiating contact and without worry. (22, 23)

17. Dependent partner lists decisions made without consulting others for reassurance or agreement. (24, 25)

18. List the legitimate needs that each partner can expect the other to fulfill. (26)

19. Discuss how support from others outside the relationship can actually benefit the relationship (e.g., decreases the need for partner support, broadens social support network, and affirms self in ways that cannot or will not be satisfied by the partner).

20. Encourage the dependent partner to set goals for independence and to discuss how independence builds self-esteem and makes a relationship more interesting.

21. Reinforce the dependent partner's reports of progress in independence, decision-making, assertiveness, and resilience in the face of disapproval from friends or family.

22. Encourage the dependent partner to take increasingly larger ventures away from home on his/her own (e.g., to store, gym, social outing, overnight trips).

23. Assign the dependent partner to increase time spent at work or play without partner contact.

24. Encourage the dependent partner to make decisions on his/her own (i.e., without input from other partner) (or assign "Making Your Own Decisions" in the *Adult Psychotherapy Homework Planner*, 2nd ed. by Jongsma).

25. Have the nondependent partner provide positive feedback about good decisions made unilaterally by the dependent partner.

26. Ask each partner to list the legitimate needs that could be fulfilled by the other partner (or assign "How Can We Meet Each

Other's Needs and Desires?" in the *Adult Psychotherapy Homework Planner*, 2nd ed. by Jongsma).

19. List the legitimate rights that each partner has within the relationship. (27)

27. Ask each partner to list the legitimate rights that each has within the relationship.

20. Verbalize negative automatic thoughts associated with assertiveness, being alone, or refusing to meet others' needs. (28)

28. Explore the dependent client's automatic thoughts associated with assertiveness, being alone, or not meeting others' needs.

21. Replace negative thoughts about independence with healthy, positive self-talk. (29)

29. Assist the dependent partner in developing positive self-talk to replace negative thoughts about independence that precipitate fear and desperation.

22. Attend assertiveness training class. (30)

30. Refer the dependent partner to assertiveness training classes to learn ways to get his/her own needs met in a healthy, direct manner and to say no without guilt or fear of rejection.

___. _____   ___. _____
_____   _____
___. _____   ___. _____
_____   _____
___. _____   ___. _____
_____   _____

DIAGNOSTIC SUGGESTIONS

ICD-9-CM	*ICD-10-CM*	*DSM-5* Disorder, Condition, or Problem
311	F32.9	Unspecified Depressive Disorder
300.4	F34.1	Persistent Depressive Disorder
296.xx	F32.x	Major Depressive Disorder, Single Episode
296.xx	F33.x	Major Depressive Disorder, Recurrent Episode
301.6	F60.7	Dependent Personality Disorder
301.82	F60.6	Avoidant Personality Disorder
_____	_____	_____
_____	_____	_____

DEPRESSION DUE TO
RELATIONSHIP PROBLEMS

BEHAVIORAL DEFINITIONS

1. Feeling blue.
2. Difficulties in concentrating.
3. Lack of interest in sexual interactions.
4. Difficulty in sleeping, or sleeping too much.
5. Lack of energy.
6. Withdrawal from social activities.
7. Low self-esteem.
8. Feelings of hopelessness.
9. Suicidal thoughts and/or behavior.
10. Feelings of guilt, especially because of relationship problems related to the depression.
11. Movement retardation or acceleration (slowed activity or pacing).
12. Recurrent crying spells.
13. Inability to resolve grief.
14. Belief that relationship problems are the cause of depression.
15. History of relationship problems prior to the depression.
16. History of some precipitating event in the relationship that was very destructive (e.g., verbal abuse, physical abuse, discovery of action by other partner that led to distrust).

—. _____
   _____

—. _____
   _____

—. _____
   _____

LONG-TERM GOALS

1. Increase the partners' general level of satisfaction with relationship.
2. Reduce the client's depressed mood and increase his/her energy level.
3. Increase the client's self-esteem.
4. Recognize factors that led to the client's depressed feelings and cope with them in a manner that makes relapse less likely.

__. _____
   _____
   _____
__. _____
   _____
   _____
__. _____
   _____

SHORT-TERM OBJECTIVES

▽ 1. Describe overall level of satisfaction with the relationship. (1)

▽ 2. Complete relationship assessment instruments. (2)

▽ 3. Verbalize own level of commitment to remain in the relationship. (3)

▽ 4. Describe extent of own love and caring for the other partner. (4)

▽ 5. Identify sources of depressed mood and related depressive symptoms, focusing on the

THERAPEUTIC INTERVENTIONS

1. Explore each partner's thoughts and feelings concerning the relationship. ▽

2. Have each partner complete some standardized assessment of relationship satisfaction (e.g., *Spanier Dyadic Adjustment Scale* or *Couples Satisfaction Inventory* by Funk & Rogge). ▽

3. Have each partner describe his/her commitment to the relationship and/or complete a standardized commitment to relationship scale (e.g., *Commitment Scale* by Broderick & O'Leary). ▽

4. Have each partner articulate and/or complete an assessment of love/caring for the other partner (e.g., *Positive Feelings Questionnaire* by O'Leary, Fincham, & Turkewitz). ▽

5. Assess the extent to which each partner believes relationship problems preceded the depression. ▽

role of conflicts within the relationship. (5, 6, 7)

6. Have each partner describe whether and why he/she believes the depression was caused by problems in the relationship such as verbal and/or physical aggression. Ask whether there have been instances of physical aggression from or toward the partner such as slapping, hitting, or shoving. ▽

7. Have the client rank in order of importance all the factors that are making him/her depressed. ▽

▽ 6. Complete standardized measures of depression and suicidal ideation. (8)

8. Administer standardized measures of depression and hopelessness (such as *Beck Depression Inventory* or *Beck Hopelessness Scale*) and provide feedback on the results. ▽

▽ 7. Implement a plan of preventative action to be used if suicidal thoughts become frequent. (9)

9. Develop plan of action with client about who to call if hopeless feelings are becoming magnified, and arrange for 24-hour coverage with clear instructions to client about how to reach help quickly. ▽

▽ 8. Verbalize an understanding of how anger and depression interact. (10)

10. Teach the partners how individuals with depression often become angry quickly and make hostile comments to people they love. ▽

▽ 9. Reduce the frequency of critical, angry expressions that are related to a general state of depression. (11)

11. Ask the partner with depression to monitor self and minimize hostile comments to the other partner. ▽

▽ 10. Describe instances of sharing depressed feelings in a controlled, limited manner that is sensitive to not alienating self from others. (12, 13)

12. Encourage sharing of depressed feelings in therapy session and, on a limited basis, with significant others. ▽

13. Have client verbally outline appropriate reliance on significant others (friends and family) to minimize alienation of the client from friends. ▽

11. Use prayer, meditation, and/or attendance at religious services if doing so seems to have provided benefit in the past. (14)

▽ 12. Apologize and offer restitution to other partner for past nonsupportive behavior. (15)

▽ 13. Engage in positive interaction with the other partner. (16, 17)

14. Describe instances of verbal and physical affection between self and other partner. (18)

▽ 15. Reduce the frequency of hostile comments related to dissatisfaction with the other partner. (19, 20)

16. As a means of increasing awareness, identify instances of self issuing negative, hostile comments. (21, 22)

14. Encourage the use of religious services, spiritual writings, and prayer if those have proven useful in the past to relieve depression and/or if client seems desirous of beginning such endeavors.

15. Encourage the partner who has been nonsupportive to apologize and make some restitution for lack of support. ▽

16. Assign each partner to give positive, supportive comments to the other on a daily basis. ▽

17. Help the partners list thoughtful, kind acts that each partner would appreciate and then assign each to engage in at least one caring gesture toward the other each day (or assign "How Can We Meet Each Other's Needs and Desires" in the *Adult Psychotherapy Homework Planner,* 2nd ed. by Jongsma). ▽

18. If the level of anger and hostility has subsided, assign the partners to be verbally and physically affectionate to each other each day.

19. Have the partner without depression refrain from making hostile, counterproductive comments to the other partner out of frustration with his/her depression. ▽

20. Provide feedback to both partners regarding the extent of negativity and hostility that exists in their communication. ▽

21. If the therapist's requests to avoid negativity prove ineffective, provide audio or videotaped feedback to the partners to illustrate the hostility displayed in the session.

22. If the therapist's request to avoid negativity prove ineffective, encourage adjunctive individual sessions to each partner to address the anger and hostility.

▽ 17. Cooperate with a medication evaluation by a physician. (23)

23. If the relationship problems have subsided but the depression has not, refer the partner with depression to a psychiatrist or other physician for a medication evaluation. ▽

▽ 18. Take prescribed antidepressant medication at times ordered by physician and report therapeutic impact and any side effects. (24, 25, 26)

24. Encourage the partner with depression to take medication regularly and monitor for side effects and effectiveness. ▽

25. Educate the depressed partner on the common side effects of various antidepressant medications (such as nausea, anxiety and nervousness, insomnia, dry mouth, or diminished sexual arousal), but note that these often go away during the first few weeks of medication. ▽

26. If the depressed partner is unresponsive to antidepressant medication, have him/her discuss lack of responsiveness with physician and raise the issue of changing dosage and/or medication. ▽

▽ 19. Partner with depression utilizes "behavioral activation" to overcome depression. (27)

27. Engage the depressed partner in "behavioral activation" by scheduling activities that have a high likelihood for pleasure and mastery (or assign "Identify and Schedule Pleasant Activities" in the *Adult Psychotherapy Homework Planner*, 2nd ed. by Jongsma); use rehearsal, role-playing, or role reversal as needed to assist adoption in the client's daily life; review and reinforce success. ▽

▽ 20. Depressed partner identifies and replaces cognitive self-talk that supports depression. (28, 29, 30)

28. Assist the depressed partner in developing an awareness of his/her automatic thoughts that reflect a depressogenic schema. ▽

29. Assign the depressed partner to keep a daily journal of automatic thoughts associated with depressive feelings (e.g., "Negative Thoughts Trigger Negative Feelings" in the *Adult Psychotherapy Homework Planner*, 2nd ed. by Jongsma or "Daily Record of Dysfunctional Thoughts" in *Cognitive Therapy of Depression* by Beck, Rush, Shaw, & Emery). ▽

30. Assign behavioral experiments in which depressive automatic thoughts are treated as hypotheses/predictions; reality-based alternative hypotheses/predictions are generated; and both are tested against the client's past, present, and future experiences. ▽

▽ 21. Verbalize an awareness of the frequency with which critical, hopeless, and pessimistic self-talk is engaged in. (31)

31. If the depressed partner continues to engage in pessimistic self-talk regarding self, partner, and the future, confront and highlight these negative expressions. ▽

▽ 22. Make positive statements to self and others about the future. (32, 33)

32. Teach the depressed partner to replace negative self-talk with positive messages regarding self, partner, and the future of the relationship (or assign "Positive Self-Talk" in the *Adult Psychotherapy Homework Planner*, 2nd ed. by Jongsma). ▽

33. Reinforce the depressed partner's verbalizations of hope and self-esteem-enhancing thoughts. ▽

▽ 23. Practice problem-solving techniques within the session. (34)

34. Model and role-play problem-solving discussions using the following steps: (a) define the problem (with the help of the

therapist); (b) generate many solutions, even if some are not practical, encouraging creativity; (c) evaluate the pros and cons of the proposed solutions; (d) select and implement a solution; (e) evaluate the outcome and adjust actions if necessary. ▽

▽ 24. Identify at least one instance since the last session when the partners made cooperative use of problem-solving techniques learned in session. (35)

35. Review and reinforce the partners' reported instances of successfully implementing problem-solving techniques at home since the last session (or assign "Applying Problem-Solving to Interpersonal Conflict" in the *Adult Psychotherapy Homework Planner,* 2nd ed. by Jongsma). ▽

—. _____
_____

—. _____
_____

—. _____
_____

—. _____
_____

—. _____
_____

—. _____
_____

DIAGNOSTIC SUGGESTIONS

ICD-9-CM	*ICD-10-CM*	*DSM-5* Disorder, Condition, or Problem
309.0	F43.21	Adjustment Disorder, With Depressed Mood
V62.82	Z63.4	Uncomplicated Bereavement
300.4	F34.1	Persistent Depressive Disorder
296.xx	F32.x	Major Depressive Disorder, Single Episode
296.xx	F33.x	Major Depressive Disorder, Recurrent Episode
V61.12	Z69.12	Encounter for Mental Health Services for Perpetrator of Spouse or Partner Violence, Physical
995.81	Z69.11	Encounter for Mental Health Services for Victim of Spouse or Partner Violence, Physical
V61.10	Z63.0	Relationship Distress with Spouse or Intimate Partner
_____	_____	_____
_____	_____	_____

DEPRESSION INDEPENDENT
OF RELATIONSHIP PROBLEMS

BEHAVIORAL DEFINITIONS

1. Pervasive feeling of sadness and dissatisfaction with life.
2. Difficulties in concentrating.
3. Lack of interest in sexual interactions.
4. Difficulty in sleeping, or sleeping too much.
5. Lack of energy.
6. Withdrawal from social activities.
7. Low self-esteem or feelings of worthlessness.
8. Feelings of hopelessness.
9. Suicidal thoughts and/or behavior.
10. Feelings of guilt, especially because relationship problems may seem to be due to depression.
11. Movement retardation or acceleration (slowed activity or pacing).
12. Chronic or recurrent feelings of depression.
13. Unable to resolve grief.

—. _____
  _____

—. _____
  _____

—. _____
  _____

---

*Partner-assisted therapy has been used successfully both in Europe and the United States, and there have been studies that show the effectiveness of dyadic approaches to the reduction of depression in males and females. In short, a sensitive, empathetic partner can be of great value in partner-assisted therapy for depression. On the other hand, a partner who is prone to being critical can undermine therapy, even if the overall relationship is satisfactory. Thus, a careful, accurate assessment of the potential for support or harm by the partner's participation in some or all of the therapy sessions is crucial to the success of the therapy.

LONG-TERM GOALS

1. Reduce depression and increase energy level.
2. Increase self-esteem.
3. Recognize why grief is prolonged; resolve grief; and return to normal, non-depressed functioning.
4. Recognize factors that have led to depression and cope with them in a manner that makes relapse less likely.
5. Develop positive attitudes and beliefs that make relapse less likely.
6. Capitalize on the support and positive feedback of the partner and his/her understanding of depression to increase self-esteem and make relapse less likely.

—. _____

   _____

—. _____

   _____

—. _____

   _____

SHORT-TERM OBJECTIVES

▽ 1. Identify sources of depressed mood and related depressive symptoms. (1, 2)

▽ 2. List changes that could be made in external causative factors that could result in improved mood. (3)

▽ 3. Complete standardized measures of depression, suicidal ideation, and relationship satisfaction and process feedback about the results. (4)

THERAPEUTIC INTERVENTIONS

1. Ask the client to list all the factors that seem to make him/her depressed. ▽

2. Have the client rank in order of importance the factors that are making him/her depressed. ▽

3. Explore changes that can be made in external causative factors (e.g., friend conflict, employment, or family issues) that could result in improved mood. ▽

4. Administer standardized measures of depression, hopelessness (e.g., *Beck Depression Inventory*, *Beck Hopelessness Inventory*) and relationship (e.g., *Couples*

Satisfaction Inventory by Funk & Rogge); review results with the client. ▽

▽ 4. Verbally understand and agree upon a plan of preventative action to be used if suicidal thoughts become frequent and intense. (5)

5. Develop a plan of action with the client about who to call if hopeless feelings are becoming magnified, and arrange for 24-hour coverage at these times with clear instructions about how to reach help quickly. ▽

▽ 5. Identify possible genetic and family-of-origin factors that relate to a vulnerability to depression. (6, 7)

6. Assign the client to create a family tree with brief descriptions of the mental health of each family member and notations about whether they experienced depression. ▽

7. Discuss family risk and genetic liability for depression, but emphasize the equally important roles that psychological and environmental factors play in preventing and coping with depression even when hereditary risk factors are high. ▽

▽ 6. Describe instances of verbalized anger toward the other partner for his/her perceived lack of support or withdrawal during a depressive episode. (8)

8. Discuss with both partners how individuals with depression often become angry quickly and make hostile comments to people they love; encourage the depressed client to monitor self and minimize such hostile comments. ▽

▽ 7. Verbalize a plan for appropriate sharing of depressed feelings with family and friends. (9, 10)

9. Encourage the depressed partner to share depressed feelings in therapy sessions and, on a limited basis, with significant others, to help them understand the factors that lead to depression (while being careful to not alienate self from others by constant negativity). ▽

10. Have the depressed client verbally outline appropriate

reliance on significant others (friends and family) to minimize alienation of the client from friends. ▽

8. Use prayer, meditation, and/or attendance at religious services when such seems to have provided benefit in the past. (11)

11. Encourage use of religious services, spiritual writings, and prayer if these have proven useful in the past for alleviation of feelings of hopelessness or worthlessness, and/or if the client seems desirous of beginning such endeavors.

▽ 9. Take antidepressant medication as prescribed by physician. (12)

12. Assess the depressed partner for a history of mania present along with depressive episodes; when antidepressant medication appears appropriate for unipolar depression, make referral to psychiatrist or other physician for medication; encourage the client to take medication regularly. ▽

▽ 10. Report side effects and effectiveness of medication. (13, 14, 15)

13. Educate the partners on the common side effects of various antidepressant medications (such as nausea, anxiety and nervousness, insomnia, dry mouth, or decreased sexual arousal), but note that these often go away during the first few weeks of medication. ▽

14. Monitor the depressed client for side effects and effectiveness of antidepressant medications; report to physician. ▽

15. If the depressed partner is unresponsive to antidepressant medication, have him/her discuss lack of responsiveness with the physician and raise the issue of changing dosage and/or medication. ▽

11. Verbalize an understanding of alternatives to antidepressant medication, if not responsive to the medication. (16)

16. If the depressed client is unresponsive to other medications, discuss the option of electro-convulsive shock therapy; review the positive effects that such treatments have had on patients who have been unresponsive to antidepressants.

▽ 12. Engage in some daily activity that involves interactions with others. (17)

17. Assign the depressed partner to make a certain number of social contacts (e.g., lunch meetings, visits, couple activities) per week that requires taking care of one's appearance. ▽

▽ 13. When possible, use the support of the other partner through phone contact during day. (18)

18. Assign the depressed partner to make a certain number of contacts with the other partner per week at his/her work, provided that such contacts are permitted by the employer, and the partner is supportive. ▽

▽ 14. Engage in physical activity (walk, jog, work out in gym, ride bicycle) to help overcome depressed feelings. (19)

19. Assist the depressed partner in planning regular physical activities (e.g., walking, jogging, working out in a gym); when appropriate, involve the other partner in these activities. ▽

▽ 15. Have the depressed partner identify and replace cognitive self-talk that supports depression. (20, 21, 22)

20. Assist the depressed partner in developing an awareness of his/her automatic thoughts that reflect a depressogenic schema. ▽

21. Assign the depressed partner to keep a daily journal of automatic thoughts associated with depressive feelings (e.g., "Negative Thoughts Trigger Negative Feelings" in the *Adult Psychotherapy Homework Planner*, 2nd ed. by Jongsma or "Daily Record of Dysfunctional Thoughts" in *Cognitive Therapy of Depression* by Beck, Rush, Shaw, & Emery). ▽

▽ 16. Report instances of making positive statements to self and others about the future. (23)

22. Assign behavioral experiments in which depressive automatic thoughts are treated as hypotheses/predictions, reality-based alternative hypotheses/predictions are generated, and both are tested against the client's past, present, and future experiences. ▽

23. Encourage the depressed partner to engage in positive self-talk; reinforce verbalizations of hope- and self-esteem-enhancing thoughts (or assign "Positive Self-Talk" in the *Adult Psychotherapy Homework Planner*, 2nd ed. by Jongsma). ▽

▽ 17. Partner with depression utilizes "behavioral activation" to overcome depression. (24)

24. Engage the depressed partner in "behavioral activation" by scheduling activities that have a high likelihood for pleasure and mastery (or assign "Identify and Schedule Pleasant Activities" in the *Adult Psychotherapy Homework Planner*, 2nd ed. by Jongsma). Use rehearsal, role-playing, or role reversal as needed to assist adoption in the client's daily life; review and reinforce success. ▽

▽ 18. Partner without depression verbalizes an understanding that the depressed partner's depression or aversive behaviors are not to be taken personally. (25)

25. Educate the partner without depression that the depressed partner's mood and aversive behaviors are symptomatic of clinical depression. ▽

▽ 19. Partner without depression holds realistic expectations for the depressed partner's functioning. (26)

26. Encourage the partner without depression to adjust expectations to the severity of the other partner's depression-impaired functioning. ▽

20. Read books on coping with depression. (27)

27. Recommend that the partners read self-help books on coping with depression (e.g., *The Feeling Good Handbook* or *Ten Days to Self-Esteem* by Burns, *The Cognitive Behavioral Workbook for Depression* by Knaus & Ellis, or *The Depression Workbook* by Copeland & McKay).

__. _____   __. _____
    _____   _____
__. _____   __. _____
    _____   _____
__. _____   __. _____
    _____   _____

DIAGNOSTIC SUGGESTIONS

ICD-9-CM	*ICD-10-CM*	*DSM-5* Disorder, Condition, or Problem
309.0	F43.21	Adjustment Disorder, With Depressed Mood
V62.82	Z63.4	Uncomplicated Bereavement
300.4	F34.1	Persistent Depressive Disorder
296.xx	F32.x	Major Depressive Disorder, Single Episode
296.xx	F33.x	Major Depressive Disorder, Recurrent Episode
301.83	F60.3	Borderline Personality Disorder
_____	_____	_____
_____	_____	_____

DISILLUSIONMENT WITH RELATIONSHIP

BEHAVIORAL DEFINITIONS

1. Feelings of being "out of touch" with other partner (i.e., distant, detached, and/or resentful).
2. Trend toward going own way in life, with decreasing sharing of activities, interests, and communication between self and other partner.
3. Fears by one or both partners that relationship will deteriorate to the point of separation or divorce.
4. Arguments or distance created by failed attempts to jointly attend to needs of relationship.
5. Blaming other partner for past personal and relationship disappointments.
6. Making almost no future plans because of arguments or distance in the relationship.
7. Expectations of the self, partner, and/or relationship that lead to negative outcomes (e.g., frustrations, disappointments, depression, anxiety, anger).
8. Increasing preoccupation with past personal and relationship disappointments.
9. Thoughts of what it would be like to be out of relationship with partner.

—. _____
   _____
   _____

—. _____
   _____
   _____

—. _____
   _____

LONG-TERM GOALS

1. Partners rededicate selves to meeting each other's needs and attending to each other's interests.

2. Partners recognize pros and cons of current relationship and commit to actively building on the positive aspects of that relationship.
3. Renegotiate the relationship contract to increase its helpfulness for current coping needs.
4. Commit to improve coping by working together as a team.

—. _____

_____

—. _____

_____

—. _____

_____

SHORT-TERM OBJECTIVES

1. Each partner identifies own attitude about making changes to resolve the relationship dissatisfaction. (1)

2. List the current strengths and weaknesses of the relationship. (2, 3)

3. Each partner list three changes he/she will make to improve the relationship. (4)

THERAPEUTIC INTERVENTIONS

1. Administer "Stages of Change" questionnaire (Prochaska et al., 1994) to determine which of the four stages of change (precontemplation, contemplation, action, maintenance) best describes each partner's current approach to the relationship dissatisfaction; discuss the results in conjoint session.

2. Ask both partners to describe the strengths of their current relationship.▽

3. Ask both partners to describe the elements of their current relationship that they would like to improve.

4. Have each partner list three ways that he/she could change to cause improvement in those elements of the relationship that he/she would like to improve, and express commitment to the relationship and change.▽

▽ 4. Identify the ways in which each partner's individual and relationship developmental history may be impacting current functioning. (5, 6)

5. Have partners trace important events in their individual developmental history that may relate to their current style of interacting and that could adversely affect their current functioning with their partner. ▽

6. Have partners trace important events in their relationship developmental history that may relate to their current style of interacting and that could adversely affect their current functioning with their partner. ▽

▽ 5. Elucidate the original relationship contract, including both explicit and implicit expectations. (7, 8)

7. Ask partners to describe what their stated expectations were of each other (i.e., the explicit relationship contract). ▽

8. Ask partners to describe what their unspoken expectations were of each other (i.e., the implicit relationship contract). ▽

▽ 6. Verbalize the pros and cons of the original relationship contract. (9, 10)

9. Explore the ways in which the original relationship contract (both implicit and explicit) has benefitted each partner. ▽

10. Explore the negative aspects in the partners' original relationship contract that have led to conflict, disappointment, or frustration. ▽

7. Agree to discard the explicit or implicit expectations in the relationship that have led to conflict, disappointment, or frustration. (11)

11. Encourage each partner to agree to eliminate expectations that have been sources of conflict, disappointment, or frustration.

8. Identify the ways in which the relationship contract either evolved or needed to evolve but didn't. (12, 13)

12. Explore how the partners' relationship contract has evolved over time.

13. Explore the ways that the partners' relationship contract

needed to change but never did change.

9. Each partner states the ways in which his/her personal and relationship dreams have been fulfilled and dashed. (14, 15)

14. Have each partner identify his/her personal dreams, and discuss the ways in which they have been fulfilled and ways in which they have remained unfulfilled.

15. Ask partners to identify the dreams they had for their relationship, and discuss the ways in which these have been fulfilled and ways in which they have remained unfulfilled.

▽ 10. Express gratitude to each other for dreams realized, and acceptance or forgiveness for dreams unfulfilled. (16)

16. Explore the need for partners to express gratitude to each other for dreams that were realized and to let go of resentment over dreams that remained unfulfilled. ▽

11. Verbalize acceptance of the continuities and disruptions of their lives together by narrating two contrasting versions of their life history. (17, 18)

17. Have partners tell their life story together, emphasizing the predictability and continuities of their shared life.

18. Have partners retell their life story, emphasizing the surprises, choices, sacrifices, and unpredictability of their shared life.

12. Identify the impact, on both emotions and coping, of viewing their lives as predictable or unpredictable. (19)

19. Help the partners compare and contrast the two versions of their past lives and relationship, emphasizing the impact their emotional and coping responses have on the two versions.

13. Identify the security of viewing their life story as predictable and the excitement and need for each other that accompanies life as unpredictable. (20, 21)

20. Have the partners add chapters to each version of their life story, envisioning their future.

21. Help the partners discuss the pros and cons of both versions of their future chapters, emphasizing the security of predictability and the need for

▽ 14. Accept responsibility for disappointing decisions by recognizing that they reflected the best that each could do at the time, giving up a pattern of blame of the partner. (22, 23)

▽ 15. Elucidate the stressful life circumstances over the years that have necessitated coping. (24)

▽ 16. Verbalize empathy with the other partner's attempts to cope, and describe the negative impact the partner's coping has had on oneself. (25, 26, 27, 28)

▽ 17. Agree to begin to coordinate coping with life's stressors "as a team." (29, 30)

each other during times of unpredictability.

22. Reframe past decisions that led to disappointments as being the best decisions that could be made, considering contextual factors that influenced the choices. ▽

23. Have each partner take personal responsibility for disappointing decisions, thereby reducing blame of the other partner. ▽

24. Foster acceptance of each other by having partners discuss the life circumstances that have forced them to cope (e.g., changing social expectations, changing gender roles, family life-cycle changes). ▽

25. Reframe current problems as a natural outgrowth of the partners' individual attempts to cope with changes forced on them by life's circumstances. ▽

26. Foster acceptance of each other by having partners discuss how their individual attempts to cope with life's stressors have led to current difficulties. ▽

27. Ask the listening partner to empathize with speaker's point of view regarding coping. ▽

28. After the listener has empathized, have him/her explain the impact the speaker's coping had, and how it forced him/her to cope with speaker's coping attempt. ▽

29. Reframe current problems as resulting from partners being out-of-sync with each other in coping. ▽

▽ 18. Report on recent improvements in communication. (31)

▽ 19. Identify current needs and resources. (32, 33)

▽ 20. Catalog needs that will be met within the relationship and those that will be met outside of the relationship. (34)

21. Write a new relationship contract to redefine relationship roles and expectations. (35)

22. Strategize together about meeting future challenges to the relationship. (36, 37)

▽ 23. Identify support systems that already exist that could be used to assist in the renewal of the relationship. (38)

30. Help partners agree to begin working on coping "as a team" to get more in sync. ▽

31. Remediate communication problems, as necessary, with targeted interventions (see the chapter on Communication in this *Planner*). ▽

32. Have both partners identify their current needs. ▽

33. Have both partners identify what each is willing to give to the relationship. ▽

34. Have each partner identify the needs that he/she would like to have met within the relationship, and those that he/she would like to have met outside of the relationship. ▽

35. Have partners hold a "constitutional convention" to re-evaluate their relationship contract, specifying what expectations, rights, and responsibilities each agrees to.

36. Ask partners to generate a list of challenges that they anticipate contending with in the future (e.g., retirement, moving, health problems).

37. Using the agreements detailed in the new relationship contract, have the couple plan for their future "as a team."

38. Discuss support systems outside of the relationship that are already in place that can help the partners renew the vitality of their relationship (e.g., friends, self-help and support groups, religious community). ▽

▼ 24. Identify support systems that could be added to assist in the renewal of the relationship. (39)

39. Discuss support systems outside of the relationship that can be added to help the partners renew the vitality of their relationship (e.g., friends, self-help and support groups, religious community). ▼

__. _____

_____

__. _____

_____

__. _____

_____

__. _____

_____

__. _____

_____

__. _____

_____

DIAGNOSTIC SUGGESTIONS

ICD-9-CM	_ICD-10-CM_	_DSM-5_ Disorder, Condition, or Problem
309.0	F43.21	Adjustment Disorder, With Depressed Mood
305.00	F10.10	Alcohol Use Disorder, Mild
303.90	F10.20	Alcohol Use Disorder, Moderate or Severe
300.4	F34.1	Persistent Depressive Disorder
296.xx	F32.x	Major Depressive Disorder, Single Episode
296.xx	F33.x	Major Depressive Disorder, Recurrent Episode
V61.10	Z63.0	Relationship Distress with Spouse or Intimate Partner
_____	_____	_____
_____	_____	_____

EATING DISORDERS

BEHAVIORAL DEFINITIONS

1. Rapid consumption of large quantities of food in a short time, followed by self-induced vomiting and/or use of laxatives due to fear of weight gain.
2. Extreme weight loss (and amenorrhea in females), with refusal to maintain a minimal healthy weight due to very limited ingestion of food and high frequency of secretive self-induced vomiting, inappropriate use of laxatives, and/or excessive strenuous exercise.
3. Preoccupation with body image related to grossly unrealistic assessment of self as being too fat or strong denial of recognizing self as emaciated.
4. An irrational fear of becoming overweight.
5. Fluid and electrolyte imbalance due to eating disorder.
6. Avoidance of expressions of affection with partner.
7. Avoidance of sexual interaction with partner.
8. Arguments over dieting, binging, and purging.
9. Chronic or recurrent depression (partner with eating disorder).
10. Chronic or recurrent depression (partner without eating disorder).
11. Lack of communication.
12. Intermittently explosive interchanges between the partners.

—. _____

  _____

---

*The family approaches like that of Russell, Szmuukler, Dare, & Eisler (1987) and le Grange, Crosby, Rathouz, & Leventhal (2007) have fared reasonably well and are recommended by Wilson, Grillo, & Vitousek (2007). However, the approaches of Russell and colleagues and le Grange and colleagues are not couple-based but family-based, and the teenage patients were not married or in committed relationships. Cognitive behavior therapy is the treatment of choice for bulimia nervosa and binge eating disorder, and a specific form of family therapy is recommended for anorexia nervosa (Wilson, Grillo, & Vitousek, 2007), but we cannot recommend couple-based treatment for eating disorders based on assessment of evidence-based outcomes. However, couple-based approaches might be used with individuals with sub-threshold symptomatology problems of an eating disorder nature.

—. _____
   _____
—. _____
   _____

LONG-TERM GOALS

1. Increase both partners' understanding of eating disorders.
2. Restore normal eating patterns, body weight, balanced fluid and electrolytes, and realistic perception of body size.
3. Reduce conflict over problems of eating.
4. Increase support of partner without eating disorder for partner with eating disorder.
5. Increase positive communication between the partners.
6. Increase expressions of affection between the partners.
7. Increase frequency of sexual interactions between the partners.

—. _____
   _____
—. _____
   _____
—. _____
   _____

SHORT-TERM OBJECTIVES

1. Describe the current eating problems of the partner with eating disorder. (1, 2)

2. Identify those factors previous to, outside of, and within the relationship that cause or maintain the eating disorder. (3, 4)

THERAPEUTIC INTERVENTIONS

1. Ask each partner to describe the eating patterns of the partner with the eating disorder.

2. Ask the partners to describe the purging patterns of the partner with the eating disorder.

3. Ask the partners to list the factors that they believe are causing the eating problems (or assign "How Fears Control My Eating" in the *Adult Psychotherapy Homework Planner*, 2nd ed. by Jongsma).

3. Read factual material about prevalence, course, and treatment of eating disorders. (5)

4. Partner with eating disorder accepts referral to a physician for physical examination. (6)

5. Partner without eating disorder verbalizes encouragement and appreciation, praises assets, and recognizes accomplishments of other partner. (7, 8)

6. Verbalize an understanding of risks and potential benefits of appetite-suppressant medication and antidepressant medication to treat eating disorders. (9, 10, 11)

7. Accept referral to a physician for medication evaluation and take any medication ordered. (12)

4. Ask the partner without the eating disorder to list the ways that he/she may be contributing to the exacerbation and/or maintenance of the other partner's eating problems.

5. Assign treatment-related reading to the partners (e.g., *Eating Disorders*, brochure #94-3477, NIMH, 1994).

6. Refer the partner with eating disorder to a physician to assess physical health and future risks.

7. Educate the partners regarding the central role that low self-esteem plays in the development and maintenance of eating disorders.

8. Discuss the need for the partner without the eating disorder to provide the other partner with supportive feedback to enhance his/her self-esteem.

9. Review current evidence with the partners about the role of appetite-suppressant medication in treating eating disorders.

10. Review current evidence with the partners about the risk involved with use of psychostimulant medication in treating eating disorders.

11. Review current evidence with the partners about the role of antidepressant medication in treating eating disorders.

12. Arrange for a medication evaluation and monitor the effectiveness of any psychotropic medication ordered.

8. Partner without eating disorder identifies feelings of anger, concern, and helplessness about the other partner's eating disorder. (13)

9. Partner with eating disorder verbalizes acceptance of responsibility for maintaining a balanced and healthy diet. (14)

▼ 10. Partner with the eating disorder identifies, challenges, and replaces self-talk and beliefs that promote the eating disorder. (15, 16, 17)

13. Have the partner without the eating disorder describe the ways that he/she experiences conflict and anger over the other partner's eating disorder.

14. Obtain commitment from the partner with the eating disorder to accept responsibility for changing problematic eating patterns and attitudes; ask the partner to keep a record of food consumed along with associated thoughts and feelings (or assign "A Reality Journal: Food, Weight, Thoughts, and Feelings" in the *Adult Psychotherapy Homework Planner*, 2nd ed. by Jongsma).

15. Assign the client to self-monitor and record food intake, thoughts, and feelings (or assign "A Reality Journal: Food, Weight, Thoughts, and Feelings" in the *Adult Psychotherapy Homework Planner*, 2nd ed. by Jongsma or "Daily Record of Dysfunctional Thoughts" in *Cognitive Therapy of Depression* by Beck, Rush, Shaw, & Emery); process the journal material to challenge maladaptive patterns of thinking and behaving, and replace them with adaptive alternatives. ▼

16. Assist the client in developing an awareness of his/her automatic thoughts and underlying assumptions, associated feelings and actions that lead to maladaptive eating and weight control practices (e.g., poor self-image, distorted

body image, perfectionism, fears of failure and/or rejection, fear of sexuality). ▽

17. Assist the client in the identification of negative cognitive messages (e.g., catastrophizing, exaggerating) that mediate his/her dysfunctional eating behavior, then train the client to establish realistic cognitive messages regarding food intake and body size (or assign "Fears Beneath the Eating Disorder" from the *Adolescent Psychotherapy Homework Planner*, 2nd ed. by Jongsma, Peterson, & McInnis). ▽

11. Partner without the eating disorder commits to avoid monitoring and criticizing other partner's eating (and purging) habits. (18)

18. Obtain a commitment from the partner without the eating disorder to minimize attempts to control the eating behavior of the other partner.

12. Identify the specific role that perfectionism plays in a relationship and in sexual interaction. (19, 20)

19. Discuss with the partners the roles that high standards and perfectionism play in the life of the partner with the eating disorder.

20. Review with the partners how perfectionism may interfere with various aspects of their relationship, including communication and sexual functioning.

13. Partner with eating disorder identifies the type of positive feedback most desired from other partner to help build self-esteem. (21)

21. Have the partner with the eating disorder describe in some detail the specific positive feedback that he/she most desires from the other partner to help build self-esteem during efforts to overcome the eating disorder.

__. _____   __. _____
     _____   _____
__. _____   __. _____
     _____   _____
__. _____   __. _____
     _____   _____

DIAGNOSTIC SUGGESTIONS

ICD-9-CM	_ICD-10-CM_	_DSM-5_ Disorder, Condition, or Problem
303.90	F10.20	Alcohol Use Disorder, Moderate or Severe
305.00	F10.10	Alcohol Use Disorder, Mild
307.1	F50.02	Anorexia Nervosa, Binge-Eating/Purging Type
307.1	F50.01	Anorexia Nervosa, Restricting Type
307.51	F50.2	Bulimia Nervosa
307.50	F50.9	Unspecified Feeding or Eating Disorder
296.xx	F32.x	Major Depressive Disorder, Single Episode
296.xx	F33.x	Major Depressive Disorder, Recurrent Episode
V61.10	Z63.0	Relationship Distress with Spouse or Intimate Partner
_____	_____	_____
_____	_____	_____

FINANCIAL CONFLICT

BEHAVIORAL DEFINITIONS

1. Arguments over the amount of money spent by one partner.
2. Arguments over the priorities regarding spending money.
3. Critical comments about a partner not making enough money.
4. Arguments over the amount of money to be saved.
5. Feelings of being left out of decision-making regarding the allocation of money.
6. Suspicions that the other partner is secretively spending money without mutual consent.
7. Arguments over the need to save money for retirement.
8. Arguments over "legitimate" methods of reporting income for tax purposes.
9. Arguments over the need to shop for the best possible price on an item.

__. _____
   _____
__. _____
   _____
__. _____
   _____

LONG-TERM GOALS

1. Develop open and honest communication between the partners about the budgeting of all money.
2. Reduce arguments over how money is spent and how much should be saved.
3. Arrive at long-term financial plans for spending, saving, and investing money.
4. Reach mutual agreement regarding the amount of time each partner is expected to be involved in gainful employment.

5. Accept contrasting opinions regarding the need to work and save money, provided the differences do not adversely affect the family.

6. Address individual problems within the relationship that may interfere with finances (e.g., alcohol dependence, substance abuse, manic depressive disorder, occupational problem).

—. _____
   _____

—. _____
   _____

—. _____
   _____

SHORT-TERM OBJECTIVES	THERAPEUTIC INTERVENTIONS
▽ 1. Increase awareness of the sources of the other partner's anger and disappointment regarding money acquisition and use. (1, 2)	1. Ask each partner to describe his/her angry feelings about how money is spent. ▽
	2. Ask each partner to describe his/her disappointments regarding money. ▽
▽ 2. Identify and share priorities as to how money should be spent. (3)	3. Have each partner itemize his/her priorities regarding how money should be spent. ▽
▽ 3. Identify the differences in financial priorities that exist between self and the other partner. (4)	4. Explore with the partners whether there are basic differences over priorities in the budgeting of money. ▽
4. Identify family-of-origin style of living and use of money, and state their impact on current financial attitudes. (5)	5. Have the partners describe how decisions were made about spending money and what money was spent on in their families of origin and how that history influences their current attitudes about finances.
5. Describe the future income, saving, and spending expectations that existed when relationship began. (6)	6. Ask the partners to describe the expectations they had at the beginning of their relationship regarding amount of money they would have and how it would be spent and saved.

▽ 6. Verbalize whether parents influence current financial decisions. (7)

7. Have each partner explain whether his/her parents influence current financial decisions; help the couple resolve any conflicts over parental influence and the need for family boundaries. ▽

▽ 7. Agree to set financial goals and to make budgetary decisions cooperatively with partner, without undue reaction to family pressure. (8)

8. Encourage cooperative, partnership-based financial planning that is free from undue family influence. ▽

▽ 8. Practice listening effectively to the other partner regarding differing financial ideas and possible solutions to these conflicts. (9, 10, 11)

9. Have each partner practice listening without interruption to the other partner's views about financial and budgetary goals. ▽

10. After the partner has listened without interrupting, ask him/her to paraphrase what the other partner said about what the financial problem is. ▽

11. Model and role-play applying problem-solving to the financial problem using the following steps: (a) define the financial problem; (b) generate many solutions, even if some are not practical, encouraging creativity; (c) both partners evaluate the pros and cons of the proposed solutions; (d) both partners agree on, select, and implement a solution; (e) both partners evaluate the outcome and adjust actions if necessary. ▽

▽ 9. Report on implementing agreed-upon changes in the handling of finances. (12)

12. Review and reinforce the partners' reported instances of successfully applying problem-solving techniques to their financial conflicts at home since the last session (or assign "Applying Problem-Solving to Interpersonal Conflict" in the *Adult Psychotherapy Homework Planner,* 2nd ed. by Jongsma). ▽

▽ 10. Verbalize an agreement regarding the need for each partner to work. (13, 14, 15)

13. Ask the partners to describe their employment situations at the time they first met. ▽

14. Explore with the partners the expectations each had regarding his/her own employment once they were married, and what employment expectations each held for the other. ▽

15. Facilitate an agreement between the partners regarding the current need for each to work versus the value placed on one staying home to manage the household and family responsibilities. ▽

▽ 11. Agree on how a balance will be reached between the need for child care and the need for income production. (16, 17)

16. If the couple has children, have each partner describe what he/she expected in terms of employment for self and the other partner once they had children. ▽

17. Facilitate an agreement between the partners regarding child-care needs and income needs (recommend the partners read *Work-Life Balance for Dummies* by Mumford & Lockette or *The One Minute Manager Balances Work and Life* by Blanchard, Edington, & Blanchard). ▽

▽ 12. Agree on steps to begin coping with expenses (and debt-retirement demands) exceeding income. (18)

18. Review with the partners the need for filing for bankruptcy, applying for welfare, and/or obtaining credit counseling. ▽

▽ 13. Develop a written plan for current budget and future finances. (19, 20)

19. If financial planning is needed, refer couple to a professional planner (see *Consumer Reports*, 1998, for qualifications of a financial planner), or have the partners write a current budget and long-range savings and investment plan (or assign "Plan a Budget" in the *Adult Psychotherapy Homework Planner*, 2nd ed. by Jongsma). ▽

20. If budgeting information is a primary need, refer the partners to *Family Economics Review,* published by the U.S. Department of Agriculture (Superintendent of Documents, U.S. Government Printing Office, Washington, D.C. 20402) for information regarding household expense allocations. ▽

14. Verbalize feelings about one partner exercising virtually exclusive control over the couple's finances and financial decisions. (21)

21. Ask each partner to describe the ways that he/she feels controlled by the other partner when all financial decisions are made by only one of the partners.

▽ 15. Agree on how financial control and decision-making should be shared. (22)

22. Facilitate an agreement between the partners on how they can cooperatively make financial decisions, with each partner's ideas being respected. ▽

▽ 16. Implement mutual decision-making regarding the management of money in daily living. (23)

23. Reinforce changes in managing money that reflect responsible planning, compromise, and respectful cooperation. ▽

▽ 17. Verbalize conflicts over the issue of control by one partner that goes far beyond finances. (24, 25, 26)

24. Assess whether one partner attempts to restrict the other in contacts with family, friends, and/or enhancement of educational/vocational skills. ▽

25. If general control of one partner is a problem, address this issue directly as potential psychological abuse (see chapters on Psychological Abuse or Intimate Partner Violence in this Planner). ▽

26. Explore the specific control that one partner has over the finances of the partnership and the degree of feeling that the other has about it. ▽

▽ 18. State the extent to which any individual behavioral or personality disorder interferes with financial issues in the family. (27, 28)

27. During individual sessions, assess whether a personality or behavioral disorder of either partner interferes with financial issues in the family. ▽

28. If assessment reveals that an individual disorder (e.g., alcohol abuse, substance abuse, or occupational problem) interferes with financial solidarity, refer the individual to the appropriate services. ▽

—. _____   —. _____

_____   _____

—. _____   —. _____

_____   _____

—. _____   —. _____

_____   _____

DIAGNOSTIC SUGGESTIONS

ICD-9-CM	_ICD-10-CM_	_DSM-5_ Disorder, Condition, or Problem
309.24	F43.22	Adjustment Disorder, With Anxiety
309.0	F43.21	Adjustment Disorder, With Depressed Mood
309.28	F43.23	Adjustment Disorder, With Mixed Anxiety and Depressed Mood
303.90	F10.20	Alcohol Use Disorder, Moderate or Severe
305.00	F10.10	Alcohol Use Disorder, Mild
304.30	F12.20	Cannabis Use Disorder, Moderate or Severe
296.xx	F31.1x	Bipolar I Disorder, Manic
307.51	F50.2	Bulimia Nervosa
V62.2	Z56.9	Other Problem Related to Employment
V61.10	Z63.0	Relationship Distress with Spouse or Intimate Partner
301.7	F60.2	Antisocial Personality Disorder
301.81	F60.81	Narcissistic Personality Disorder
301.4	F60.5	Obsessive-Compulsive Personality Disorder
301.6	F60.7	Dependent Personality Disorder

_____ _____ _____

_____ _____ _____

INFIDELITY

BEHAVIORAL DEFINITIONS

1. One partner engages in sexual behavior (e.g., penile-vaginal intercourse, oral sex, anal sex) that violates the explicit or implicit expectations of the relationship.
2. One partner engages in nonsexual behavior that involves sharing intimate time, feelings, and/or thoughts with an extramarital partner, and secrecy that violates the explicit or implicit expectations of the relationship.

__. _____
   _____
__. _____
   _____
__. _____
   _____

LONG-TERM GOALS

1. Partners agree on appropriate emotional, social, and sexual boundaries with others (e.g., acceptable and prohibited behavior).
2. Hurt partner indicates a willingness to attempt to engage in a process of forgiveness and to begin rebuilding a trusting relationship.
3. Partners attempt to meet each other's emotional and physical needs.
4. Partners verbally express empathy toward each other and demonstrate shared responsibility for reconstructing the relationship.
5. Partners explicitly agree on values to be exercised in the reconstructed relationship.
6. Clients agree to separate and terminate the relationship after a respectful analysis of what led to the breaking of the commitment to faithfulness.

—. _____
_____

—. _____
_____

—. _____
_____

SHORT-TERM OBJECTIVES

▼ 1. Verbally commit to (a) relationship therapy, (b) ambivalence therapy, or (c) separation therapy. (1, 2)

2. Both partners agree to make no threats nor take any action to hurt themselves or others. (3, 4)

THERAPEUTIC INTERVENTIONS

1. Establish the type of treatment that will be conducted by describing and agreeing on (a) relationship therapy (i.e., the affair will end and the goal will be to salvage the relationship); (b) ambivalence therapy (i.e., the goal will be to clarify the future of the relationship and the affair); or (c) separation therapy (i.e., either client is determined to end the relationship, and the goal is to separate under the best possible terms). ▼

2. Negotiate a "noncollusion contract" with both partners, stipulating that the therapist will not agree to secrecy with either partner, thus establishing the therapist's role as working for the mutual well-being of the couple. ▼

3. Ask the partners to agree (a) not to make threats regarding own safety; (b) not to make threats about the safety of others; and (c) to stop discussing difficult topics at home if either partner believes that the discussion is beginning to escalate out-of-control; ask them to avoid deep discussions at home about the

affair or future of the relationship during the first phase of treatment.

4. Assess for suicidality and homicidality by asking each client individually if they have any thoughts, intent, or means to hurt themselves or others.

▽ 3. Practice the use of the "Pause, Calm, and Think" (i.e., time-out) technique to modulate anger. (5, 6)

5. Teach partners the "Pause, Calm, and Think" technique: *Pause* the conversation (i.e., letting the other partner know that you want to pause the discussion); *Calm down* (e.g., focusing on diaphragmatic breathing, counting to 10, focusing on calming self down); *Think* (e.g., taking responsibility for ways in which you are making the conflict worse; planning ways to respond in a mindful, nonescalating manner instead of an automatic, escalating manner; examining thinking by asking self "How TRUE is this thought?" "Is it about JUST THIS SITUATION?" "Will it HELP me get what I want?"). ▽

6. Using role-playing, practice using "Pause, Calm, and Think" within the session with situations from a real-life experience of the couple and then assign at-home practice. ▽

▽ 4. Verbalize and then write about the feelings generated by the affair. (7, 8, 9, 10, 11)

7. In individual sessions with the partners, ask each to discuss emotions elicited by the affair (guilt, anger, shame, ambivalence). ▽

8. If emotional volatility is high, in individual sessions ask each partner to write a letter to the

other conveying the emotions elicited by the affair. ▽

9. In individual sessions, ask each partner to read his/her letter and discuss emotions, bringing out softer emotions (e.g., vulnerability, hurt, regret) and positive feelings toward partner. ▽

10. In an individual session, counsel the participating partner that the hurt partner will be most open to listening to the participating partner if she/he can clearly and considerately convey (a) insight into the meaning of his/her behavior, and (b) authentic contrition for any harm to the hurt partner and to the relationship. ▽

11. Ask each partner to revise his/her letter and to read letter in subsequent conjoint session. ▽

▽ 5. Ask partners to discuss emotions elicited by the affair using the two overarching communication skills: "Be Clear" and "Be Considerate." (12, 13, 14)

12. In a conjoint session, provide guidelines for discussing the affair: (a) be clear (i.e., be specific, share thoughts and feelings, pay attention, ask clarifying questions, summarize content and feelings); and (b) be considerate (i.e., include positives, show consideration when expressing negatives, let partner know that one is listening even if one disagrees, reserve judgment). ▽

13. Ask the partners to discuss feelings and thoughts about the affair and ask them to rate how well they did being clear. ▽

14. Ask the partners to discuss feelings and thoughts about the affair and ask them to rate how well they did being considerate. ▽

6. Verbalize an understanding of common reactions to traumatic events by reviewing the symptoms of Major Depressive Disorder and Posttraumatic Stress Disorder. Identify which symptoms the hurt partner is experiencing. (15)

▽ 7. Hurt partner uses anxiety-management techniques to deal with intrusive thoughts about the affair. (16)

▽ 8. Employ communication skills to express hurt and understanding around affair-related intrusive thoughts. (17)

▽ 9. Each partner constructs and implements a self-change plan regarding coping with emotion-evoking situations. (18, 19)

15. Normalize the hurt partner's experience by giving the partners handouts of common reactions to trauma (e.g., symptoms of Major Depressive Disorder and Post-traumatic Stress Disorder) and assessing which symptoms the hurt partner may be experiencing.

16. Teach and model anxiety-management techniques to enable the hurt partner to cope with intrusive thoughts (e.g., setting aside "worry" times; keeping a journal; using a thought-stopping exercise in which client says "Stop" to self and then substitutes a pleasant, relaxing thought for a disturbing one; using diaphragmatic breathing, where client focuses on slow breathing while concentrating on the diaphragm and silently saying the word "calm" during exhalation). ▽

17. Ask the hurt partner to describe intrusive thoughts about the affair; have the offending partner listen empathically and supportively, using the communication skills of being clear and considerate. ▽

18. Teach the partners the five steps of a Self-Change Plan: (1) Describe the behavior to be changed; (2) Examine the pros and cons of the current behavior; (3) Set a goal, describing as precisely as possible what is to happen; (4) Create an Action Plan, pinpointing a specific plan for enacting the goal; and (5) Evaluate enacting of the plan. Have the partners practice this in session on an emotion-evoking behavior that each would like to change. ▽

19. Ask the partners to make a global evaluation of how they did on implementing the action plan before the next session. The rating scale is 0 = didn't think about it or do it; 1 = thought about it; 2 = gave it a weak try; 3 = tried, partially succeeded; and 4 = did a great job. Ask them to jot down short answers to the following: What did we actually do? What positives resulted? What negatives resulted? What do we need to do from here?▽

▽ 10. Ask the partners to generate factors that they believe contributed to the affair. (20, 21)

20. Ask the partners to generate factors that set the context for the affair from the following domains: couple factors, external factors, individual factors from each partner.▽

21. Ask both partners to describe their beliefs regarding monogamy, need for excitement, escapism, romantic love, admiration, and growth. Ask how these beliefs may have made an affair more likely.▽

▽ 11. Create a summary and formulation of the affair. (22)

22. Ask the partners to summarize their understanding of how and why the affair happened.▽

▽ 12. List the strengths and needs of the relationship and of selves as individuals and how those needs can be met. (23, 24)

23. Assess the current strengths and needs of relationship via interviews and/or questionnaires (e.g., *Couples Satisfaction Inventory* [Funk & Rogge], *Marital Satisfaction Inventory – Revised* [Snyder], *Conflicts and Problem-Solving Scales* [Kerig], *Sexual History Form* [LoPiccolo], *Revised Conflict Tactics Scale* [Straus et al.]); provide feedback regarding test results.▽

24. Have each partner list what changes each would like to feel more loved, respected, or committed; requests should be brief, and ask for observable increases in positive behavior rather than decreases in negative behavior (or assign "How Can We Meet Each Other's Needs and Desires?" in the *Adult Psychotherapy Homework Planner,* 2nd ed. by Jongsma). ▽

▽ 13. Describe pre-affair relationship functioning. (25)

25. Assess the couple's pre-affair functioning by asking each partner for relationship history. Questions could include: "How did the two of you meet?" "What attracted you to each other?" "What qualities or characteristics did you find that you liked about your partner?" "How did the two of you decide to get married?" "How was the adjustment after you got married?" "What have been the highs and lows during dating and your marriage prior to this affair?" ▽

▽ 14. Complete the "Catch Your Partner Pleasing You" exercise at home and bring the list to the next session. (26)

26. Increase caring behaviors and counter negative selective attention by assigning clients the "Catch Your Partner Pleasing You" exercise (i.e., client records at least one positive behavior each day by partner, and at least one by self). ▽

▽ 15. Identify and list behavioral changes for self and partner that would enhance the relationship. (27, 28)

27. Assign each partner to list changes for self and the other that would improve the relationship (e.g., modified instructions for the "Areas of Change" questionnaire [Weiss & Birchler] or assign "Positive and Negative Contributions to the Relationship: Mine and Yours"

in the *Adult Psychotherapy Homework Planner*, 2nd ed. by Jongsma) and then review and discuss the lists in session. ▽

28. Assign each partner to analyze the list of behaviors to be performed by self and the partner that would benefit the relationship; prioritize the list from least to greatest in terms of the effort, trust, and sacrifice each behavior would require (e.g., using "Cost/Benefit Analysis" by Birchler & Weiss). Assign mutual enactment of the behaviors, requiring the least amount of trust and commitment first, following later with those of greater cost. ▽

▽ 16. List relationship issues that contribute to dissatisfaction and unhappiness and agree to address these in future conjoint sessions. (29)

29. Devise and enact a treatment plan for addressing specific couple problems (such as communication issues or sexual dissatisfaction) by reviewing pertinent sections of this *Planner*, negotiating the plan with clients, and executing appropriate interventions. ▽

▽ 17. Verbalize a healthy understanding of forgiveness as a process, not a one-time event. (30, 31, 32, 33, 34).

30. Ask partners to share their definitions of and thoughts about forgiveness. ▽

31. Give the partners Baucom, Snyder, & Gordon's (2008, p. 285) handout listing what forgiveness is ("a process; a release from being dominated by negative thoughts, feelings, and behaviors; a chance to learn about and gain more understanding of your partner, your relationship, and yourself") and what forgiveness is not ("forgetting; reconciliation; an immediate event; a one-time event"). ▽

32. Ask partners to discuss their fears or apprehensions about forgiveness. ▽

33. Ask partners to discuss (a) the repercussions of not forgiving, and (b) the potential payoffs of forgiving. ▽

34. Challenge maladaptive beliefs about forgiveness (e.g., forgiveness implies weakness, condones the affair). ▽

▽ 18. Process a decision regarding reasons for and against remaining in the relationship. (35, 36)

35. Ask partners to discuss the following questions: "Why did we choose to get together?" "How have we developed and matured as individuals and as a unit over the years?" "What are our strengths/accomplishments as a couple?" "What struggles have we survived or surmounted over the years? What are the challenges?" "How does the affair fit into the entire tapestry of our relationship?" ▽

36. Provide partners Baucom, Snyder, & Gordon's (2008, p. 304) handout detailing "Factors to Consider in Reaching a Decision about Your Relationship" and ask them to discuss each item within the session (i.e., domains of "Evaluating Your Partner," "Evaluating Your Relationship," "Evaluating Yourself," and "Evaluating Your Relationship with the Environment, Including Other People"). ▽

▽ 19. Clarify what level of trust exists for various aspects of the relationship. (37)

37. Ask each partner to answer the following questions (Baucom et al., p. 321) "I trust you to _____," "I trust you with _____," "[Right now,] I don't trust you to _____," "[Right now,] I don't trust you

with _____," "I have some but
not full trust regarding _____." ▽

20. Devise and carry out personally
meaningful rituals that aid
relationship healing and
symbolize moving forward
together. (38, 39, 40)

38. Using brainstorming techniques,
help partners devise an appropriate ritual to signify that the
offending partner takes responsibility for the affair and asks for
forgiveness, and that forgiveness
is granted by the hurt partner.

39. Using brainstorming techniques,
help the partners devise an appropriate ritual to signify their mutual
recommitment to an explicitly
monogamous relationship.

40. Help the partners devise a plan
for reclaiming places, people, or
events tarnished by the affair.

___. _____   ___. _____

_____   _____

___. _____   ___. _____

_____   _____

___. _____   ___. _____

_____   _____

DIAGNOSTIC SUGGESTIONS

ICD-9-CM	_ICD-10-CM_	_DSM-5_ Disorder, Condition, or Problem
309.24	F43.22	Adjustment Disorder, With Anxiety
309.0	F43.21	Adjustment Disorder, With Depressed Mood
309.28	F43.23	Adjustment Disorder, With Mixed Anxiety and Depressed Mood
296.xx	F31.xx	Bipolar I Disorder
296.xx	F32.x	Major Depressive Disorder, Single Episode
296.xx	F33.x	Major Depressive Disorder, Recurrent Episode
V61.10	Z63.0	Relationship Distress with Spouse or Intimate Partner
309.81	F43.10	Posttraumatic Stress Disorder

_____ _____ _____

_____ _____ _____

INTERNET SEXUAL USE

BEHAVIORAL DEFINITIONS

1. One partner has been secretly using Internet pornography for voyeuristic sexual pleasure.
2. Partner is distressed by knowledge that mate uses Internet images for sexual gratification.
3. Partner feels that the intimate relationship has been violated by the mate's Internet use, but not in-person involvement with someone on the Internet.
4. Partner feels frustrated that sexual involvement within the primary relationship is not enough.
5. Partner expresses a belief that the mate's Internet sexual involvement may be indicative of, or lead to, in-person sexual involvements.
6. Partner demonstrates anxiety about the mate's Internet sex viewing.
7. Partner cannot sleep through the night due to concern about the mate's Internet pornography use.
8. Partner expresses jealousy regarding the mate's Internet pornography viewing.
9. Partner verbalizes anger toward the mate for Internet pornography use.
10. Partner is considering a separation.
11. Partner now checks the home computer daily to attempt to monitor the mate's past Internet usage.

__. _____

_____

---

*The use of pornography was the subject of intense criticism by feminists in the 1980s, such as Andrea Dworkin, who wrote *Pornography: Men Possessing Women*. There are many correlational and experimental studies that addressed the purported link between use of pornography and sexual assault, but the link has not been well established. On the other hand, the use of pornographic materials by partners in a marriage is a topic that has received relatively little attention, and a recent book, *Sex and Love in Intimate Relationships* (2008), published by the American Psychological Association, had only two pages listed in the index for the term pornography. Further, Stern and Handel (2001) indicated that researchers are divided on whether the use of the Internet for sexual purposes is a blessing or a problem.

—. _____

_____

—. _____

_____

LONG-TERM GOALS

1. Partners agree on what is acceptable use, if any, of Internet sexual material.
2. Partners agree on appropriate boundaries regarding sexual and emotional behavior with others.
3. Partners agree on acceptable use of sexually explicit, non-Internet material such as magazines, DVDs, and movies.
4. The partner who used the Internet sexual material apologizes for any hurt caused to the partner.
5. The partner who used the Internet for sexual gratification understands the perceived threat that his or her partner feels because of the use of the Internet for sexual gratification.
6. Partners agree to work together to rebuild their relationship.
7. Partners agree to separate after discussing the ways that the relationship cannot be repaired and how the use of sexual material in the past, or continuing into the present, makes the relationship not tolerable for one partner.

—. _____

_____

—. _____

_____

—. _____

_____

SHORT-TERM OBJECTIVES	THERAPEUTIC INTERVENTIONS
1. Increase open communication about sexual matters. (1, 2, 3)	1. Ask each partner to describe what has been pleasing about the sexual relationship, now and in the past.
	2. Ask each partner to describe aspects of the sexual relationship

2. Verbalize an understanding of the extent to which the Internet is used for sexual interest and gratification by males and females in the United States. (4, 5)

3. Clarify personal moral position on the viewing of sexually explicit material. (6)

4. Verbalize the extent to which the use of Internet content for sexual gratification is an issue that either partner can accept. (7, 8, 9)

that they would like to see changed.

3. Ask each partner to describe any aspect of the sexual relationship that has been negative.

4. Review the most recent survey data with clients about the use of Internet sexual material by males and females in the United States (e.g., in a nationally representative U.S. sample, Buzzell (2005) found that found 25% of males and 4% of females use Internet pornography while Salwen, O'Leary, Jose, Foran, & Kar (2010) found that 82% of college males and 16% of college females used the Internet for sexual purposes).

5. Review research regarding women's reactions to the discovery of information that their husbands use Internet sexual material.

6. Explore the partners' specific moral views independent of what may be a normative or usual practice for a population regarding viewing the Internet's sexually explicit material.

7. Ask each partner if there are conditions under which some use of sexually explicit material on the computer, in a video, or in print is acceptable.

8. Make clear that the use of Internet material for sexual use is a personal decision of the partners, even though the therapists may differ on whether they believe that use of sexually explicit material on the Internet

5. Describe the use of sexually explicit Internet material for sexual purposes in the past. (10)

6. Therapist describes his or her interpretation of the data regarding the use of sexually explicit material and its impact on relationships in general. (11)

7. Discuss the normative use of sexual fantasies by males and females. (12)

8. The user of the sexually explicit Internet material verbalizes an understanding of the extent of hurt caused in the partner from the use of Internet material. (13)

has any place in a marriage or close relationship.

9. Facilitate a discussion and problem-solving session (if disagreement exists between partners) to reach a resolution regarding whether the use of Internet or other sexually explicit material, together or individually, is acceptable to this couple or not.

10. Ask each partner if they ever have used sexually explicit Internet material together in the past either at home, or in a hotel/motel, and if they would ever have an interest in doing so.

11. To encourage open and honest communication, the therapist describes his or her interpretation of any data related to the use of Internet sexually explicit material and its likely impact on a relationship.

12. Describe data regarding sexual fantasies by males and females; ask the partners to share their indulgence in sexual fantasizing and any beliefs about whether it is a moral issue (or assign "Journal of Sexual Thoughts, Fantasies, Conflicts" in the *Adult Psycho-therapy Homework Planner*, 2nd ed. by Jongsma).

13. Ask the user of the Internet sexual material to describe the ways in which the partner feels hurt and disappointed about the actions involving Internet sexual content; ask the other partner to share feelings of hurt and betrayal experienced as a result of the partner's secret use of Internet pornography.

9. The user of the Internet sexually explicit material verbalizes an understanding that partners often feel anxious and betrayed by use of such material. (14)

10. Partners agree to not lock the computer and to make all files available to both partners. (15)

11. The user of the Internet for sexual gratification commits to a course of action that is acceptable to both partners. (16, 17, 18).

14. Ask the user of the Internet sexual material to describe the ways in which the partner feels threatened by the use of sexually explicit materials on the Internet; ask the partner to add any feelings the other partner failed to verbalize.

15. The past user of the Internet for sexual purposes makes clear that the computer is not locked and files are made available to both individuals through various passwords known to both individuals.

16. Ask the user of the Internet sexual material to commit to a course of action regarding the use of sexually explicit material that will be acceptable to the partner.

17. If there are major differences between the partners regarding use of sexually explicit materials, there may have to be an acknowledgement of this possible unresolved difference and a need to discuss whether this is a difference that can be accepted or whether it will lead to a split in the relationship.

18. Outline a course of behavior for the partner who used Internet sexual content designed to rebuild the trust of the hurt partner (e.g., offending partner signs a pledge to stop Internet sex use, offending partner agrees to not delete the history of Internet sites visited in the future so the other partner can review the use history to verify no sexual sites were visited, download a program that blocks sexual content from being

viewed, offending partner agrees to keep private use of the Internet to a minimum, place the computer in a common area of the house easily seen by all members of the household, etc.).

12. Partners agree that the sexually explicit material will be hidden from children and that they will not have access to such files and content. (19, 20, 21)

19. If the use of Internet sexual content is to continue, the user of the Internet for sexual purposes agrees to use the computer in a fashion that children and adolescents will not be able to see that such files have been used and will not be able to have access to such files.

20. Have the partners discuss how either of them can gain access to the home computer and encourage the sharing of passwords to facilitate the promotion of trust.

21. Assist the partner who feels wronged by the other partner's past use of the Internet to focus on the current behavior of the other partner rather than thinking about blaming the other partner for past wrongs.

13. Verbalize an increased level of trust in the partner who used the Internet for sexual purposes. (22, 23)

22. Assist the partner who feels wronged by the other partner's use of Internet sexual material to focus on things that can be done daily by each to convey caring (or assign "How Can We Meet Each Other's Needs and Desires?" in the *Adult Psychotherapy Homework Planner*, 2nd ed. by Jongsma).

23. Ask the partner who used the Internet for sexual purposes to convey feelings of being attracted emotionally and sexually to the other partner;

check with the other partner as to what means of affection and intimacy are acceptable as the relationship is being repaired.

14. Verbalize feelings of attraction to the partner. (24)

24. Ask the partners to discuss how and why they feel attracted to one another.

15. Partners agree on a path to renewed intimacy between them. (25, 26, 27)

25. Request that the partners, especially the user of the Internet, convey how sexual interactions with the partner are positive.

26. Ask the injured partner to describe any boundaries that are placed on sexual interaction as they rebuild the relationship; explore as to what will be necessary before the boundaries can be removed and normal sexual interaction gradually resumed.

27. Request that the partners, especially the user of the Internet, convey loving and caring to the other partner.

16. Offending partner discloses any unmet needs that the Internet sex was used to satisfy. (28, 29)

28. Explore with the offending partner any needs that were being met through Internet sex and whether those needs can reasonably be met within the relationship with the partner.

29. Explore the offending partner's attitude toward women as sexual objects and whether this contributes to the use of pornography; probe as to where this treatment of women might have been learned in the family of origin and whether the offending partner wants to change this view (or assign "Factors Influencing Negative Sexual Attitudes" in the *Adult*

Psychotherapy Homework Planner, 2nd ed. by Jongsma).

17. Couple amicably agrees to separate if no agreement can be reached about Internet use for sexual gratification. (30)

30. Should there be unresolved differences about the use of sexually explicit materials via the Internet or other sources, explore whether a separation is unavoidable.

__. _____

_____

__. _____

_____

__. _____

_____

__. _____

_____

__. _____

_____

__. _____

_____

DIAGNOSTIC SUGGESTIONS

ICD-9-CM	ICD-10-CM	DSM-5 Disorder, Condition, or Problem
309.24	F43.22	Adjustment Disorder, With Anxiety
309.0	F43.21	Adjustment Disorder, With Depressed Mood
309.28	F43.23	Adjustment Disorder, With Mixed Anxiety and Depressed Mood
296.2x	F32.x	Major Depressive Disorder, Single Episode
296.3x	F33.x	Major Depressive Disorder, Recurrent Episode
V61.10	Z63.0	Relationship Distress with Spouse or Intimate Partner
301.7	F60.2	Antisocial Personality Disorder
301.6	F60.7	Dependent Personality Disorder
_____	_____	_____
_____	_____	_____

INTIMATE PARTNER VIOLENCE (IPV)— INTIMATE TERRORISM[1]

BEHAVIORAL DEFINITIONS

1. Intentional infliction of physical pain or injury on partner, or any action perceived by partner as having that intent (e.g., pushing, shoving, slapping, grabbing, poking, hair-pulling, scratching, pinching, restraining, shaking, throwing, biting, kicking, hitting with fist, hitting with an object, burning, poisoning, stabbing, applying force to throat, cutting off air supply, holding under water, using a weapon, forced sex).
2. Intentional infliction of psychological pain or injury on partner, or any action perceived by partner as having that intent (e.g., berating; disparaging; degrading; humiliating; interrogating; restricting ability to come and go freely; obstructing access to law enforcement, legal, protective, or medical resources; threatening; harming people/things that victim cares about; restricting access to or use of economic resources; isolating from family, friends, or social support resources; stalking).
3. Fear of continuing physical injury or emotional abuse resulting from assaultive acts, threats, intimidation, or berating by abusive partner.

__. _____
   _____
__. _____
   _____
__. _____
   _____

---

[1]Therapists should be cautioned to thoroughly understand the controversies and contraindications of conjoint approaches to abuse (see McCollum & Stith, 2009; McMahon & Pence, 1996; O'Leary, 1996) before attempting to use the suggestions summarized in this chapter.

LONG-TERM GOALS

1. Eliminate all physical aggression in the relationship.
2. Establish safety plan for victim (i.e., concrete plan detailing cues for danger and steps that will be taken to enhance safety).
3. Eliminate all emotional abuse and coercion in the relationship.
4. Examine the pros and cons of remaining in the relationship.

__. _____
   _____
   _____
__. _____
   _____
   _____
__. _____
   _____

SHORT-TERM OBJECTIVES	THERAPEUTIC INTERVENTIONS
1. Describe the frequency, impact, and function of intimate partner violence (IPV). (1, 2)	1. Have both partners privately and confidentially complete the *Revised Conflict Tactics Scale* (CTS2; Straus, Hamby, Boney-McCoy, & Sugarman).
	2. Privately interview each partner about IPV, including (a) antecedents, (b) impact, (c) function, (d) fear, (e) safety issues, (f) extent of psychological coercion or abuse, (g) openness to discuss issues dyadically, and (h) resistance to disclose or discuss violence.
2. Both partners agree to attend individual and/or conjoint sessions as directed by the therapist. (3)	3. If IPV appears out-of-control and/or one partner is fearful of the other, discuss why individual treatment (to eliminate IPV and increase respectful behavior in the relationship) is necessary before conjoint sessions are possible.

3. Both partners cooperate openly with a substance abuse evaluation. (4)

4. If either partner has committed acts of physical or psychological abuse, he/she agrees to sign a nonviolence, nonintimidation contract. (5)

5. Both partners verbalize behavioral definitions of physical, psychological, and sexual abuse. (6)

6. Victim of abuse verbalizes a plan for avoidance or escape if violence erupts or becomes imminent. (7, 8, 9)

4. Assess clients for the presence of chemical dependence in either partner and for its contribution to the abusive behavior pattern.

5. Have both partners sign a contract stipulating that no abusive behavior will occur, regardless of purported provocation of partner.

6. Assist the couple in defining physical, emotional, and sexual abuse in concrete, behavioral terms (e.g., (a) physical— pushing shoving, punching, slapping, grabbing, scratching, throwing objects, biting, using a weapon; (b) emotional— berating; humiliating; interrogating; restricting ability to come and go freely; threatening; isolating from family, friends, or social support resources; (c) sexual—physically forcing or coercing sex acts, engaging in sexual contact when partner was unable to consent [e.g., was asleep, under the influence of alcohol or drugs]).

7. Privately establish a safety plan for victim (i.e., identification of violence cues and resources for assistance; prearrangement of items necessary for escape, such as extra car keys and escape money; and a plan of where to go and what to do if violence erupts).

8. Privately provide the telephone number of local victim services to the victim (ensuring that it is provided in a manner that will not elicit violence from the partner).

7. Both partners identify the behaviors that typically signal the escalation toward violence. (10, 11, 12)

▼ 8. Practice the use of the "Pause, Calm, and Think" (i.e., time-out) technique to modulate anger. (13, 14)

9. Establish a plan for what each partner will do if the nonviolence contract is violated (e.g., call police, leave the situation, arrange for a separation).

10. Assist partners in identifying the behavioral, cognitive, and affective cues of being at low levels of anger (0–30 on a 0–100 scale), moderate levels of anger (31–50 on a 0–100 scale), the danger zone of anger (51–70 on a 0–100 scale), and the extreme zone of anger, where emotional and/or physical violence becomes more likely (71–100 on a 0–100 scale).

11. Train partners to recognize and label emotions other than anger, and to identify emotions that often precede/accompany anger (e.g., hurt, disappointment, sadness).

12. Assign anger-tracking homework that identifies the situations that trigger anger as well as the thoughts and behaviors that occur during anger-eliciting situations (see "Anger Journal" in the *Adult Psychotherapy Homework Planner*, 2nd ed. by Jongsma).

13. Teach partners the "Pause, Calm, and Think" technique: *Pause* the conversation (i.e., letting the other partner know that you want to pause the discussion); *Calm down* (e.g., focusing on diaphragmatic breathing, counting to 10, focusing on calming self down); *Think* (e.g., taking responsibility for ways in which you are making the conflict worse;

pertinent sections of this *Planner*, negotiating a plan with the partners, and executing appropriate interventions.

▽ 19. Partners verbalize an understanding that forgiveness is not a one-time event but a process. (37, 38)

37. Ask the couple to review and discuss Baucom, Snyder, & Gordon's (2008, p. 285) handout listing what forgiveness is ("a process; a release from being dominated by negative thoughts, feelings, and behaviors; a chance to learn about and gain more understanding of your partner, your relationship, and yourself") and what forgiveness is not ("forgetting; reconciliation; an immediate event; a one-time event"). ▽

38. Ask partners to discuss (a) their fears or apprehensions about forgiveness, (b) the repercussions of not forgiving, and (c) the potential payoffs of forgiving. ▽

20. Partners identify negative communication patterns that facilitate aggression and then role-play positive alternative styles of communication. (39, 40)

39. Assist the partners in identifying negative communication patterns that accompany and/or increase the likelihood of physical aggression (e.g., blaming partner for all problems, fast reciprocation of partner's anger, contempt or lack of respect for partner, defensiveness; resistance/refusal to change, coercive control, etc.).

40. Using role-playing and behavior rehearsal, teach the partners positive communication skills (e.g., problem-solving skills, use of "I" statements and listening skills, etc.); assign homework on implementing these skills (e.g., "Applying Problem-Solving to Interpersonal Conflict" in the *Adult Psychotherapy Homework Planner,* 2nd ed. by Jongsma).

—. _____   —. _____
   _____   _____
—. _____   —. _____
   _____   _____
—. _____   —. _____
   _____   _____

DIAGNOSTIC SUGGESTIONS

ICD-9-CM	_ICD-10-CM_	_DSM-5_ Disorder, Condition, or Problem
309.3	F43.24	Adjustment Disorder, With Disturbance of Conduct
305.00	F10.10	Alcohol Use Disorder, Mild
312.34	F63.81	Intermittent Explosive Disorder
296.xx	F32.x	Major Depressive Disorder, Single Episode
296.xx	F33.x	Major Depressive Disorder, Recurrent Episode
V61.10	Z63.0	Relationship Distress with Spouse or Intimate Partner
995.82	T74.31XA	Spouse or Partner Psychological Abuse, Confirmed, Initial Encounter
995.82	T74.31XD	Spouse or Partner Psychological Abuse, Confirmed, Subsequent Encounter
995.82	T74.11XA	Spouse or Partner Violence, Physical, Confirmed, Initial Encounter
995.82	T74.11XD	Spouse or Partner Violence, Physical, Confirmed, Subsequent Encounter
V61.12	Z69.12	Encounter for Mental Health Services for Perpetrator of Spouse or Partner Psychological Abuse
995.81	Z69.11	Encounter for Mental Health Services for Victim of Spouse or Partner Psychological Abuse
309.81	F43.10	Posttraumatic Stress Disorder
301.7	F60.2	Antisocial Personality Disorder
301.83	F60.3	Borderline Personality Disorder
301.81	F60.81	Narcissistic Personality Disorder

_____ _____ _____

_____ _____ _____

PARTNER VIOLENCE—SITUATIONAL (BI-DIRECTIONAL) COUPLE VIOLENCE[1]

BEHAVIORAL DEFINITIONS

1. Nonaccidental use of physical force by both partners during conflict (e.g., throwing objects at partner, pushing, grabbing, hitting).

—. _____

   _____

—. _____

   _____

—. _____

   _____

LONG-TERM GOALS

1. Eliminate all physical aggression in the relationship.
2. Eliminate all emotional abuse and coercion in the relationship.

—. _____

   _____

—. _____

   _____

---

[1]A more expansive description of the interventions summarized in this chapter can be found in LaTaillade, Epstein, & Werlinich, 2006; Mitnick & Heyman, 2009; and Stith & McCullom, 2009. Therapists should be cautioned to thoroughly understand the controversies and contraindications of conjoint approaches to abuse (see O'Leary, 1996; McMahon & Pence, 1996) before attempting to use the suggestions summarized in this chapter.

—. _____

_____

SHORT-TERM OBJECTIVES

THERAPEUTIC INTERVENTIONS

1. Describe the frequency, impact, and function of intimate partner violence (IPV). (1, 2)

1. Have both couples privately and confidentially complete the Revised Conflict Tactics Scale (CTS2; Straus, Hamby, Boney-McCoy, & Sugarman).

2. Privately interview each partner about IPV including (a) antecedents, (b) impact, (c) function, (d) fear, (e) safety issues, (f) extent of psychological coercion or abuse, (g) openness to discuss issues dyadically, and (h) resistance to disclose or discuss violence.

2. Both partners agree to attend individual and/or conjoint sessions as directed by the therapist. (3, 4)

3. If violence arises out of conflict (versus control) and neither partner is fearful of the other, discuss why eliminating IPV should be the first treatment focus.

4. Discuss how IPV is the riskiest, most out-of-control end of their conflict continuum and recommend that conjoint and individual sessions be used to help them best keep conflict from escalating to a dangerous level.

▽ 3. Verbalize an understanding of anger as an adaptive physiological response to fight a perceived threat. (5, 6, 7)

5. Educate the partners that the purpose of anger control is not to eliminate anger, because anger is an important, natural signal that something important is at stake. ▽

6. Educate the partners that anger motivates the body's general response to fight a perceived

threat and that the form these responses take can either help or hurt one's self and the relationship. ▽

7. Educate the partners that the goals of anger control are first to recognize the importance of a provocative situation, and then to manage anger in a way that strengthens rather than weakens the relationship. ▽

▽ 4. Identify the short- and long-term pros and cons of their current style of expressing anger. (8, 9)

8. Have each partner write down and then read aloud what he/she currently does when angry and what the pros (gains) and cons (negative consequences) are in the short term. ▽

9. Have each partner write down and then read aloud what he/she currently does when angry and what the pros (gains) and cons (negative consequences) are in the long term. ▽

▽ 5. Identify successful and unsuccessful anger-management strategies of the past and their consequences. (10, 11)

10. Ask how each partner has tried to manage or de-escalate his/her anger in ways that have worked well in the past. ▽

11. Ask how each partner has tried to manage or de-escalate his/her anger in ways that have been counterproductive. ▽

▽ 6. Identify the "mutual trap" whereby one partner's anger-management strategy is misinterpreted and leads to mutual anger escalation and risk of IPV. (12)

12. Help partners identify ways in which one's de-escalation strategies have been perceived as a provocation by the other (e.g., male partner's leaving the room during a conflict is perceived as "he is ignoring and disrespecting me" by the female partner). ▽

▽ 7. Ask both partners to sign a nonviolence, nonintimidation contract. (13)

13. Have both partners sign a contract stipulating that no aggressive behavior will occur, even when feeling angry. ▽

▽ 8. Both partners identify the behaviors that typically signal the escalation toward violence. (14, 15, 16)

14. Assist the partners in identifying the behavioral, cognitive, and affective cues of being at low levels of anger (0–30 on a 0–100 scale), moderate levels of anger (31–50 on a 0–100 scale), the danger zone of anger (51–70 on a 0–100 scale), and the extreme zone of anger, where emotional and/or physical aggression becomes more likely (71–100 on a 0–100 scale). ▽

15. Train partners to recognize and label emotions other than anger, and to identify emotions that often precede anger. ▽

16. Assign anger-tracking homework that identifies the situations that trigger anger as well as the thoughts and behaviors that occur during anger-eliciting situations (see "Anger Journal" in the *Adult Psychotherapy Homework Planner*, 2nd ed. by Jongsma). ▽

▽ 9. Verbalize recognition of the gradations of anger cues in the three channels of anger (i.e., affective, cognitive, and behavioral). (17)

17. Assist partners in identifying the behavioral, cognitive, and affective cues of being at low levels of anger (0–30 on a 0–100 scale), moderate levels of anger (31–50 on a 0–100 scale), the danger zone of anger (51–70 on a 0–100 scale), and the extreme zone of anger, where emotional and/or physical violence becomes more likely (71–100 on a 0–100 scale). ▽

▽ 10. Identify the degree of anger (on a scale of 0–100) that in the past has led to destructive expressions of anger and lack of control. (18, 19, 20)

18. Inquire at what levels anger has been constructive and destructive in the past. ▽

19. Inquire at what level of anger effective control over behavior begins to erode. ▽

20. Identify at what level of anger the management skills should be exercised. ▽

▽ 11. Practice the use of the "Pause, Calm, and Think" (i.e., time-out) technique to modulate anger. (21, 22)

21. Teach partners the "Pause, Calm, and Think" technique: *Pause* the conversation (i.e., letting the other partner know that you want to pause the discussion); *Calm down* (e.g., focusing on diaphragmatic breathing, counting to 10, focusing on calming self down); *Think* (e.g., taking responsibility for ways in which you are making the conflict worse; planning ways to respond in a mindful, nonescalating manner instead of an automatic, escalating manner; examining thinking by asking self "How TRUE is this thought?" Is it about JUST THIS SITUATION? Will it HELP me get what I want?"). ▽

22. Practice using "Pause, Calm, and Think" within the session with situations from a real-life experience of the couple and then assign at-home practice. ▽

12. Both partners agree not to use in-session material as a weapon outside of the session. (23)

23. Educate the partners regarding the negative impact on the therapy process of being critical or angry with the other partner for what he/she says in a session; solicit an agreement for partners not to punish one another for what is said in a session.

13. Both partners agree to abide by the therapist's directions if the session process becomes destructive. (24)

24. Educate the partners regarding the need for each to respect the other in sessions, especially when feelings become strong; emphasize the therapist's responsibility for maintaining control of the session and for

14. Both partners verbalize negative effects of IPV on each partner, on the relationship, and on their children. (25, 26)

15. Ask each partner to write a plan that provides several alternatives to aggressive behavior when anger is triggered. (27, 28, 29, 30)

▽ 16. Each partner constructs and implements a self-change plan regarding reduction of conflict-escalating behaviors. (31, 32)

interrupting destructive patterns of interaction.

25. Have each partner describe any history of psychological and/or physical victimization each may have experienced in childhood; probe the effects this had on them as a victim (e.g., modeling, excusing, rage, etc.).

26. Ask each partner about the destructive consequences that he/she thinks that IPV has currently (or can have) on each partner and on their children.

27. Educate the partners regarding the differences between nonassertive, assertive, and aggressive communication.

28. Use guided discovery with each partner regarding the function of IPV in their relationship and identify nonaggressive means to accomplish such goals.

29. Assign each partner to list several alternative behaviors to abuse when anger is felt (e.g., using "Pause, Calm, and Think," calling a friend, taking a walk, writing out feelings, deep breathing).

30. Process recent examples of escalating behaviors and review alternative behaviors that were available to the partners (or assign "Alternatives to Destructive Anger" in the *Adult Psychotherapy Homework Planner*, 2nd ed. by Jongsma).

31. Teach the partners the five steps of a Self-Change Plan: (1) Describe the behavior to be changed; (2) Examine the pros and cons of the current behavior;

(3) Set a goal, describing as precisely as possible what is to happen; (4) Create Action Plan, pinpointing a specific plan for enacting the goal; and (5) Evaluate enacting of plan. Have the partners practice this in session on a conflict-escalating behavior that each would like to change.▽

32. Ask the partners to make a global evaluation of how they did on implementing the action plan before the next session. The rating scale is 0 = didn't think about it or do it; 1 = thought about it; 2 = gave it a weak try; 3 = tried, partially succeeded; and 4 = did a great job. Ask them to jot down short answers to the following: What did we actually do? What positives resulted? What negatives resulted? What do we need to do from here?▽

17. Ask partners to report instances where feelings of anger were expressed in a controlled, assertive, respectful manner. (33)

▽ 18. Both partners identify negative communication patterns that facilitate IPV. (34)

▽ 19. Both partners role-play situations wherein they can practice positive communication skills. (35)

33. Highlight and reinforce assertive behaviors in session and reports of successful assertiveness between sessions.

34. Identify negative behaviors and communication patterns that accompany and/or increase the likelihood of IPV (e.g., blocking exit from a room, withdrawal, raising voices, touching or getting too close to each other when anger is escalating, fast reciprocation of partner's anger).▽

35. Using role-playing and behavior rehearsal, teach the partners positive communication skills (e.g., problem-solving skills, use of "I" statements and listening skills, etc.); assign homework on

implementing these skills (e.g., "Applying Problem-Solving to Interpersonal Conflict" in the *Adult Psychotherapy Homework Planner*, 2nd ed. by Jongsma). ▽

—. ————————————   —. ————————————
   ————————————   ————————————
—. ————————————   —. ————————————
   ————————————   ————————————
—. ————————————   —. ————————————
   ————————————   ————————————

DIAGNOSTIC SUGGESTIONS

ICD-9-CM	*ICD-10-CM*	*DSM-5* Disorder, Condition, or Problem
309.4	F43.25	Adjustment Disorder, With Mixed Disturbance of Emotions and Conduct
305.00	F10.10	Alcohol Use Disorder, Mild
303.90	F10.20	Alcohol Use Disorder, Moderate or Severe
300.4	F34.1	Persistent Depressive Disorder
296.xx	F32.x	Major Depressive Disorder, Single Episode
296.xx	F33.x	Major Depressive Disorder, Recurrent Episode
V61.10	Z63.0	Relationship Distress with Spouse or Intimate Partner
995.82	T74.31XA	Spouse or Partner Psychological Abuse, Confirmed, Initial Encounter
995.82	T74.31XD	Spouse or Partner Psychological Abuse, Confirmed, Subsequent Encounter
995.82	T74.11XA	Spouse or Partner Violence, Physical, Confirmed, Initial Encounter
995.82	T74.11XD	Spouse or Partner Violence, Physical, Confirmed, Subsequent Encounter
V61.12	Z69.12	Encounter for Mental Health Services for Perpetrator of Spouse or Partner Psychological Abuse
995.81	Z69.11	Encounter for Mental Health Services for Victim of Spouse or Partner Psychological Abuse

——————— ——————— ————————————————

——————— ——————— ————————————————

INTOLERANCE[1]

BEHAVIORAL DEFINITIONS

1. Consistently rigid attitude on the part of one or both partners that one's own behavior, beliefs, opinions, feelings, and attitudes are right and that the other partner's behavior, beliefs, feelings, and opinions are wrong.
2. Frequent critical comments directed toward the partner for minor traits or habits that could be overlooked.
3. Frequent arguments or disagreements that cause excessive tension.
4. Disagreements that are not restricted to specific problems but are interpreted as symbols of global problems (e.g., partner's personality, lack of love or respect).
5. Attempts to resolve problems result in more tension and conflict than the original problems.
6. Efforts to coercively change partner's behavior that in turn produce coercive responses from the partner, thus causing the relationship to get stuck in a blaming cycle.
7. Expressions of affect that consist almost exclusively of protective emotions such as anger and vengeance, rather than empathy-enhancing emotions such as hurt and fear.

___. _____
   _____
___. _____
   _____
___. _____
   _____

---

[1]A more expansive description of the interventions summarized in this chapter of the *Treatment Planner* can be found in Jacobson & Christensen (1997); Greenberg & Johnson (1988); Watzlawick, Weakland, & Fisch (1974); and Haley (1987).

LONG-TERM GOALS

1. Develop an attitude of acceptance toward each other, forgiveness toward shortcomings, and tolerance toward unique personality and behavior traits.
2. Allow for differences of opinion, beliefs, and feelings without undue and ongoing conflict.
3. Recognize that each partner's problem behaviors are understandable ways of coping with the current relationship environment.
4. Express the underlying softer feelings that promote understanding rather than the more aggressive protective emotions that promote defensiveness and retaliation.
5. Accept the central differences in each other's approach to problems and the world.
6. Increase the meeting of some personal needs outside of the relationship and decrease the exclusive reliance on the partner.

__. _____
_____

__. _____
_____

__. _____
_____

SHORT-TERM OBJECTIVES

▽ 1. Express, verbally and in writing, overall level of relationship dissatisfaction and the specific areas of dissatisfaction. (1)

▽ 2. Identify the strengths and needs of the relationship. (2)

THERAPEUTIC INTERVENTIONS

1. Assess the current level of relationship satisfaction, using interview and/or self-report instruments (e.g., Couples Satisfaction Inventory by Funk and Rogge, Relationship Satisfaction Questionnaire by Burns & Sayers, or the Marital Satisfaction Inventory-Revised by Snyder); provide feedback regarding test results. ▽

2. Have the partners identify the strengths and needs of the relationship via interviews and questionnaires (e.g., *Revised Conflict Tactics Scale* by

Straus et al., *Conflicts and Problem-Solving Scales* by Kerig, or the *Sexual History Form* by LoPiccolo); provide feedback regarding test results. ▽

▽ 3. Describe the origination, development, and present state of the relationship. (3, 4)

3. Assess the current developmental stage of the relationship (e.g., early marriage, parents of young children, long-term marriage); ask the partners to list changes they have noted in their relationship as they moved from one stage to the next. ▽

4. Assess the history of the relationship. Appropriate questions might be: "How did the two of you meet?" "What attracted you to each other? "What qualities or characteristics did you find that you liked about your partner?" "How did the two of you decide to get married?" "What have been the highs and lows during dating and your marriage?" ▽

▽ 4. State the degree of dissatisfaction with the marriage and own thoughts or actions taken toward breaking off the relationship. (5)

5. Assess the steps each partner has taken toward divorce, using the *Marital Status Inventory* by Weiss & Cerreto and by interviews with each partner about his/her sense of hope and vision for the future of the relationship. ▽

▽ 5. Identify current problem areas and changes that self and the other partner could make to improve the relationship. (6, 7)

6. Have partners identify the current problem areas in the relationship. ▽

7. Assign each partner to list changes for self and the other that would improve the relationship (e.g., modified instructions for the "Areas of Change" questionnaire [Weiss and Birchler] or assign "Positive and Negative Contributions to the

Relationship: Mine and Yours" in the *Adult Psychotherapy Homework Planner*, 2nd ed. by Jongsma); review and discuss the lists in session. ▼

6. Identify the core themes of arguments that evoke intolerant responses. (8)

8. Help the partners identify the core themes (e.g., closeness/distance, respect, responsibility, power differentials) that underlie their most intolerant, affectively charged arguments. ▼

7. Identify process by which partners become increasingly polarized. (9)

9. Ask the partners to discuss the ways in which their behavior in response to the core themes has become increasingly polarized (e.g., the closeness seeker becomes clingier while the distancer becomes more withdrawn). ▼

8. Identify the "mutual trap" whereby one partner's response (e.g., withdrawal) evokes the other partner's response (e.g., demand for closeness) and vice versa. (10)

10. Assist the partners in identifying the "mutual trap" underlying their communication problems, whereby one partner's solution to the core theme (e.g., demanding more time together) triggers the other's solution (e.g., withdrawal) and vice versa. ▼

9. Identify instances in which the definition of, or reaction to, a problem has become the main issue; agree to refocus on the problem itself. (11)

11. Assist the partners in identifying instances where their definition of, or reaction to, a problem became the main issue; help them refocus on the original problem using problem-solving skills (i.e., pinpoint the problem, generate multiple possible solutions, list the pros and cons of each possible solution, select a solution for enactment, implement the solution, review the results and modify as necessary). ▼

10. Verbalize an understanding that each partner is reacting in understandable, but ultimately

12. Provide the partners with feedback on their strengths and weaknesses, highlighting those

self-defeating, ways to the other's behavior. (12, 13)

qualities of each that were either strengths or tolerated as weaknesses and which are now perceived as problems. ▽

13. Teach that each partner's emotional and behavioral reactions are understandable, given their respective perceptions of the problem. "Bill believes that sex brings the two of you closer together, so if there is conflict, he thinks that sex might get things back on the right track. But Andrea, you believe that sex starts long before the bedroom and comes after conflict is resolved. So you both end up feeling hurt and angry." ▽

▽ 11. Each partner acknowledges trying to force the other to change to meet the former's expectations. (14)

14. Emphasize that the more each partner tried to force the other to change, the worse their relationship problems became; discuss each partner's perspective on this idea. ▽

▽ 12. Each partner agrees to practice more acceptance of the other's unique feelings, beliefs, behaviors, and opinions. (15, 16)

15. Suggest to the partners that healing will only occur when they return to where all couples start relationships — by acknowledging the other's strengths and tolerating the other's weaknesses; discuss each partner's perspective on this idea. ▽

16. Present the equation "Pain + Accusation = Relationship Discord; Pain − Accusation = Acceptance" (Jacobson & Christensen); have the couple discuss the implications of the equation for their relationship (i.e., mindful accepting of relationship hurts can be more productive than angrily focusing on change or retribution). ▽

▽ 13. Avoid blame and mind reading of partner by speaking only about own thoughts and feelings. (17)

▽ 14. Verbalize an understanding that soft emotions, such as hurt and vulnerability, precede hard/ protective emotions, such as anger and resentment. (18, 19, 20)

15. Identify the ways in which central trait differences between self and partner create friction. (21, 22)

16. Verbally accept the inevitability of trait differences and discuss how to move toward acceptance of each other. (23)

17. Encourage each partner to express him/herself in terms of own thoughts and feelings (using "I" messages), and to not presume to know or speak for the other's thoughts and feelings. ▽

18. Discuss the difference between "hard" (i.e., protective) emotions such as anger, retribution, and resentment, and "soft" (i.e., vulnerable) emotions such as hurt, insecurity, and fear. ▽

19. When the client expresses a hard emotion, have him/her identify the soft emotion that underlies the hard emotion. ▽

20. Have the listener practice empathy by paraphrasing or reflecting the other partner's disclosure of soft emotions that underlie the more easily expressed hard emotions. ▽

21. Guide the partners in discussing central trait differences between them, and the ways these differences have been causing problems (e.g., one partner is solution-oriented and one is expression-oriented).

22. Guide the partners in discussing an event that will be occurring in the near future. Have them identify the ways behavioral and emotional problems resulting from their central trait differences will likely cause difficulty.

23. Encourage the partners to accept the inevitability of their trait differences; have them discuss what they can do to reduce the level of conflict, given that the

trait differences are not going to go away.

17. Track and discuss successful adaptation to the central trait differences. (24)

24. When the partners report that they handled a problem well at home, have them specifically elucidate what they thought or did differently that caused the situation to improve; reinforce the successful acceptance of each other.

18. Track and discuss unsuccessful adaptations to the behavioral trait differences. (25)

25. When partners report that a situation went poorly at home, have them specifically elucidate their respective thoughts, behaviors, and hard emotions (e.g., anger, contempt) that contributed to the difficulty; ask each partner what he/she could have done to practice more acceptance of the other partner.

▽ 19. Each partner constructs and implements a self-change plan regarding an intolerance evoking situation. (26, 27)

26. Teach the partners the five steps of a Self-Change Plan: (1) Describe the behavior to be changed; (2) Examine the pros and cons of the current behavior; (3) Set a goal, describing as precisely as possible what is to happen; (4) Create Action Plan, pinpointing a specific plan for enacting the goal; and (5) Evaluate enacting of the plan. Have the partners practice this in session on an area that has evoked intolerance that each would like to change. ▽

27. Ask the partners to make a global evaluation of how they did on implementing the action plan before the next session. The rating scale is 0 = didn't think about it or do it; 1 = thought about it; 2 = gave it a weak try; 3 = tried, partially succeeded; and 4 = did a great job. Ask them to jot

▽ 20. Demonstrate acceptance by describing the conflict as an external "thing," rather than blaming the other partner. (28)

▽ 21. Demonstrate acceptance by describing positive aspects of the other partner's problem behavior. (29, 30, 31)

▽ 22. Demonstrate acceptance of the problem pattern by admitting the inevitability of its reoccurrence, and by practicing the reoccurrence in session. (32, 33)

down short answers to the following: What did we actually do? What positives resulted? What negatives resulted? What do we need to do from here?▽

28. Reframe the problematic interactional patterns as an external problem (an "it"), rather than as the fault of either partner; ask each partner to reflect on how this change reduces defensiveness, hurt, and anger.▽

29. Have one partner describe the positive features of the other's problematic behavior (i.e., the ways the other partner's behavior actually serves a positive function in the relationship).▽

30. If a partner has difficulty finding positive features, reframe the other partner's problematic behavior in terms of how it balances the client's behavior (e.g., a hyper-responsible man may get involved with a spontaneous woman).▽

31. Explain to both of the partners that they each are bringing only one part of the balancing act to the relationship; ask each whether there is anything that he/she can learn from the other partner's opposite, but balancing, behavior that formerly has been upsetting to him/her.▽

32. Explain to clients that no matter how they try to improve, they will sometimes fall back into their well-practiced, old patterns; advise them to prepare for this and to not be too surprised or disappointed when the inevitable

occurs; ask them what each can do to reverse this relapse into old patterns. ▽

33. Have the couple practice falling back into their old patterns in session; ask each partner to express his/her thoughts and feelings, with the therapist emphasizing the naturalness of each person's perspective and response. ▽

▽ 23. Increase understanding of the problem pattern by demonstrating it when not upset. (34, 35)

34. Assign each partner to enact or practice his/her problematic behaviors (e.g., Bill asking for sex following a tense time, even if he doesn't want sex) several times during the week, to get a sense of the pattern when he/she is not already upset. ▽

35. Assign each partner to let the other in on the practiced problematic behaviors soon after the argument ensues, to prevent further escalation. ▽

▽ 24. Practice problem enactment and discussion of soft emotions following the "practiced" demonstration. (36, 37)

36. Have the partners take turns practicing problematic behaviors in session; review and discuss the emotional reactions. ▽

37. Review and discuss the emotional reaction to the practicing homework in the subsequent session. ▽

25. Identify acceptable resources outside the relationship for meeting some important personal needs. (38)

38. Help the partners identify acceptable ways of satisfying needs outside of the relationship, to reduce the pressure on the relationship to meet all of their core needs.

26. Practice alternative, constructive means for satisfying important personal needs within the relationship. (39, 40)

39. Help the partners list ways in which they could satisfy needs arising from their soft emotions (e.g., relief from hurt or fear)

within the relationship, without resorting to destructive, hard emotion-laced escalation (or assign "How Can We Meet Each Other's Needs and Desires?" in the *Adult Psychotherapy Home-work Planner*, 2nd ed. by Jongsma).

40. Help clients rehearse, in session, alternative means of meeting needs arising from their soft emotions.

__. _____   __. _____
    _____   _____
__. _____   __. _____
    _____   _____
__. _____   __. _____
    _____   _____

DIAGNOSTIC SUGGESTIONS

ICD-9-CM	*ICD-10-CM*	*DSM-5* Disorder, Condition, or Problem
309.4	F43.25	Adjustment Disorder, With Mixed Disturbance of Emotions and Conduct
309.3	F43.24	Adjustment Disorder, With Disturbance of Conduct
305.00	F10.10	Alcohol Use Disorder, Mild
296.xx	F32.x	Major Depressive Disorder, Single Episode
296.xx	F33.x	Major Depressive Disorder, Recurrent Episode
V61.10	Z63.0	Relationship Distress with Spouse or Intimate Partner
V61.12	Z69.12	Encounter for Mental Health Services for Perpetrator of Spouse or Partner Violence, Physical
995.81	Z69.11	Encounter for Mental Health Services for Victim of Spouse or Partner Violence, Physical
301.7	F60.2	Antisocial Personality Disorder
301.83	F60.3	Borderline Personality Disorder
301.50	F60.4	Histrionic Personality Disorder
_____	_____	_____
_____	_____	_____

JEALOUSY[1]

BEHAVIORAL DEFINITIONS

1. Concerns about loss of partner's affection, attention, and love to a rival.
2. Obsessive thoughts and/or frequent accusations about one's partner being with another person and being verbally and/or physically intimate with that person.
3. Monitoring of partner's activities (e.g., mileage, appointments, travel, money spent) based on the suspicion that the partner is having an affair.
4. Controlling actions to restrict the activity of the partner (e.g., demanding partner stay at home; limiting the amount of money available to partner) based in fear of losing the partner's attention.
5. Feelings of anger regarding a perceived loss of face to friends and family because partner did not show enough loyalty or attention to self.
6. Periodic angry outbursts directed at partner.
7. Blaming their partner for not being trustworthy or honest.
8. Depressive feelings regarding perceived loss of partner's attention, affection, and love.
9. Fear of being left alone and not being able to cope.
10. General anxiety and periodic physiological symptoms such as sleep disturbance, rapid heartbeat, tightness of chest, sweating, shortness of breath, dizziness, shakiness, and an empty feeling in the stomach.

__. _____
   _____
   _____
__. _____
   _____
   _____
__. _____
   _____

---

[1]If the level of jealousy is especially high, it may be advantageous for the therapist to see the jealous partner individually for at least a brief course of therapy before couple therapy is started. This especially may be the case with jealousy that immediately follows the discovery of an affair, or in cases of jealousy with paranoid qualities.

LONG-TERM GOALS

1. Eliminate jealous thoughts and unfounded accusations of unfaithfulness.
2. Eliminate controlling behaviors.
3. Eliminate critical and angry comments associated with jealousy.
4. Eliminate revengeful actions by the jealous partner (damaging property, destroying pictures of men/women who remind the jealous partner of the perceived rival).
5. Restore feelings of trust.

—. _____
   _____
—. _____
   _____
—. _____
   _____

SHORT-TERM OBJECTIVES

THERAPEUTIC INTERVENTIONS

1. Clarify and identify the jealous and controlling behaviors in the relationship. (1, 2)

1. In individual sessions, ask both partners to describe jealous thoughts/behaviors of the jealous partner.

2. In individual sessions, ask both partners to describe the controlling behaviors of the jealous partner.

2. Describe any history of and reasons for affairs. (3, 4)

3. In individual sessions, ask each partner about current or past affairs.

4. Ask the partners to summarize their understanding of how and why the past affair happened.

▽ 3. Verbalize an understanding of forgiveness as a process, not a one-time event. (5, 6, 7, 8, 9)

5. Ask the partners to share their definitions of and thoughts about forgiveness. ▽

6. Provide a copy of Baucom, Snyder, & Gordon's (2009, p. 285) handout listing what

forgiveness is ("a process; a release from being dominated by negative thoughts, feelings, and behaviors; a chance to learn about and gain more understanding of your partner, your relationship, and yourself") and what forgiveness is not ("forgetting; reconciliation; an immediate event; a one-time event"). ▽

7. Ask the partners to discuss their fears or apprehensions about forgiveness. ▽

8. Ask the partners to discuss (a) the repercussions of not forgiving and (b) the potential payoffs of forgiving. ▽

9. Challenge maladaptive beliefs about forgiveness (e.g., forgiveness implies weakness, condones the affair, excuses the affair, etc.). ▽

▽ 4. Process a decision regarding reasons for and against remaining in the relationship. (10, 11)

10. Ask both partners to discuss the following questions: "Why did we choose to get together?" "How have we developed and matured as individuals and as a unit over the years?" "What are our strengths/ accomplishments as a couple?" "What struggles have we survived or surmounted over the years?" "What are the challenges?" "How does the past affair fit into the entire tapestry of our relationship?" ▽

11. Provide partners with Baucom, Snyder, & Gordon's (2009, p. 304) handout detailing "Factors to Consider in Reaching a Decision about Your Relationship" and ask them to discuss each item within the

session (i.e., domains of "Evaluating Your Partner," "Evaluating Your Relationship," "Evaluating Yourself," and "Evaluating Your Relationship with the Environment, Including Other People"). ▽

▽ 5. Clarify what level of trust exists for various aspects of the relationship. (12)

12. Ask each partner to complete the following statements (Baucom et al., 2009, p. 321) "I trust you to _____," "I trust you with _____," "[Right now,] I don't trust you to _____," "[Right now,] I don't trust you with _____," "I have some but not full trust regarding _____." ▽

6. Verbalize a differentiation between the rational and irrational feelings of jealousy. (13)

13. Ask both partners to describe what seem to be the rational and irrational aspects of the jealous partner's thoughts/behaviors.

7. Verbalize and then write about the feelings generated by the jealousy. (14, 15, 16, 17, 18)

14. Ask each partner to discuss emotions elicited by jealousy (guilt, anger, shame, ambivalence).

15. If emotional volatility is high, in individual sessions ask each partner to write a letter to the other. The letter will convey the emotions evoked by the jealousy.

16. In individual sessions, ask each partner to read his/her letter and discuss emotions, bringing out softer emotions (e.g., vulnerability, hurt, regret) and positive feelings toward partner.

17. In individual sessions, counsel the jealous partner that the nonjealous partner will be most open to listening if he/she can clearly and considerately convey (a) insight into the meaning of his/her behavior, and (b) authentic contrition for the harm

to the nonjealous partner and to the relationship.

18. Ask each partner to revise his/her letter and to read letter in subsequent conjoint session.

▽ 8. Ask partners to discuss emotions elicited by the jealousy using the two overarching communication skills: "Be Clear" and "Be Considerate." (19, 20, 21)

19. In conjoint session, provide guidelines for discussing the jealousy: (a) be clear (i.e., be specific, share thoughts and feelings, pay attention, ask clarifying questions, summarize content and feelings); and (b) be considerate (i.e., include positives, show consideration when expressing negatives, let partner know that one is listening even if one disagrees, reserve judgment).▽

20. Ask partners to discuss feelings and thoughts about the jealousy and ask them to rate how well they did being clear.▽

21. Ask partners to discuss feelings and thoughts about the jealousy and ask them to rate how well they did being considerate.▽

▽ 9. Jealous partner to use anxiety-management techniques to deal with intrusive jealous thoughts. (22)

22. Teach and model anxiety-management techniques to enable jealous partner to cope with intrusive thoughts (e.g., setting aside "worry" times; keeping a journal; using a thought-stopping exercise in which client says "Stop" to self and then substitutes a pleasant, relaxing thought for a disturbing one; using diaphragmatic breathing, where client focuses on slow breathing while concentrating on the diaphragm and silently saying the word "calm" during exhalation).▽

▽ 10. Employ communication skills to express hurt and understanding around jealousy-related intrusive thoughts. (23)

▽ 11. Each partner constructs and implements a self-change plan regarding coping with emotion-evoking situations (including jealousy). (24, 25)

12. Ask partners to generate factors that they believe contributed to the jealousy. (26, 27, 28)

23. Ask jealous partner to describe intrusive thoughts about the jealousy; have non-jealous partner listen empathically and supportively, using communication skills of being clear and considerate. ▽

24. Teach partners the five steps of a Self-Change Plan: (1) Describe the behavior to be changed; (2) Examine the pros and cons of the current behavior; (3) Set a goal, describing as precisely as possible what is to happen; (4) Create Action Plan, pinpointing a specific plan for enacting the goal; and (5) Evaluate enacting of the plan. Have the partners practice this in session on an emotion-evoking behavior each would like to change. ▽

25. Ask the partners to make a global evaluation of how they did on implementing the action plan before the next session. The rating scale is 0 = didn't think about it or do it; 1 = thought about it; 2 = gave it a weak try; 3 = tried, partially succeeded; and 4 = did a great job; ask them to jot down short answers to the following: What did we actually do? What positives resulted? What negatives resulted? What do we need to do from here? ▽

26. Ask the jealous partner to elaborate on hurts from past and current partners that have fueled feelings of jealousy and distrust.

27. Ask the partners to generate factors that set the context for the jealousy from the following domains: couple factors (e.g., not

sharing intimate thoughts with each other), external factors (e.g., working long hours with an attractive colleague), and individual factors (e.g., family-of-origin experiences with infidelity) from each partner.

28 Ask each partner to describe his/her beliefs regarding monogamy, need for excitement, escapism, romantic love, admiration, and growth; have the partners discuss how these beliefs may have made jealousy more likely.

▽ 13. List the strengths and needs of the relationship and of selves as individuals and how those needs can be met. (29, 30)

29. Assess current strengths and needs of the partners' relationship via interviews and/or questionnaires (e.g., *Couples Satisfaction Inventory* by Funk & Rogge, *Marital Satisfaction Inventory – Revised* by Snyder, *Conflicts and Problem-Solving Scales* by Kerig, *Sexual History Form* by LoPiccolo, *Revised Conflict Tactics Scale* by Straus et al.); provide feedback regarding test results. ▽

30. Have each partner list what changes each would like to feel more loved, respected, or committed; requests should be brief, and ask for observable increases in positive behavior rather than decreases in negative behavior (or assign "How Can We Meet Each Other's Needs and Desires?" in the *Adult Psychotherapy Homework Planner,* 2nd ed. by Jongsma). ▽

▽ 14. Describe the history of relationship functioning. (31)

31. Assess functioning by asking each partner for relationship history; Questions could include: "How did the two of you meet?"

"What attracted you to each other?" "What qualities or characteristics did you find that you liked about your partner?" "How did the two of you decide to get married?" "How was the adjustment after you got married?" "What have been the highs and lows during dating and your marriage?"▽

15. Create jealousy timeline for current relationship. (32)

32. Beginning with their first meeting, draw a timeline and have partners rate the level of jealousy between 0 (no jealousy) and 100 (most jealousy ever experienced); ask partners to elaborate on the events/contexts that are related to major increases and decreases in jealousy from their first meeting until the present.

▽ 16. Complete the "Catch Your Partner Pleasing You" exercise at home and bring the list to the next session. (33)

33. Increase caring behaviors and counter negative selective attention by assigning clients the "Catch Your Partner Pleasing You" exercise (i.e., client records at least one positive behavior each day by partner, and at least one by self).▽

▽ 17. Identify and list behavioral changes for self and partner that would enhance the relationship. (34, 35)

34. Assign each partner to list changes for self and the other that would improve the relationship (e.g., modified instructions for the "Areas of Change" questionnaire by Weiss & Birchler or assign "Positive and Negative Contributions to the Relationship: Mine and Yours" in the *Adult Psychotherapy Homework Planner,* 2nd ed. by Jongsma); review and discuss the lists in session.▽

35. Assign each partner to analyze the list of behaviors to be

performed by self and the partner that would benefit the relationship; prioritize the list from least to greatest in terms of the effort, trust, and sacrifice each behavior would require (e.g., using "Cost/Benefit Analysis" by Weiss). Assign mutual enactment of the behaviors, requiring the least amount of trust and commitment first, following later with those of greater cost. ▽

18. List relationship issues that contribute to dissatisfaction and unhappiness and agree to address these in future conjoint sessions. (36)

36. Devise and enact a treatment plan for addressing specific couple problems (such as communication issues or sexual dissatisfaction) by reviewing pertinent sections of this *Planner*, negotiating plan with clients, and executing appropriate interventions.

19. Jealous partner list behaviors that can be changed by other partner to minimize jealousy. (37)

37. Have jealous partner list and prioritize what he/she would like the other partner to do to minimize own feelings of jealousy.

20. Discuss requests made by the jealous partner and come to an agreement about the behavioral changes that seem reasonable to help minimize jealousy. (38, 39)

38. Encourage the jealous partner to reconsider some requests for change he/she has made regarding partner that may be self-defeating or overly demanding.

39. Encourage the partners to jointly conclude which behaviors would be reasonable for reaching a goal of minimizing jealousy.

▽ 21. Using problem-solving techniques, negotiate rules regarding each partner's interaction with others in social situations. (40)

40. Using problem-solving techniques (e.g., define the problem specifically, generate at least two solutions, weigh the pros/cons of each solution before choosing one solution, enact a

solution, evaluate the results, modify the solution if necessary); negotiate rules about how partners should behave when around other people, the degree of individual freedom each should have, and behaviors that are explicitly permitted and explicitly prohibited. ▽

__. _____   __. _____
  _____   _____

__. _____   __. _____
  _____   _____

__. _____   __. _____
  _____   _____

DIAGNOSTIC SUGGESTIONS

ICD-9-CM	ICD-10-CM	DSM-5 Disorder, Condition, or Problem
309.4	F43.25	Adjustment Disorder, With Mixed Disturbance of Emotions and Conduct
309.3	F43.24	Adjustment Disorder, With Disturbance of Conduct
305.00	F10.10	Alcohol Use Disorder, Mild
296.xx	F31.xx	Bipolar I Disorder
296.xx	F32.x	Major Depressive Disorder, Single Episode
296.xx	F33.x	Major Depressive Disorder, Recurrent Episode
V61.10	Z63.0	Relationship Distress with Spouse or Intimate Partner
V61.12	Z69.12	Encounter for Mental Health Services for Perpetrator of Spouse or Partner Violence, Physical
995.81	Z69.11	Encounter for Mental Health Services for Victim of Spouse or Partner Violence, Physical
301.7	F60.2	Antisocial Personality Disorder
301.83	F60.3	Borderline Personality Disorder
301.81	F60.81	Narcissistic Personality Disorder
_____	_____	_____
_____	_____	_____

JOB STRESS

BEHAVIORAL DEFINITIONS

1. Lack of respect for, and resultant lack of support of, supervisor.
2. Worry stemming from employer's threats to replace higher-salaried people with lower-salaried individuals through plant move or layoffs.
3. Frustration and helplessness stemming from competing company's product that could replace mainstay product of the partner's employer.
4. Anxiety caused by highly critical supervisor.
5. Anxiety stemming from employer's reduction of salaries due to decreasing profits.
6. Fear of being unable to master employer's new computer software system.
7. Concern and anger stemming from being moved to a less desirable office (e.g., one with less space, no windows).
8. Depression caused by being fired or laid off.
9. Inability to get along with peers at work.
10. Anxiety, frustration, and/or anger stemming from the belief that own excellence and hard work is neither recognized nor rewarded.
11. Intermittent depression, low energy, and sleep disturbance.
12. Lack of interest in sexual interactions.
13. Anger and intermittently explosive behavior.
14. Unable to find permanent employment.
15. Employment hours were reduced resulting in less income.

___. _____

_____

___. _____

_____

___. _____

_____

LONG-TERM GOALS

1. Increase positive coping behaviors to reduce negative effects of work stress.
2. Increase positive attitudes about job and/or job alternatives.
3. Begin the process of searching for new and more desirable employment.
4. Obtain further training and/or retraining in work-related skills.
5. Reduce depressed mood and sleep disturbance while increasing energy level.
6. Reduce anger and terminate explosive outbursts at work and at home.

—. _____

_____

—. _____

_____

—. _____

_____

SHORT-TERM OBJECTIVES

▽ 1. Identify sources of irritability, depressed mood, and related depressive symptoms. (1, 2, 3, 4)

THERAPEUTIC INTERVENTIONS

1. Assist the stressed partner in listing all the work-related factors that make him/her depressed, angry, or discouraged. ▽

2. Have the stressed partner rank in order the employment factors that are most significant in causing his/her depression. ▽

3. Develop a plan with the stressed partner to address coping (e.g., increased recreational diversions, relaxation and deep-breathing techniques, physical exercise, assertiveness training, job transfer) with the most important work-related stressors. ▽

4. Have the stressed partner rank in order the perceived causes (and associated factors) of depression. ▽

▽ 2. Identify sources of anger. (5, 6, 7, 8)

5. Have the stressed partner list all of the job-related factors that make him/her angry. ▽

6. Ask the stressed partner to rank in order the most important job-related factors that make him/her angry. ▽

7. Develop a plan to resolve (e.g., increased communication, assertiveness training, problem pinpointing/resolution training) causes for anger. ▽

8. Have the other partner rank in order the perceived causes (and associated factors) of anger in the job-stressed partner. ▽

▽ 3. Explore whether some other mental health problem is the primary cause for unhappiness. (9)

9. Explore with the partners whether some other individual problem (e.g., chronic depression, alcohol abuse, or sleep disorder) may be the primary cause for unhappiness. ▽

4. Use antidepressant or anti-anxiety medication as prescribed by physician. (10)

10. Refer the stressed partner to a physician for medication, and encourage him/her to take medication regularly.

▽ 5. Consider a medical leave of absence from work responsibilities. (11, 12)

11. Explore with the stressed partner the advantages and disadvantages of taking medical leave. ▽

12. Obtain input from the other partner about the advantages and disadvantages of medical leave. ▽

▽ 6. Assess and articulate own ability to handle technical requirements of job. (13, 14)

13. Ask the stressed partner to obtain feedback about job performance from supervisor and peers, if doing so is practical. ▽

14. Have the partner assess his/her ability to perform the technical aspects of the job. ▽

▽ 7. Enlist support of partner to help cope with job stress. (15, 16)

8. Contact agencies that provide instruction and training in areas relevant to current job. (17, 18)

9. Commit to further instruction and/or training to enhance job skills. (19)

10. Attend classes to obtain further education and vocational training or obtain information on computer-assisted home-teaching packages that would enhance job skills. (20, 21)

▽ 11. Make positive statements to self and others about the future. (22, 23, 24, 25)

15. Have the other partner advise the stressed partner on how he/she can best support him/her during the next few months to assist in coping with job stress. ▽

16. Explore whether the partner can help the stressed partner's situation by providing more financial support. ▽

17. Refer the stressed partner to an agency that could provide assessment and/or job-skill training.

18. Refer the stressed partner to an educational institution with curriculum that could enhance job skills and/or enable the partner to obtain new degree or certificate.

19. Have the stressed partner verbally commit to further training or education.

20. Support and reinforce the stressed partner in efforts to pursue further training through an educational institution or via computer-assisted home instruction.

21. Explore with the stressed partner possible alternative jobs that would be available upon completion of a course of study.

22. Assign the stressed partner to make one positive statement to someone at work each day about the work and/or work environment. ▽

23. Assign the other partner to tell the stressed partner something positive about work each day. ▽

24. Assign the other partner to support the stressed partner's

affirming of positive aspects of work and to add own positive perspective on the stressed partner's work. ▽

25. Explore the stressed partner's cognitions for self-defeating messages that lead to feelings of hopelessness and helplessness; assist the partner in replacing these negative thoughts with more realistic, energizing thoughts that lead to constructive actions (or assign "A Vocational Action Plan" in the *Adult Psychotherapy Homework Planner,* 2nd ed. by Jongsma). ▽

▽ 12. Decrease critical and complaining comments at work and at home. (26, 27, 28)

26. Advise the stressed partner to avoid making negative comments about work to colleagues. ▽

27. Assign the other partner to provide support and reinforcement for the stressed partner's decreasing negative comments about work. ▽

28. Have the stressed partner and the other partner list advantages of reducing complaining and critical comments about the work situation. ▽

13. Make some acceptable changes in work space to enhance physical and emotional aspects of working environment. (29, 30, 31)

29. Explore with the partner possible acceptable ways of making his/her work space or office more pleasant and attractive.

30. Encourage the partner to take something attractive to work to decorate his/her office (e.g. picture, poster, clock).

31. Encourage the partner to clean his/her office and arrange things neatly.

▽ 14. Limit time on work activities to allow for family time. (32, 33)

15. Read sources regarding family and work balance. (34)

32. Assist the partners in reviewing their weekly schedules in order to set aside recurring family time.▽

33. Ask the partners to agree to say "no" gracefully when family priorities are threatened.▽

34. Read the following: *Work-Life Balance for Dummies* by Mumford & Lockette, *The One Minute Manager Balances Work and Life* by Blanchard, Edington, & Blanchard, or *First Things First* by Covey, Merrill, & Merrill.

—. _____

_____

—. _____

_____

—. _____

_____

—. _____

_____

—. _____

_____

—. _____

_____

DIAGNOSTIC SUGGESTIONS

ICD-9-CM	*ICD-10-CM*	*DSM-5* Disorder, Condition, or Problem
309.24	F43.22	Adjustment Disorder, With Anxiety
309.0	F43.21	Adjustment Disorder, With Depressed Mood
309.28	F43.23	Adjustment Disorder, With Mixed Anxiety and Depressed Mood
300.4	F34.1	Persistent Depressive Disorder
300.02	F41.1	Generalized Anxiety Disorder
296.xx	F32.x	Major Depressive Disorder, Single Episode
296.xx	F33.x	Major Depressive Disorder, Recurrent Episode
301.82	F60.6	Avoidant Personality Disorder
301.6	F60.7	Dependent Personality Disorder
_____	_____	_____
_____	_____	_____

LIFE-CHANGING EVENTS

BEHAVIORAL DEFINITIONS

1. Individual distress (e.g., anxiety, depression) following an environmental event that requires adaptation (e.g., employment change, relocation, serious illness, etc.).
2. Increased relationship distress due to perceived inability to support each other emotionally during a transition marked by significant stress.
3. Increased relationship distress due to arguments resulting from the transition.
4. Relationship distress caused by a change in employment situation (i.e., new responsibilities, increased travel, new employer, and/or changes in compensation).
5. Relationship distress caused by the diagnosis of a significant chronic illness of their child.
6. Relationship distress caused by a move to a new community and resultant severing of existing social support network and need for establishing a new one.
7. Relationship distress caused by deterioration in health or debilitating injury and resulting in significant changes in lifestyle.

__. _____
   _____
__. _____
   _____
__. _____
   _____

LONG-TERM GOALS

1. Resolve negative feelings and relationship conflict generated by the life-changing event, making adaptive responses to the situation that foster individual and relationship growth.

2. Adapt to the life-changing event by using personal, relationship, and social resources.
3. Recognize the difference between transition problems that can be changed and those that cannot.
4. Strengthen the relationship by being accepting of, and supportive of, each other.
5. As a couple, seek social supports to help buffer negative effects of the transition.

—. _____
   _____

—. _____
   _____

—. _____
   _____

SHORT-TERM OBJECTIVES	**THERAPEUTIC INTERVENTIONS**
1. Describe the life-changing event and its impact on each partner and the relationship. (1, 2)	1. Have each partner define the life-changing event and its meaning to him/her individually and to the relationship.
	2. Determine whether the event was expected or unexpected.
▽ 2. Verbalize acceptance of the fact that change is inevitable in everyone's life. (3)	3. Normalize the process of change in everyone's life by reviewing common changes that occur in the various developmental stages of life. ▽
▽ 3. Each partner identifies the stage of change in adapting to current life-changing event. (4)	4. Administer "Stages of Change" questionnaire (Prochaska et al., 1994) to determine which of the four stages of change (pre-contemplation, contemplation, action, or maintenance) best describes each partner's current adaptation to the transition; review and discuss the results with partners. ▽

▽ 4. List ways of coping with the change that have been positive and productive. (5)

▽ 5. List ways of coping with the change that have been negative and counterproductive. (6)

▽ 6. Identify the positive and negative aspects of the life change. (7)

▽ 7. Describe the anxiety and stress that the life-changing event has produced. (8)

▽ 8. Identify the pros and cons of the life-changing event for self individually. (9, 10)

▽ 9. Identify the pros and cons of the life-changing event for the relationship. (11, 12)

▽ 10. Describe the day-to-day changes that the life-changing event will precipitate. (13)

5. Ask each partner to describe his/her ways of coping with the current stressor that are productive. ▽

6. Ask each partner to describe his/her ways of coping with the current stressor that are counterproductive. ▽

7. Have partners discuss the positive and negative aspects of the life-changing event. ▽

8. Teach that anxiety and strain are normal responses when coping with both good and bad life-changing events (e.g., the birth of a child, diagnosis of an illness, a job layoff). ▽

9. Ask one partner to describe how the life-changing event may have positive effects for him/her individually, and have the other partner respond using supportive listener skills (i.e., paraphrasing, reflecting). ▽

10. Ask one partner to describe how the life-changing event may have negative effects for him/her individually, and have the other partner respond using supportive listener skills (i.e., paraphrasing, reflecting). ▽

11. Ask each partner to describe how the life-changing event may have positive effects on the relationship. ▽

12. Ask each partner to describe how the life-changing event may have negative effects on the relationship. ▽

13. Help the partners identify the concrete, day-to-day changes that the life-changing event will require. ▽

▽ 11. Identify goals for short-term changes to be made in adapting to the current situation. (14)

▽ 12. Identify goals for long-term changes to be made in adapting to the current situation. (15)

▽ 13. Increase use of empathic listening skills in response to the other partner, stating what behaviors the partner could increase and those he/she could decrease in order to be supportive. (16, 17)

▽ 14. Identify support systems outside of the relationship that are currently available or can be added to assist in coping with the change. (18)

▽ 15. Increase the use of individualized stress-reducing activities. (19, 20)

▽ 16. Increase the use of shared stress-reducing activities. (21)

▽ 17. Identify those problems that can be controlled, and those that must be accepted and adapted to. (22)

14. Help each partner identify changes that will have to be made by self in the short term. ▽

15. Help each partner identify changes that have to be made by self for the long term. ▽

16. Have each partner describe what supportive behaviors he/she could increase during the transition, and have other partner respond using supportive listener skills. ▽

17. Have each partner describe what negative behaviors he/she could decrease during the transition, and have other partner respond using supportive listener skills. ▽

18. Explore the support systems already in place outside of the relationship that can aid both partners in coping (e.g., friends, self-help and support groups, religious organizations). ▽

19. Teach personal relaxation techniques (e.g., diaphragmatic breathing, progressive relaxation) that can be used as coping mechanisms, to deal with the stress of life-changing events. ▽

20. Encourage each partner to commit to regular individual stress-reducing activities (e.g., relaxation techniques, exercise, music, hobbies). ▽

21. Encourage both partners to commit to regular couple stress-reducing activities (e.g., foot rubs, social engagements, walks, sex, shared hobbies). ▽

22. Help the partners identify which problems are within their control and which problems to which they need to adapt. ▽

▼ 18. Pinpoint the changes that will be required in the personal, relational, and social domains. (23)

19. Using brainstorming techniques develop at least two solutions to each change that is required. (24, 25)

20. Agree to a specific plan for enacting the selected solutions. (26)

▼ 21. Validate and empathize with other partner's feelings regarding the difficulty of accepting a problem that cannot be changed or controlled. (27, 28, 29)

23. To set stage for solving problems within partners' control, have them pinpoint adaptations required in the personal, relational, and social domains. ▼

24. Teach partners to brainstorm at least two solutions for each problem before trying to solve the problem, and have them practice this in session.

25. Teach partners to evaluate the pros and cons of the brain-stormed solutions, and have them practice this in session.

26. Teach partners to make a specific, pinpointed plan for each solution, including a time in the future to evaluate the progress on the solution; have them practice this in session.

27. For problems outside partners' control, role-play support and acceptance by having one person "vent" about difficult aspects of coping with the transition and ask the listener to practice validation skills (i.e., conveying that he/she understands and can empathize with the speaker's feelings, even if he/she does not agree). ▼

28. When dealing with problems out-side the partners' control instruct them to avoid trying to solve the external problem, but instead support each other and problem-solve how they can accept the unchangeable problem. ▼

29. If understanding or problem-solving is at an impasse, have partners switch places and then discuss the issue from the other's perspective. ▼

▽ 22. Describe what in six months could be the best possible outcome to the life-changing event. (30)

▽ 23. Increase the frequency of mutually enjoyable activities with partner to promote relationship support and harmony. (31)

30. Ask the partners to envision themselves six months from now and to describe their functional adaptation to the transition. ▽

31. Assist the partners in identifying pleasant activities each would enjoy engaging in together; assign the partners to schedule regular positive activities with each other during the stressful transition period (or assign each partner to complete and then share the homework exercise "Identify and Schedule Pleasant Activities" in the *Adult Psychotherapy Home-work Planner*, 2nd ed. by Jongsma). ▽

__. _____   __. _____

_____   _____

__. _____   __. _____

_____   _____

__. _____   __. _____

_____   _____

DIAGNOSTIC SUGGESTIONS

ICD-9-CM	*ICD-10-CM*	*DSM-5* Disorder, Condition, or Problem
309.24	F43.22	Adjustment Disorder, With Anxiety
309.0	F43.21	Adjustment Disorder, With Depressed Mood
309.28	F43.23	Adjustment Disorder, With Mixed Anxiety and Depressed Mood
305.00	F10.10	Alcohol Use Disorder, Mild
303.90	F10.20	Alcohol Use Disorder, Moderate or Severe
300.4	F34.1	Persistent Depressive Disorder
296.xx	F32.x	Major Depressive Disorder, Single Episode
296.xx	F33.x	Major Depressive Disorder, Recurrent Episode
V61.10	Z63.0	Relationship Distress with Spouse or Intimate Partner
_____	_____	_____
_____	_____	_____

LOSS OF LOVE/AFFECTION

BEHAVIORAL DEFINITIONS

1. Infrequent verbalizations of caring.
2. No verbalizations of love.
3. Overt questioning of own love for partner.
4. Absence of acts of kindness or thoughtfulness.
5. Little or no affectionate touching or kissing.
6. Infrequent sexual interaction.
7. Little time spent with partner on social or recreational activities.
8. Infrequent communication with partner regarding intimate matters.
9. Little planning for future events and activities with partner.
10. Avoidance of partner (e.g., often arrives home late at night, preferring work and coworkers over partner).

__. _____
   _____

__. _____
   _____

__. _____
   _____

LONG-TERM GOALS

1. Overcome reasons for lack of caring and increase verbal, behavioral, and physical expressions of kindness, affection, and sexual intimacy.
2. Increase communication about all issues.
3. Increase acts of kindness and thoughtfulness with partner.
4. Increase time spent together in social and recreational activities.
5. Increase overall feelings and expressions of love and caring between the partners.

6. Increase amount of physical intimacy and satisfying sexual interaction with partner.

—. _____
   _____

—. _____
   _____

—. _____
   _____

SHORT-TERM OBJECTIVES

▽ 1. Identify reasons for lack of caring by partner. (1, 2, 3)

▽ 2. Begin to make restitution to partner for past wrongs. (4, 5, 6)

THERAPEUTIC INTERVENTIONS

1. Have each partner list the reasons that caring has eroded in the relationship (or assign "Positive and Negative Contributions to the Relationship: Mine and Yours" in the *Adult Psychotherapy Homework Planner,* 2nd ed. by Jongsma).▽

2. Review with the partners the reasons for the erosion of caring.▽

3. Address the possible need for individual therapy to help the partners cope with any individual problems that interfere with the development of caring in the relationship.▽

4. Obtain a commitment from both partners to make restitution for respective wrongs and transgressions in the relationship.▽

5. If one partner's actions have caused the other to experience jealousy, obtain a commitment from that partner to work especially hard at reassuring the other of his/her commitment to the relationship.▽

6. Have the partners provide feedback to each other about

▽ 3. Verbalize an understanding of forgiveness as a process, not a one-time event. (7, 8, 9, 10, 11)

specific actions that will help build mutual trust. ▽

7. Ask the partners to share their definitions of and thoughts about forgiveness. ▽

8. Provide a copy of Baucom, Snyder, & Gordon's (2009, p. 285) handout listing what forgiveness is ("a process; a release from being dominated by negative thoughts, feelings, and behaviors; a chance to learn about and gain more understanding of your partner, your relationship, and yourself") and what forgiveness is not ("forgetting; reconciliation; an immediate event; a one-time event"). ▽

9. Ask the partners to discuss their fears or apprehensions about forgiveness. ▽

10. Ask the partners to discuss (a) the repercussions of not forgiving and (b) the potential payoffs of forgiving. ▽

11. Challenge maladaptive beliefs about forgiveness (e.g., forgiveness implies weakness, condones the affair, excuses the affair, etc.). ▽

4. Read books on the process of forgiving another person. (12)

12. Recommend that the partners read a book on forgiveness (e.g., *Forgive and Forget: Healing the Hurts We Don't Deserve* by Smedes or *Forgiveness Is a Choice: A Step-by-Step Process for Resolving Anger and Restoring Hope* by Enright).

▽ 5. Commit to moving forward and to letting go of past issues. (13)

13. Obtain a verbal commitment between the partners and the therapist to attempt to move forward and to put past issues behind them, at least for a specified period. ▽

6. Increase eye contact with the partner. (14, 15)

▽ 7. Decrease critical comments toward the other partner. (16, 17. 18)

▽ 8. Increase positive verbal communication with the other partner. (19, 20, 21)

▽ 9. Increase acts of kindness and helpfulness toward the other

14. Teach the partners to maintain eye contact with each other while speaking and listening.

15. Provide feedback to the partners about the extent to which each maintains eye contact with the other.

16. Educate the partners regarding the very negative impact of making critical and hostile comments to each other in therapy sessions or at home. ▽

17. Obtain a commitment from the partners to minimize critical and hostile comments toward each other (or assign "Alternatives to Destructive Anger" in the *Adult Psychotherapy Homework Planner,* 2nd ed. by Jongsma). ▽

18. Advise the partners that individual therapy may be needed as an adjunct or precursor to conjoint therapy, especially if expressions of anger by one or both partners in conjoint sessions cannot be contained. ▽

19. Assist each partner in identifying the types of positive feedback that are pleasing to the other partner (e.g., some partners care about feedback about attire, while others regard such comments as irrelevant). ▽

20. Using behavior-rehearsal techniques, have the partners make positive comments about each other and about each other's positive behaviors. ▽

21. Reinforce attempts by clients to be verbally supportive of each other. ▽

22. Assist each partner in identifying the types of kind or helpful

partner (e.g., complete a task for the partner, run an errand for the partner). (22, 23, 24)

behaviors that are pleasing to the other partner (e.g., some partners care about getting the house cleaned, while others do not care much about that). ▽

23. Obtain an agreement from the partners regarding specific helpful, thoughtful gestures each will perform during the week (or assign "How Can We Meet Each Other's Needs and Desires?" in the *Adult Psychotherapy Homework Planner,* 2nd ed. by Jongsma). ▽▽

24. Reinforce attempts by the partners to engage in nonverbal and nonphysical affectionate gestures, such as doing a chore with or for the partner. ▽

▽ 10. Increase expressions of praise, compliments, recognition, and gratitude to the other partner. (25, 26)

25. Prompt mutual expressions of praise, compliments, recognition, and gratitude by the partners during and between therapy sessions; assign the partners to log the giving and receiving of such comments as a means of reinforcing the process. ▽

26. Monitor the partners' progress in mutually reinforcing each other and provide support for this effort. ▽

▽ 11. Identify activities that self and the partner would enjoy together. (27)

27. Have the partners describe social and recreational activities that they might like to do together. ▽

▽ 12. Engage in pleasurable social and recreational activities with the partner. (28, 29)

28. Facilitate an agreement between the partners regarding a specific plan for some social or recreational activities together, even if they feel somewhat reluctant to do so initially. ▽

29. Obtain feedback about how each partner felt during the mutual activity, and assist in helping expand such activities where possible. ▽

▽ 13. Acknowledge that in unsatisfactory relationships changes in feelings generally follow changes in behavior. (30)

30. Educate the partners about the usual course of change, emphasizing that initial changes in behaviors generally lead to subsequent changes in feelings and attitudes. ▽

▽ 14. Verbalize realistic, attainable time goals for expression of feelings of affection, and intimacy. (31, 32)

31. Educate the partners regarding the need for patience when seeking changes in positive relationship feelings. ▽

32. Assist the partners in setting realistic goals about changes in caring and love. ▽

15. Express commitment to not verbally coerce partner into sexual activities; acknowledge that sexual activities should be mutually agreed upon. (33, 34)

33. Advise the partners that forced sexual activities often backfire, with coercion by one partner frequently leading to resentment and withdrawal by the other.

34. Obtain a commitment from both the partners (and especially from the partner who has been the most frequent initiator of sexual activity) to only initiate and engage in sexual actions that are mutually agreed upon.

▽ 16. Verbalize an understanding that positive sexual interchanges generally follow when other aspects of the relationship improve. (35)

35. Explain to the partners that sexual satisfaction in marital and long-term relationships often increases naturally even without direct attention to the sexual relationship (unless there are specific sexual dysfunctions) when other aspects of the relationship, such as communication and nonsexual expressions of caring, improve. ▽

▽ 17. Implement the techniques of sensate focus to increase the giving and receiving of physical pleasure. (36, 37)

36. If both partners are willing, teach them the techniques of sensate focus, where each partner alternates between giving and receiving sensual pleasure (or assign "Journaling the Response to Non-demand, Sexual Pleasuring [Sensate Focus]" in the

*Adult Psychotherapy Homework
Planner,* 2nd ed. by Jongsma). ▽

37. Monitor, review, and discuss the
partners' feelings surrounding
their increase in physically
intimate contact. ▽

▽ 18. Read educational material
regarding human sexuality and
techniques of pleasuring. (38)

38. Assign the partners to read,
either independently or together
material on sexual relationships
(e.g., *Sexual Awareness* by
McCarthy & McCarthy,
Rekindling Desire by McCarthy
& McCarthy, or *The Gift of Sex*
by Penner & Penner). ▽

__. _____   __. _____

_____   _____

__. _____   __. _____

_____   _____

__. _____   __. _____

_____   _____

DIAGNOSTIC SUGGESTIONS

ICD-9-CM	*ICD-10-CM*	*DSM-5* Disorder, Condition, or Problem
309.0	F43.21	Adjustment Disorder, With Depressed Mood
309.24	F43.22	Adjustment Disorder, With Anxiety
309.28	F43.23	Adjustment Disorder, With Mixed Anxiety and Depressed Mood
296.2x	F32.x	Major Depressive Disorder, Single Episode
296.3x	F33.x	Major Depressive Disorder, Recurrent Episode
V61.10	Z63.0	Relationship Distress with Spouse or Intimate Partner
V61.12	Z69.12	Encounter for Mental Health Services for Perpetrator of Spouse or Partner Violence, Physical
995.81	Z69.11	Encounter for Mental Health Services for Victim of Spouse or Partner Violence, Physical
301.83	F60.3	Borderline Personality Disorder

_____   _____   _____

_____   _____   _____

MIDLIFE TRANSITION PROBLEMS

BEHAVIORAL DEFINITIONS

1. Depressed mood and irritability.
2. Periodic crying spells.
3. Sleep disturbance.
4. Conflict between commitment to partner versus desire to be with another partner.
5. Conflict between staying in current job versus attempting to get another job.
6. Conflict over changing careers.
7. Conflict over goals (e.g., time spent with family members versus time on job versus time with friends).
8. Conflict over religious values and practices.
9. Concern about declining opportunity to have another sexual partner.
10. Concern about perceived decline in physical attractiveness.

__. _____
   _____

__. _____
   _____

__. _____
   _____

LONG-TERM GOALS

1. Reduce symptoms of depression and anxiety related to ambiguity of direction and values in life.
2. Resolve the conflict that precipitated the midlife crises.
3. Increase focus on living in accordance with specified goals and clarified values.
4. Recognize advantages that usually come only with maturity.

5. Become connected or reconnected to partner, family members, employment, and/or religious community.
6. Rediscover an appreciation for and commitment to the existing intimate relationship.

__. _____
   _____
   _____
__. _____
   _____
   _____
__. _____
   _____
   _____

SHORT-TERM OBJECTIVES

1. Describe the mismatch between life goals and accomplishments that seem to trigger midlife transition difficulties. (1)

2. Cooperate with an assessment of midlife transition difficulties by completing the *Midlife Crisis Scale*. (2)

▽ 3. Verbalize the thoughts that are associated with anxiety and worry over the future. (3, 4)

▽ 4. Organize a list of thoughts, behaviors, actual outcomes, and desired outcomes via situational analysis of midlife transition-problem experiences. (5, 6)

THERAPEUTIC INTERVENTIONS

1. Ask the client experiencing midlife transition difficulties to describe the mismatch between life goals and accomplishments.

2. Ask the client experiencing midlife transition difficulties to complete the *Midlife Crisis Scale* (Hermans & Oles); provide feedback to the client as to test results.

3. Probe for the client's cognitive distortions that lead to anxiety and uneasiness. ▽

4. Assign the client homework to track events/thoughts that precipitate anxious and depressed feelings (for use in situational analyses). ▽

5. Demonstrate how to organize a situational analysis. Have the client choose from his/her homework specific midlife problem-eliciting situations and tell what his/her interpretations/ cognitions were, what his/her behavior was, and what the actual outcome of the situation was. ▽

6. As the concluding step in the situational analysis, have the client describe what his/her

▽ 5. Verbalize thoughts that were unhelpful, global, or inaccurate, and then state more beneficial self-talk. (7, 8)

6. Articulate the values and goals for living a meaningful life using Covey's four human needs and the approach taken to fulfill those needs. (9, 10, 11, 12, 13)

desired outcome was in the specified situation.▽

7. Help the client determine whether each thought was (a) accurate, (b) anchored to the specific situation, and (c) helpful in getting the desired outcome.▽

8. If any thoughts are not accurate, anchored, and helpful in getting the desired outcome, have the client rework the thoughts so they meet criteria (for example, "I only get to have sex with one woman for the rest of my life" can become "I'm fortunate to have sex regularly with someone who loves and respects me").▽

9. Ask the partners to read First Things First (Covey, Merrill, & Merrill), which posits that cross-cultural wisdom literature contains four key human needs "to live, to love, to learn, to leave a legacy."

10. Ask the partners to consider their approach to fulfilling the need "to live" ("Our physical need for such things as food, clothing, economic well-being, health," Covey et al., p. 45) by having them write and discuss (a) their past and current goals for meeting financial needs, and (b) the pros and cons of their current approach.

11. Ask the partners to consider their approach to fulfilling the need "to love" ("Our social need to relate to other people, to belong, to love, to be loved," Covey et al., p. 45) by having them write and discuss (a) their past and current goals for having rich, satisfying relationships with others, and (b) the pros and cons of their current approach.

12. Ask the partners to consider their approach to fulfilling the need "to learn" ("Our mental need to develop and to grow," Covey et al., p. 45) by having them write and discuss (a) their past and current goals for learning, growing, and being open to new experiences and skills, and (b) the pros and cons of their current approach.

13. Ask the partners to consider their approach to fulfilling the need "to leave a legacy" ("Our spiritual need to have a sense of meaning, purpose, personal congruence, and contribution," Covey et al., p. 45) by having them write and discuss (a) their past and current goals for having a sense of direction and purpose, and (b) the pros and cons of their current approach.

7. Identify developmental history of goals held for self and perceived expectations of others for self. (14, 15, 16)

14. Have each partner describe his/her goals and wishes as a late teen and young adult in the areas of (a) to live, (b) to love, (c) to learn, and (d) to leave a legacy; how have these changed over the years?

15. Have each partner describe the goals and wishes his/her parents had for him/her.

16. Have each partner describe perceived goals that the other partner had for him/her.

8. Each partner describes goals he/she has had for the other partner. (17)

17. Obtain feedback from each partner regarding goals and wishes he/she has for the other.

9. Describe goals that have remained unfulfilled and the feelings associated with that lack of fulfillment. (18)

18. Have each partner describe his/her unfulfilled goals; assist each partner in identifying the feelings associated with failure to attain those goals.

10. Verbalize acceptance that some goals cannot be attained. (19)

11. List realistic, meaningful alternative goals for future attainment and steps needed to reach them. (20, 21, 22, 23)

▽ 12. Each partner constructs a self-change plan to accomplish an articulated goal. (24, 25).

19. Assist the client in identifying goals that probably are not realistically attainable and that must be accepted as such; review and discuss the client's feelings associated with this reality.

20. Have the client list goals that are still realistically attainable and plans he/she has to reach them; clarify why these goals are meaningful and of value to self, partner, and the relationship.

21. Assign the client to consult other individuals whom he/she respects regarding possible alternative goals for himself/herself and their value.

22. Obtain feedback from each partner about the perceived value of alternative goals to self and to the relationship.

23. Assist the client in determining the likelihood of attaining alternative goals; ask the client to lay out steps necessary to attain these new goals.

24. Teach the partners the five steps of a Self-Change Plan (1) Describe the behavior to be changed; (2) Examine the pros and cons of the current behavior; (3) Set a goal, describing as precisely as possible what is to happen; (4) Create an Action Plan, pinpointing a specific plan for enacting the goal; and (5) Evaluate enacting of the plan. Have the partners practice this in session on an articulated goal that each would like to achieve. ▽

25. Ask the partners to make a global evaluation of how they did on implementing the action plan before the next session. The rating scale is 0 = didn't think about it

or do it; 1 = thought about it;
2 = gave it a weak try; 3 = tried,
partially succeeded; and 4 = did a
great job. Ask them to jot down
short answers to the following:
What did we actually do? What
positives resulted? What negatives
resulted? What do we need to do
from here?▽

13. Identify the advantages that
    come with maturity. (26, 27)

26. Have partners describe attributes
    of an older individual whom
    he/she respects.

27. Help the partners identify
    advantages that usually come
    with maturity (e.g., less
    impulsive judgments, greater
    experiential wisdom, broader
    views of values in life, knowledge
    of more lifestyle alternatives,
    more concern about others).

14. Verbalize acceptance of own
    aging and sense of peace over it.
    (27, 28)

27. Help the partners identify
    advantages that usually come
    with maturity (e.g., less
    impulsive judgments, greater
    experiential wisdom, broader
    views of values in life, knowledge
    of more lifestyle alternatives, and
    more concern about others).

28. Explore and resolve the client's
    possible feelings of anxiety and
    fatalistic depression related to
    aging, including fear of physical
    deterioration and/or declining
    health.

15. Identify steps that could be
    taken to increase current or
    future financial security. (29)

29. Ask the partners to create and
    enact self-change plans related to
    financial security.

16. Clarify and articulate the
    beneficial value of giving more
    time to family relationships. (30)

30. Assist the partners in identifying
    the benefits of increased contact
    with immediate and extended
    family members and to create
    and enact self-change plans
    related to loving relationships.

17. Identify acts of kindness that could be done for others, and articulate benefits of self-sacrifice and focusing on others. (31)

18. Verbalize an understanding of the value of touching in intimate human relationships. (32)

19. Increase level of physical affection with partner. (33)

20. Increase new and interesting experiences/skills. (34)

21. Increase behaviors that provide a sense of leaving a legacy. (35, 36)

22. Articulate feelings and thoughts associated with their current employment and the vision for a future in this work or a possible

31. Assist the partners in identifying things that they might do (alone or together) for others, thereby reducing the focus on themselves; ask them to create and enact self-change plans related to helping others.

32. Teach the partners the value of touching in intimate relationships (i.e., increases partners' feelings of importance; enhances mutual feelings of closeness, warmth, caring, and security).

33. Ask the partners to create and enact self-change plans related to solidifying, improving, and/or increasing physical affection.

34. Explore what new experiences and skills might interest the partners; ask them to create and enact self-change plans related to trying new experiences (alone or together) and to learning new skills.

35. Ask the partners to consider what they would like others to say (a) about their relationship at a 50th anniversary party, and (b) about them at a 70th birthday party. Assist them in deriving lessons about the legacies they would like to leave and the behavior changes necessary to achieve that legacy.

36. Ask the partners to create and enact self-change plans related to behavioral involvements that give them a sense of meaning, purpose, personal congruence, and contribution.

37. Explore the partners' feelings associated with current employment and what impact it has on each partner and the family.

alternative employment situation. (37, 38)

38. Assist the partners in identifying possible alternative career directions and the advantages and disadvantages of each possibility for selves and the relationship.

23. Verbalize a commitment to accept current employment situation. (39)

39. Help the partners accept and commit to present employment with a sense of satisfaction and without resentment or negative self-talk regarding lack of accomplishment or future advancement.

24. State a concrete plan for exploring other career opportunities that have been identified as challenging and appropriate. (40)

40. Assist the partners in developing a plan for responsibly exploring alternative career directions while avoiding impulsive actions that could have negative long-term consequences.

__. _____
_____

__. _____
_____

__. _____
_____

__. _____
_____

__. _____
_____

__. _____
_____

DIAGNOSTIC SUGGESTIONS

ICD-9-CM	ICD-10-CM	DSM-5 Disorder, Condition, or Problem
309.0	F43.21	Adjustment Disorder, With Depressed Mood
309.24	F43.22	Adjustment Disorder, With Anxiety
309.28	F43.23	Adjustment Disorder, With Mixed Anxiety and Depressed Mood
300.4	F34.1	Persistent Depressive Disorder
296.xx	F32.x	Major Depressive Disorder, Single Episode
296.xx	F33.x	Major Depressive Disorder, Recurrent Episode
V61.10	Z63.0	Relationship Distress with Spouse or Intimate Partner

_____	_____	_____
_____	_____	_____

ONLY ONE PARTNER WILLING
TO ATTEND THERAPY

BEHAVIORAL DEFINITIONS

1. Individual distress over the relationship as evidenced by emotional (e.g., anger, tension), cognitive (e.g., blaming), and behavioral (e.g., arguing, withdrawal) difficulties.
2. Refusal by other partner to attend counseling sessions.
3. Inability of other partner to attend counseling sessions, due to work schedule conflict.

—. _____

_____

—. _____

_____

—. _____

_____

LONG-TERM GOALS

1. Improve acceptance of, and satisfaction with, the relationship, changing those things that are under one's control.
2. Enact relationship-enhancing behaviors at home.
3. Increase rewarding activities with and without partner.
4. Create and enact self-change plans.
5. Meet personal needs through rewarding activities outside the relationship.

—. _____

_____

—. _____
    _____
—. _____
    _____

SHORT-TERM OBJECTIVES

1. Invite the partner to participate in treatment sessions. (1, 2, 3)

2. Verbalize any fears about informing the partner of treatment or having him/her attend sessions. (4)

3. Give permission for therapist to invite the partner to attend counseling sessions to provide information that might be useful to the presenting client's treatment. (5)

4. Describe the origin, development, satisfaction, and present state of the relationship. (6, 7)

THERAPEUTIC INTERVENTIONS

1. Determine whether the client has asked his/her partner to attend therapy.

2. Have the client detail the context under which he/she asked the partner to attend counseling sessions (when, where, what context).

3. If appropriate, use role-playing techniques to help the client appropriately ask their partner to attend counseling sessions (for example, "I care about you, and I'm concerned that our relationship is at risk. I'm going to attend therapy to work on improving our relationship, and I'd appreciate your being willing to come with me.").

4. Assess potential dangers (such as fear of assault) of the client attempting to engage partner in therapy.

5. If the client gives permission, call the partner and invite him/her to attend sessions to provide information that might be useful to the presenting client's treatment.

6. Assess the client's history of, and satisfaction with, the relationship by conducting an interview. Appropriate questions might be:

"How did the two of you meet?"
"What attracted you to each
other?" "What qualities or
characteristics did you find that
you liked about your partner?"
"How did the two of you decide
to get married?" "What have
been the highs and lows during
dating and your marriage?" ▽

7. Assess the client's current
   relationship satisfaction using
   self-report instruments (e.g.,
   Couples Satisfaction Inventory by
   Funk & Rogge; *Relationship
   Satisfaction Questionnaire* by
   Burns & Sayers). ▽

5. Describe suspicions regarding
   whether the nonattending
   partner may be having an affair.
   (8)

8. Assess the client for the presence
   or suspicion of affairs (see
   chapters on Infidelity and
   Jealousy in this *Planner*).

▽ 6. Verbalize any incidents of
   physical, sexual, or emotional
   abuse, or intimidation by other
   partner. (9)

9. Assess the client for incidents of
   psychological, physical, or sexual
   aggression (see chapters on
   Psychological, Physical, or
   Sexual Abuse in this *Planner*),
   through inventories (e.g., *Revised
   Conflict Tactics Scale* by Straus
   et al.) and clinical interviews. ▽

▽ 7. Report any steps taken to
   dissolve the relationship. (10)

10. Assess the steps taken toward
    divorce by administering a
    questionnaire (e.g., *Marital
    Status Inventory* by Weiss &
    Cerreto) and/or by interviewing
    the client about his/her sense of
    hope and vision for the future. ▽

8. Identify the pros and cons of
   remaining in the relationship
   versus separation or divorce. (11)

11. Have the client state his/her
    point of view on (a) the pros and
    cons of preserving the relation-
    ship, and (b) the pros and cons
    of separation or divorce.

▽ 9. Identify current problem areas in
   the relationship. (12)

12. Assist the client in identifying the
    current problem areas in the
    relationship. ▽

▽ 10. Specify the problem areas that are under one's control. (13, 14)

▽ 11. Identify and implement behavioral changes for self that would enhance the relationship. (15, 16, 17)

▽ 12. Generate lists of preferred recreational activities that could be done alone, with their partner, or with others. (18)

13. Educate the client that (a) there is evidence that an individual approach to couple problems is as effective as a conjoint approach, and (b) all individual therapy can be a form of relationship therapy, because changes instigated by one partner can change the relationship system. ▽

14. Assist the client in identifying which current problems he/she has at least some influence over (e.g., communication problems, anger problems). ▽

15. Have the client list changes that he/she could make to improve the relationship; review and discuss the list with the client (or assign "How Can We Meet Each Other's Needs and Desires?" in the Adult Psychotherapy Homework Planner, 2nd ed. by Jongsma). ▽

16. Have the client rate the behaviors that he/she could perform to benefit the relationship, including estimates of both the perceived benefit and the perceived sacrifice in performing each of them (as in Weiss' *Cost/Benefit Analysis Inventory*). ▽

17. Arrange the client's list of beneficial behaviors from least to greatest in terms of the amount of sacrifice that enactment would require; ask the client to perform three to five of these behaviors per week. ▽

18. Ask the client to generate a list of desired and pleasurable activities in the following categories: (a) to be done alone, (b) to be done with partner,

(c) to be done with partner and other family members, (d) to be done with partner and nonfamily members, and (e) to be done with nonfamily members (by assigning "Identify and Schedule Pleasant Activities" in the *Adult Psychotherapy Homework Planner*, 2nd ed. by Jongsma or by administering the *Inventory of Rewarding Activities* by Weiss).▽

▽ 13. Discuss with the partner the desire to increase the frequency of engaging in rewarding activities together. (19, 20)

19. Using role-playing techniques, help the client rehearse asking his/her partner to engage in positive activities together.▽

20. Assign the client to ask the partner to engage in positive activities together, and to report his/her response at the next session.▽

▽ 14. Increase the number of rewarding activities that do not require participation by the partner. (21)

21. Assign the client to increase the frequency of behaviors from his/her list of pleasurable activities that he/she does alone or with nonfamily members; schedule these activities in the client's calendar for the week.▽

▽ 15. Each partner constructs a self-change plan regarding an important relationship-relevant event during the week. (22, 23)

22. Teach the client the five steps of a Self-Change Plan: (1) Describe the behavior to be changed; (2) Examine the pros and cons of the current behavior; (3) Set a goal, describing as precisely as possible what is to happen; (4) Create an Action Plan, pinpointing a specific plan for enacting the goal; and (5) Evaluate enacting of the plan. Have the client practice this in session on an important relationship-relevant situation that he/she would like to change.▽

23. Ask the client to make a global evaluation of how he/she did on

implementing the action plan before the next session. The rating scale is 0 = didn't think about it or do it; 1 = thought about it; 2 = gave it a weak try; 3 = tried, partially succeeded; and 4 = did a great job. Ask them to jot down short answers to the following: What did we actually do? What positives resulted? What negatives resulted? What do we need to do from here? ▽

▽ 16. Verbalize an understanding of the rationale for situational analysis. (24)

24. Describe for the client the goal of situational analysis (McCullogh) in the following manner: "Although we try to get large payoffs, like having a happy marriage, these payoffs are achieved one small situation at a time. To work toward the big goals, try to make changes in the way you think and behave in small, observable situations that have a beginning, middle, and end." Have the client repeat this rationale in his/her own words. ▽

▽ 17. Complete situational analysis homework to increase efficacy at affecting positive outcomes in situations at home. (25, 26)

25. Assign the client situational analysis homework that asks him/her to identify (a) a problematic situation (e.g., a description of the beginning, middle, and end of an observable situation), (b) three cognitions that occurred during the situation, (c) the client's behavior during the situation, (d) the actual outcome and (e) the desired outcome. ▽

26. Ask the client to read aloud from the situational analysis home-work sheet, and paraphrase his/her statements to make sure that the client understands the key elements of the situational analysis. ▽

▽ 18. Identify whether one's thoughts or conclusions promote problem resolution, are directly relevant to the situation, and are based on reality. (27)

27. Have the client state whether each thought was (a) helpful in getting the desired outcome, (b) anchored to the specific situation described (i.e., is situationally-specific, not global), and (c) accurate (i.e., overt evidence can be marshaled to support it). ▽

▽ 19. Verbalize self-talk conclusions that promote problem resolution, are directly relevant to the situation, and are based on reality. (28)

28. If any thoughts do not meet all three criteria (increase likelihood of achieving desired outcome, situationally-specific, and accurate) help the client rework the thought so that it does meet all three criteria (for example, "She's always on my back," can become "There's something happening here that she thinks is important."). ▽

▽ 20. Choose desired outcomes that are achievable. (29)

29. Have the client state whether the desired outcome was achievable (i.e., under his/her control); if not, help the client rework the desired outcome so that it is achievable (for example, "I want him to listen to me when I'm upset," can become "I want to ask him to schedule a time for us to talk about problems that we're having."). ▽

▽ 21. Verbally generate a generalizable lesson to be learned from the specific situational analysis and apply it to other situations of conflict. (30, 31)

30. Ask the client to summarize the situation by deriving a lesson to be learned from the situational analysis. ▽

31. Help the client apply the lesson to other situations. ▽

22. Verbalize an understanding that soft emotions, such as hurt and vulnerability, precede hard or protective emotions, such as anger and resentment. (32, 33)

32. Discuss with the client the difference between "hard" (i.e., protective) emotions, such as anger, retribution, and resentment, and "soft" (i.e., vulnerable) emotions, such as hurt, insecurity, and fear. ▽

33. When the client expresses a hard emotion, have him/her identify the soft emotions that underlie the hard emotion. ▽

▽ 23. Demonstrate acceptance by treating the problem as an external "thing," rather than blaming the partner. (34)

34. Reframe for the client the problematic interactional patterns as an external problem (an "it"), rather than as the fault of either partner. ▽

▽ 24. Demonstrate acceptance by listing the positive aspects of the partner's problem-causing behavior. (35, 36, 37)

35. Ask the client to describe the positive features of the partner's problematic behavior (i.e., the ways the partner's behavior actually serves a positive function in the relationship). ▽

36. If the client has difficulty finding positive features, reframe the partner's problematic behavior in terms of how it balances the client's behavior (e.g., a hyper-responsible man may get involved with a spontaneous woman). ▽

37. Explain to the client that each partner brings only one part of the balancing act to the relationship, and ask if anything can be learned from the partner's opposite, but balancing, behavior that formerly has been upsetting to the client. ▽

25. Identify resources outside the relationship that can meet important personal needs. (38)

38. Ask the client to list ways of satisfying their own needs outside of the relationship, to take pressure off the relationship to meet all his/her core needs; assign and schedule enactment of these need-satisfying activities and process any resistance or hurdles.

▽ 26. Discuss and practice alternative means (i.e., those not involving problem-causing pattern) of satisfying important personal

21. Assign the client to increase the frequency of behaviors from his/her list of pleasurable activities that he/she does alone

needs within the relationship. (21, 39, 40)

or with nonfamily members; schedule these activities in the client's calendar for the week. ▽

39. Help the client list ways that he/she could get needs arising from soft emotions (e.g., protection, relief from hurt) met within the relationship without resorting to destructive, hard emotion-laced escalation. ▽

40. Have the client role-play alternative means of satisfying needs arising from his/her soft emotions. ▽

—. _____   —. _____
   _____   _____
—. _____   —. _____
   _____   _____
—. _____   —. _____
   _____   _____

DIAGNOSTIC SUGGESTIONS

ICD-9-CM	_ICD-10-CM_	_DSM-5_ Disorder, Condition, or Problem
309.28	F43.23	Adjustment Disorder, With Mixed Anxiety and Depressed Mood
300.4	F34.1	Persistent Depressive Disorder
296.2x	F32.x	Major Depressive Disorder, Single Episode
296.3x	F33.x	Major Depressive Disorder, Recurrent Episode
V61.12	Z69.12	Encounter for Mental Health Services for Perpetrator of Spouse or Partner Violence, Physical
995.81	Z69.11	Encounter for Mental Health Services for Victim of Spouse or Partner Violence, Physical
V61.10	Z63.0	Relationship Distress with Spouse or Intimate Partner
301.83	F60.3	Borderline Personality Disorder
301.6	F60.7	Dependent Personality Disorder
301.81	F60.81	Narcissistic Personality Disorder
_____	_____	_____
_____	_____	_____

PARENTING CONFLICTS—ADOLESCENTS[1]

BEHAVIORAL DEFINITIONS

1. Frequent arguments between partners about parenting, or disagreements that interfere with effective parenting of adolescent.
2. Lack of agreement between parents regarding strategies for dealing with various types of negative adolescent behaviors.
3. Ineffective parental responses to negative adolescent behavior (i.e., efforts that do not result in the desired outcomes).
4. Inability of partners to discuss and support each other's parenting efforts.

—. _____

_____

—. _____

_____

—. _____

_____

LONG-TERM GOALS

1. Discuss and agree on the implementation of joint parenting strategies.
2. Create a positive, supportive parent-adolescent home environment.
3. Consistently reinforce positive adolescent behavior and punish negative behavior.
4. Share ideas about parenting strategies and support each other's parenting behavior.

---

[1]A more expansive description of the interventions summarized in this chapter can be found in the work of Patterson & Forgatch (1987), Forgatch & Patterson (1987), and Robin & Foster (1989).

5. Make and enforce consistent house rules.

—. _____

_____

—. _____

_____

—. _____

_____

SHORT-TERM OBJECTIVES

THERAPEUTIC INTERVENTIONS

▽ 1. Specify adolescent behavior problems. (1, 2, 3)

1. Ask the parents to describe their main concerns about the adolescent's problem behavior and its history. Therapist's questions might include: "When did the problem behavior start?" and "How has it changed across time?"▽

2. Ask the parents to specifically detail the extent of the adolescent's problem behavior. Therapist's questions might include: "How frequently and intensely does the problem behavior occur?" "How long does it last?" "In which situations does it occur?"▽

3. Identify specific areas of conflict and problem behaviors by having the parents complete questionnaire assessments such as *Issues Checklist* (Robin & Foster) or *Conflict Behavior Questionnaire* (Prinz, Foster, Kent, & O'Leary). ▽

▽ 2. Verbalize parenting philosophy and expectations for adolescent. (4)

4. Identify (a) each partner's parenting philosophy and strategy, and (b) each partner's expectations for the adolescent's

behavior (e.g., "Adolescents should never be disrespectful toward their parents.") via interviews and questionnaires such as *Family Beliefs Inventory* (Roehing & Robin) or *Parent-Adolescent Relationship Questionnaire* (Robin, Koepke, & Moye). ▽

▽ 3. Identify parenting, family, or school factors that may be contributing to the negative behavior. (5, 6, 7)

5. Assist the parents in identifying parent-adolescent behavioral patterns that may be maintaining the adolescent's behavior problem (e.g., unintentionally reinforcing problem behavior through nagging or emotional parenting). ▽

6. Identify social context factors that may be maintaining the problem (e.g., family transitions, inconsistent rules, school or social difficulties). ▽

7. Identify any parent stressors that may be maintaining the problem (e.g., unemployment, substance use, depression). ▽

▽ 4. Discuss how relationship functioning affects and is affected by parenting difficulties. (8, 9)

8. Have the parents indicate ways their relationship conflict has a negative impact on their adolescent's behavior. ▽

9. Have the parents describe how their adolescent's behavior problems impact their relationship conflict. ▽

▽ 5. Identify the strengths and weaknesses of partners working together as a team. (10, 11)

10. Using behavioral-rehearsal techniques, have the partners attempt to solve a major parenting problem; quietly observe and note skills and deficiencies. ▽

11. Review and discuss the problem-solving interaction; have partners note their strengths and

weaknesses as a parenting team (or assign "Learning to Parent as a Team" in the *Adult Psychotherapy Homework Planner*, 2nd ed. by Jongsma).▽

▽ 6. Improve parenting knowledge by reading assigned books on parenting adolescents. (12)

12. Assign the parents to read *Parents and Adolescents: Living Together. Vol. I: The Basics* and *Vol. II: Family Problem-Solving* (Patterson & Forgatch); process with the parents the principles they learned from the reading material.▽

▽ 7. Monitor adolescent's whereabouts, and identify any deficiencies in monitoring. (13, 14)

13. Assign the parents to coordinate monitoring of their adolescent's activities, keeping track of where he/she is, whom he/she is with, what they are doing, and when they will be home; assign parents to record their joint monitoring efforts.▽

14. Have the parents discuss their successes at monitoring and to identify times and situations where the monitoring needs to be improved.▽

▽ 8. Identify an adolescent behavior that partners would like to reinforce, and track its occurrence as well as antecedents and consequences. (15)

15. Have the parents identify one of their adolescent's behavior patterns that they would like to reinforce; assign them to record its occurrence every day for a week, and to note the behaviors or situations that precede it (i.e., antecedents) and follow it (i.e., consequences).▽

▽ 9. Increase the frequency of contingently reinforcing positive adolescent behavior. (16)

16. Help the parents decide on an appropriate reward (e.g., praise, use of the car, increase in allowance) to reinforce the positive behavior; have parents rehearse praising positive behavior patterns in session, and provide them with feedback.▽

▽ 10. Increase the frequency of positive social or activity-oriented interactions with the adolescent. (17, 18)

17. Assign parents to increase the amount of focused, adolescent-centered recreational activity with the adolescent experiencing difficulty. ▽

18. Assign each parent to increase the number of parent-initiated, casual, positive conversations with the adolescent experiencing difficulty. ▽

▽ 11. Identify a behavior in the adolescent that partners would like to discourage, and track its occurrence as well as antecedents and consequences. (19)

19. Ask the parents to identify one of their adolescent's problem behaviors that they would like to decrease; assign them to record its occurrence every day for a week, and to note the behaviors or situations that precede it (i.e., antecedents) and follow it (i.e., consequences). ▽

▽ 12. Establish and implement consequences (punishments) for negative adolescent behavior. (20, 21)

20. Have the parents decide on an appropriate negative consequence (e.g., loss of privilege, five-minute work chore) to contingently discourage negative behavior. ▽

21. Teach the parents to establish logical and natural negative consequences to adolescent misbehavior (e.g., break curfew → lose privilege to go out; make a mess → clean up the mess); ask them to list some of these types of natural negative consequences (punishments) that could be used with their adolescent's misbehavior. ▽

▽ 13. Each parent identifies, examines, and then pledges to terminate any negative behavior that he/she is modeling and that the adolescent is imitating. (22)

22. If the parents are modeling for the adolescent the behavior they would like to extinguish (e.g., yelling, being sarcastic), have them contract to change their own behavior before trying to change the same behavior in the adolescent. ▽

▼ 14. Check with their partner regularly concerning parenting and keep a log of these interactions. (23, 24, 25)

23. Assign the parents to confer with each other at least once a day regarding the adolescent's behavior. ▼

24. Encourage the parents to plan a mutually acceptable time to confer, to avoid casual conversations at times when arguments are likely to erupt (e.g., immediately upon arriving home in the evening). ▼

25. Instruct the partners to track their satisfaction with the daily check-ins and bring in the tracking sheet to their treatment sessions. ▼

▼ 15. Use argument-control strategies to increase the productivity of parenting conversations. (26)

26. Using modeling and behavior rehearsal, assist the partners in practicing argument control (e.g., using "Pause, Calm, and Think"; using "I" messages in place of "you" messages [see chapter on Anger in this *Planner*]); assign partners to employ these techniques to cool off during parenting discussions if either believes that the conversation is becoming unsupportive. ▼

▼ 16. Report instances of constructive and supportive conversations with partner regarding current parenting experiences. (27, 28)

27. Have the partners role-play discussions they will have when the adolescent is well-behaved; have the supportive partner ask the other what the adolescent has been doing and then support his/her parenting behaviors. ▼

28. Have the partners role-play discussions they will have when the adolescent displays negative behavior; have the supportive partner ask, in a supportive, nonthreatening manner, about the specifics of the misbehavior. ▼

▽ 17. Partners support each other's parenting. (29, 30, 31)

29. During role-playing exercises for dealing with adolescent misbehavior, have the supportive partner ask, in a supportive and nonthreatening manner, how the other partner dealt with the misbehavior and whether the supportive partner can do anything in the future to help. ▽

30. Have the partners contract to support each other's parenting by not interfering during the other's parent-adolescent interactions, and by not interfering with the other's decisions (i.e., avoiding splitting of parents' unity). ▽

31. Help the partners identify what each can do to help the other in challenging situations (e.g., when the adolescent is disrespectful). ▽

▽ 18. Discuss parenting disagreements only when discussion is likely to be constructive. (32)

32. Have the partners contract to put disagreements over parenting strategy on hold until the situation has ended and they can meet privately, and both partners are calm and able to problem-solve without accusations or defensiveness. ▽

▽ 19. Regularly discuss and problem-solve parenting strategies for handling misbehavior. (33)

33. Assign the partners to schedule parenting problem-solving discussions (see the chapter on Communication in this *Planner*) for two or three times per week. ▽

▽ 20. Use problem-solving skills with partner to resolve a parenting problem. (34, 35, 36, 37)

34. Have the partners role-play using pinpointing skills (i.e., statements that are specific, observable, and ask for increases in behavior) to specifically identify the presenting problem. ▽

35. Have the partners role-play the speaker-listener technique, where

the listener does not respond with their own thoughts until he/she has paraphrased the speaker's position to that person's satisfaction. ▽

36. Advise the partners to limit themselves to solving one problem at a time. ▽

37. Encourage each partner to generate at least two possible solutions to each of the adolescent's problem behaviors, list the pros and cons of each solution, choose a solution, enact the solution, and then review and revise the solution if effectiveness is lacking. ▽

▽ 21. Complete situational analysis homework to increase parenting efficacy. (38)

38. Assign the client situational analysis homework that asks him/her to identify (a) a problematic parenting situation (e.g., a description of the beginning, middle, and end of an observable situation); (b) three cognitions that occurred during the situation; (c) the parent's behavior during the situation; (d) the actual outcome; and (e) the desired outcome. ▽

▽ 22. Identify whether one's thoughts or conclusions promote problem resolution, are directly relevant to the situation, and are based on reality. (39)

39. Have the parent state whether each thought was (a) helpful in getting the desired outcome; (b) anchored to the specific situation described (i.e., is situationally specific, not global); and (c) accurate (i.e., overt evidence can be marshaled to support it). ▽

▽ 23. Verbalize self-talk conclusions that promote problem resolution, are directly relevant to the situation, and are based on reality. (40)

40. If any thought or conclusion fails to meet all three criteria (i.e., helpful, anchored to specific situation, accurate), help parent rework the thought so that it

does meet all three criteria (for example, "My daughter's going to be a drug addict" can become "Adolescents often experiment with marijuana."). ▽

▽ 24. Choose desired outcomes that are achievable. (41)

41. Have the client state whether the desired outcome was achievable (i.e., under his/her control). If not, help client rework the desired outcome so that it is achievable. For example, "I want my son to respect me" can become "I will set up a family meeting to discuss how I'd like members of this family to treat each other." ▽

▽ 25. Conduct regular family problem-solving meetings. (42, 43)

42. Assign parents to initiate regular family meetings for constructive problem-solving and evaluation of earlier contracts. Family meetings should be time-limited (starting with 15 minutes) and should observe set ground rules (see p. 117 of *Parents and Adolescents: Living Together. Vol. II: Family Problem-Solving* by Patterson & Forgatch). ▽

43. Family meetings should use respectful communication skills such as taking turns talking, treating each other with respect, and no lecturing (see p. 118 of *Parents and Adolescents: Living Together. Vol II: Family Problem-Solving* by Patterson & Forgatch). ▽

▽ 26. In company with partner, establish consistent house rules. (44)

44. Help the parents establish consistent house rules. Consequences for rule violation and compliance should be specified and rules can be modified and negotiated in

family meetings if necessary (or assign "Using Reinforcement Principles in Parenting" in the *Adult Psychotherapy Homework Planner*, 2nd ed. by Jongsma).▽

—. _____   —. _____

   _____   _____

—. _____   —. _____

   _____   _____

—. _____   —. _____

   _____   _____

DIAGNOSTIC SUGGESTIONS

ICD-9-CM	*ICD-10-CM*	*DSM-5* Disorder, Condition, or Problem
309.24	F43.22	Adjustment Disorder, With Anxiety
309.0	F43.21	Adjustment Disorder, With Depressed Mood
309.3	F43.24	Adjustment Disorder, With Disturbance of Conduct
309.28	F43.23	Adjustment Disorder, With Mixed Anxiety and Depressed Mood
309.4	F43.25	Adjustment Disorder, With Mixed Disturbance of Emotions and Conduct
V61.20	Z62.820	Parent-Child Relational Problem
V61.10	Z63.0	Relationship Distress with Spouse or Intimate Partner
_____	_____	_____
_____	_____	_____

PARENTING CONFLICTS—CHILDREN[1]

BEHAVIORAL DEFINITIONS

1. Frequent arguments about parenting, or disagreements that interfere with effective child-rearing.
2. Lack of agreement between parents regarding strategies for dealing with various types of child misbehaviors.
3. Ineffective parental responses to child misbehavior (i.e., efforts do not result in the desired outcome).
4. Inability of partners to discuss and support each other's parenting efforts.

—. _____
   _____

—. _____
   _____

—. _____
   _____

LONG-TERM GOALS

1. Discuss and agree on the implementation of joint parenting strategies.
2. Identify parenting and contextual factors that increase the frequency of child misbehavior.
3. Classify and respond to child misbehavior based on function.
4. Have daily casual conversations about parenting.
5. Share ideas about parenting strategies and support each other's parenting behavior.

---

[1]A more expansive description of the interventions summarized in this chapter can be found in Sanders (1992); Sanders & Dadds (1993); Sanders, Lynch, & Markie-Dadds (1994); and Sanders, Markie-Dadds, & Nicholson (1997). An excellent overview of the overlap between relationship conflict and child behavior problems can be found in Cummings & Davies (2010).

—. _____
  _____
—. _____
  _____
—. _____
  _____

SHORT-TERM OBJECTIVES

▼ 1. Discuss child problem behavior.
   (1, 2, 3, 4)

THERAPEUTIC INTERVENTIONS

1. Have parents describe their main concerns about their child's problem behavior, and review its history. Therapist's questions might include: "When did the problem behavior start?" and "How has it changed across time?" ▼

2. Ask parents to specifically detail the extent of the child's problem behavior. Therapist's questions might include: "How frequently and intensely does problem behavior occur?" "How long does it last?" "In which situations does it occur?" ▼

3. Identify specific child behavior and parenting problems by having parents complete questionnaire assessments such as the *Child Behavior Checklist* (Achenbach) and the *Parenting Scale* (Arnold, O'Leary, Wolff, & Acker). ▼

4. Identify (a) each partner's parenting philosophy and strategy, and (b) each partner's expectations for the child's behavior (e.g., three-year-olds should sit through dinner quietly). ▼

▽ 2. Identify the parenting and situational factors that may be maintaining the problem. (5, 6, 7)

3. Discuss how relationship functioning affects and is affected by parenting difficulties. (8, 9, 10, 11)

▽ 4. Verbalize an understanding of the three motives for a child's misbehavior. (12)

▽ 5. State examples of the child's misbehavior that are motivated by attention-seeking. (13)

5. Assist the parents in identifying parent-child behavioral patterns that may be maintaining the problem (e.g., unintentionally reinforcing problem behaviors through nagging or emotional parenting). ▽

6. Identify social context factors that may be maintaining the problem (e.g., family transitions, inconsistent rules, school or social difficulties). ▽

7. Identify any parent stressors that may be maintaining the problem (e.g., unemployment, substance use, depression). ▽

8. Have parents indicate ways their relationship conflict has a negative impact on their child's behavior. ▽

9. Have parents describe how their child's problem behavior impacts their relationship conflict. ▽

10. Ask the partners to attempt to solve a major parenting problem; quietly observe and note skills and deficiencies. ▽

11. Assign each parent to increase the amount of focused, child-centered positive time with the child experiencing difficulty. ▽

12. Educate parents regarding the three main motives for a child's misbehavior: attention-seeking, escape or demands, and fun-seeking. ▽

13. Help parents identify examples of attention-seeking misbehavior (i.e., misbehavior that only occurs when someone is around, and for which the child secures attention prior to performing). ▽

▽ 6. List examples of the child's misbehavior that are motivated by escape or demand. (14)

14. Help parents identify examples of demand-motivated misbehavior (i.e., misbehavior that promotes the child getting something he/she wants) and of escape-motivated misbehavior (i.e., misbehavior that promotes the child getting out of, or delaying, something he/she does not want to do). ▽

▽ 7. Identify examples of the child's misbehavior that are motivated by fun-seeking. (15)

15. Help parents identify examples of fun-motivated misbehavior (i.e., misbehavior that does not require someone to see it, and that the child attempts to hide). ▽

▽ 8. Define a behavior in the child that should be reinforced, and track its occurrence as well as antecedents and consequences. (16)

16. Ask parents to select a child behavior that they would like to reinforce; assign them to record its occurrence every day for a week, and to note the behaviors or situations that precede it (i.e., antecedents) and those that follow it (i.e., consequences). ▽

▽ 9. Identify a behavior in the child that the parents would like to discourage, and track its occurrence as well as antecedents and consequences. (17)

17. Ask parents to select a behavior that they would like to discourage; assign them to record its occurrence every day for a week and to note the behaviors or situations that precede it (i.e., antecedents) and those that follow it (i.e., consequences). ▽

▽ 10. Track and identify the functions of the child's behaviors. (18)

18. After reviewing the parents' tracking sheets, have them identify the motives for each misbehavior observed (i.e., attention-seeking, demand or escape, fun-seeking). ▽

▽ 11. Implement ignoring responses in reaction to attention-seeking behaviors by child. (19, 20)

19. Role-play purposeful ignoring and encourage parents to use this technique to discourage attention-seeking misbehavior. Warn parents that inconsistent use of technique (e.g., ignoring misbehaviors sometimes but

attending at other times) will only strengthen the misbehavior. ▽

20. Help parents formulate a plan for appropriate, function-based responses to child misbehaviors (e.g., attention = ignore; demand/escape = do not give in; fun = make the behavior less fun). ▽

▽ 12. Implement firm control in response to escape/demand behaviors of child. (21)

21. Help parents practice and troubleshoot firm, purposeful responses to demand/escape misbehavior. ▽

▽ 13. Implement commands and reprimands in response to fun-seeking behaviors by child. (22)

22. Teach parents commands and reprimands to use in response to fun-motivated misbehavior to make the behavior less fun; responses should be firm, immediate, and brief, and they should clearly state what behavior is expected from the child. Role-play implementation of these commands. ▽

▽ 14. List some natural and logical negative consequences (punishments) that could flow from specific misbehavior. (23)

23. Teach parents to establish logical and natural negative consequences to child misbehavior (e.g., refuse to eat → go hungry; make a mess → clean up the mess); ask them to list some of these types of natural negative consequences (punishments) that could be used with their child's misbehavior. ▽

▽ 15. List ways to prevent some misbehaviors by anticipating them and planning ahead. (24)

24. Have the parents list misbehavior situations that are consistently problematic; help them to identify the motivation for the misbehaviors and to brainstorm ways of preventing the misbehaviors (e.g., shorten duration of shopping trips, pack snacks for child). ▽

▽ 16. Report instances of effectively employing time-outs to deal with serious child misbehavior. (25)

25. Help parents practice and troubleshoot responding to serious misbehavior with the time-out technique (i.e., child sits

in chair with no attention for one to two minutes per year of age). ▽

▽ 17. Increase the frequency of contingently reinforcing positive child behavior. (26, 27)

26. Teach parents to notice and reinforce child's positive behaviors; have each parent practice behavior reinforcement in session, and provide feedback (or assign "Using Reinforcement Principles in Parenting" in the *Adult Psychotherapy Homework Planner*, 2nd ed. by Jongsma). ▽

27. Instruct parents in making "good behavior charts" (i.e., children earn points/tokens for appropriate behavior, and trade their points/tokens for things that they want). ▽

▽ 18. Increase frequency of positive interactions with child. (11, 28)

11. Assign each parent to increase amount of focused, child-centered positive time with the child experiencing difficulty. ▽

28. Assign each parent to increase number of casual, positive conversations with the child experiencing difficulty. ▽

▽ 19. Each parent identifies, examines, and then pledges to terminate any negative behavior that he/she is modeling and that the child is imitating. (29)

29. If parents are modeling for the child the behavior they would like to extinguish (e.g., yelling, hitting), have them contract to change their own behavior before trying to change the same behavior in the child. ▽

▽ 20. Check with partner regularly concerning parenting and keep a log of these interactions. (30, 31, 32)

30. Assign parents to confer with each other at least once a day regarding the child's behavior. ▽

31. Encourage parents to plan a mutually acceptable time to confer, to avoid having casual conversations at times when arguments are likely to erupt (e.g., immediately upon arriving home in the evening). ▽

▽ 21. Use argument-control strategies to increase the productivity of parenting conversations. (33)

▽ 22. Report instances of constructive and supportive conversations with partner regarding current parenting experiences. (34, 35, 36)

▽ 23. Agree with partner to support each other's parenting. (37, 38, 39)

32. Instruct partners to track their satisfaction with the daily check-ins and to bring in the tracking sheet to their treatment sessions. ▽

33. Assist the partners in practicing argument control (e.g., using "Pause, Calm, and Think"; using "I" messages in place of "you" messages [see chapter on Anger in this *Planner*]); assign partners to employ these techniques to cool off during parenting discussions if either believes that the conversation is becoming unsupportive). ▽

34. Help partners role-play discussions they will have when the children are well-behaved; have the supportive partner ask the other what the children have been doing and then support his/her parenting behaviors. ▽

35. Help partners role-play discussions they will have when the children are poorly behaved; have the supportive partner ask, in a supportive, nonthreatening manner, about the specifics of the misbehavior. ▽

36. During role-playing exercises for dealing with child misbehavior, have the supportive partner ask in a supportive, nonthreatening manner about how the other dealt with the misbehavior and whether the supportive partner can do anything in the future to help (or assign "Learning to Parent as a Team" in the *Adult Psychotherapy Homework Planner,* 2nd ed. by Jongsma). ▽

37. Have partners contract to support each other's parenting by not interfering during the other's parent-child interactions,

and by not interfering with the other's decisions (i.e., avoiding splitting of parents' unity).▽

38. Help partners identify what each can do to help the other in challenging situations (e.g., play with or supervise the children while the other partner is on the phone).▽

39. Have partners contract to put disagreements over parenting strategy on hold until the situation has ended and they can meet privately, and both partners are calm and able to problem-solve without accusations or defensiveness.▽

▽ 24. Regularly discuss and problem-solve parenting strategies for handling misbehavior. (40)

40. Assign partners to schedule parenting problem-solving discussions (see the chapter on Communication in this Planner) for two or three times per week.▽

▽ 25. Use problem-solving skills with partner to resolve a parenting problem. (40, 41, 42, 43)

40. Assign partners to schedule parenting problem-solving discussions for two or three times per week.▽

41. Have the partners role-play using pinpointing skills to specifically identify the problem.▽

42. Help partners role-play the speaker-listener technique, where the listener does not respond with their own thoughts until he/she has paraphrased the speaker's position to that person's satisfaction.▽

43. Advise partners to limit themselves to solving one problem at a time.▽

▽ 26. Brainstorm with partner several possible parental interventions for the misbehavior. (44)

44. Encourage each partner to generate at least two possible solutions to each of the child's problem behaviors.▽

▽ 27. Evaluate with the partner various possible solutions to the child's problematic behavior, choose one, and plan for its enactment and evaluation. (45, 46, 47)

45. Help partners role-play choosing a solution together by judging the advantages and disadvantages of each possible solution. ▽

46. Help partners plan together on how to enact solutions. ▽

47. Have partners establish a time to review the progress of the solution, and to troubleshoot the solution as necessary. ▽

▽ 28. Establish consistent house rules. (48)

48. Have parents discuss and establish consistent house rules (or assign "Using Reinforcement Principles in Parenting" in the *Adult Psychotherapy Homework Planner*, 2nd ed. by Jongsma). ▽

__. _____   __. _____
    _____   _____
__. _____   __. _____
    _____   _____
__. _____   __. _____
    _____   _____

DIAGNOSTIC SUGGESTIONS

ICD-9-CM	*ICD-10-CM*	*DSM-5* Disorder, Condition, or Problem
309.24	F43.22	Adjustment Disorder, With Anxiety
309.0	F43.21	Adjustment Disorder, With Depressed Mood
309.3	F43.24	Adjustment Disorder, With Disturbance of Conduct
309.28	F43.23	Adjustment Disorder, With Mixed Anxiety and Depressed Mood
309.4	F43.25	Adjustment Disorder, With Mixed Disturbance of Emotions and Conduct
V61.20	Z62.820	Parent-Child Relational Problem
V61.10	Z63.0	Relationship Distress with Spouse or Intimate Partner
_____	_____	_____
_____	_____	_____

PERSONALITY DIFFERENCES

BEHAVIORAL DEFINITIONS

1. One partner is introverted, whereas the other is extroverted.
2. One partner is assertive, whereas the other is passive.
3. One partner is gregarious, whereas the other prefers to be alone or only with partner.
4. One partner is religious, whereas the other is not.
5. One partner is physically active, whereas the other prefers sedentary activities.
6. One partner likes to listen to music, whereas the other does not.
7. One partner likes to watch sports, whereas the other does not.
8. One partner is independent, whereas the other is not.
9. Partners argue over choice of recreational activities.
10. One partner is much more moralistic than the other.
11. Communication is argumentative and/or avoidant.
12. Expressions of caring/love between partners have waned.

—. _____
   _____

—. _____
   _____

—. _____
   _____

LONG-TERM GOALS

1. Partners reach compromises that are acceptable to each.
2. One partner makes significant changes in style of relating.
3. Partners capitalize on their personality differences to enhance the relationship.

4. Partners accept certain personality differences and respect those differences.

—. _____

_____

—. _____

_____

—. _____

_____

SHORT-TERM OBJECTIVES

▽ 1. Describe own and partner's personality styles and differentiate long-standing personality styles from recent habitual patterns. (1, 2, 3, 4, 5)

▽ 2. Describe personality differences that have enriched the relationship. (6)

▽ 3. Acknowledge how differences in personality make social life more interesting. (7)

▽ 4. Describe personality differences that have caused conflict in the relationship. (8, 9)

THERAPEUTIC INTERVENTIONS

1. Have each partner develop a list of own personality styles that are similar to those of partner. ▽

2. Help partners differentiate between habits (i.e., changeable behaviors) and personality styles (i.e., long-standing ways of approaching the world). ▽

3. Ask each partner to develop a list of their own personality styles that differ significantly from those of their partner. ▽

4. Ask each partner to develop a list of the partner's important habits. ▽

5. Ask each partner to develop a list of their own important habits. ▽

6. Ask each partner to describe how differences between self and partner enrich the relationship. ▽

7. Help each partner identify how differences between self and partner are valuable and help in social functioning. ▽

8. Ask each partner to describe how differences between self and partner are detrimental to the relationship. ▽

5. Agree to make some changes in habitual behavior. (10)

6. Agree to attempt changing a behavior that seems to represent a long-standing personality style. (11)

7. Verbalize how personality differences in parents model very different behaviors for children. (12)

▽ 8. Verbalize acceptance of differences in personality styles between self and partner, and cite the value of some differences. (13, 14, 15, 16, 17)

9. Ask each partner to describe how differences between self and partner are detrimental to social functioning. ▽

10. Request that each partner identify and verbally commit to changing habitual patterns that are offensive to the other partner.

11. Request that each partner identify and verbally commit to changing behaviors that represent long-standing personality patterns and cause conflicts in the relationship (or assign "Positive and Negative Contributions to the Relationship: Yours and Mine" in the *Adult Psychotherapy Homework Planner*, 2nd ed. by Jongsma).

12. Help the partners understand the value of differences in the relationship for rearing children.

13. Assist the partners in understanding the value of differences in the relationship for intimate functioning. ▽

14. Assist the partners in developing an understanding of the types of behavior that are very difficult to change. ▽

15. Teach the partners about the types of personality styles that are very difficult to change. ▽

16. Assist the partners in accepting differences that can exist between them without any detriment to each other. ▽

17. Educate the partners regarding the value of their differences in personality. ▽

▽ 9. Make positive comments to partner about the differences in personality styles. (18)

10. Make positive comments to family/friends about differences in personality styles. (19)

18. Ask the partners to make comments to each other in therapy session about the value of their differences. ▽

19. Assign the partners to make comments to family/friends about the value of their differences.

__. _____

_____

__. _____

_____

__. _____

_____

__. _____

_____

__. _____

_____

__. _____

_____

DIAGNOSTIC SUGGESTIONS

ICD-9-CM	_ICD-10-CM_	_DSM-5_ Disorder, Condition, or Problem
309.0	F43.21	Adjustment Disorder, With Depressed Mood
309.24	F43.22	Adjustment Disorder, With Anxiety
309.28	F43.23	Adjustment Disorder, With Mixed Anxiety and Depressed Mood
309.4	F43.25	Adjustment Disorder, With Mixed Disturbance of Emotions and Conduct
309.3	F43.24	Adjustment Disorder, With Disturbance of Conduct
V61.10	Z63.0	Relationship Distress with Spouse or Intimate Partner
301.7	F60.2	Antisocial Personality Disorder
301.83	F60.3	Borderline Personality Disorder
301.6	F60.7	Dependent Personality Disorder
301.50	F60.4	Histrionic Personality Disorder
301.4	F60.5	Obsessive-Compulsive Personality Disorder
301.81	F60.81	Narcissistic Personality Disorder
_____	_____	_____
_____	_____	_____

PSYCHOLOGICAL ABUSE

BEHAVIORAL DEFINITIONS

1. Insults partner when alone and in front of others.
2. Swears at partner.
3. Calls partner demeaning, degrading names (e.g., lazy, sloppy).
4. Makes critical, demeaning comments about partner's body (e.g., fat, bald, ugly, skinny).
5. Makes critical and demeaning comments about partner's ability to perform his/her job.
6. Makes critical comments about partner's ability to perform roles in home (e.g., cook, fix things, clean, take care of the yard).
7. Accuses partner, without cause, of sexual promiscuity and infidelity.
8. Makes critical comments about partner's sexuality or sexual performance.
9. Makes critical statement about partner's mental health (e.g., "You are crazy," "You need a psychiatrist," "You are paranoid").
10. Threatens to do physical harm to partner.
11. Threatens to leave partner.
12. Threatens to have sex with someone else.
13. Tries to prevent partner from having contact with friends and family.
14. Tries to prevent partner from leaving home.
15. Prevents partner from using car (e.g., takes keys, removes spark plugs or wires).
16. Refuses to talk to partner for days (i.e., silent treatment).
17. Makes partner account for time.
18. Jealous of partner's time spent with other individuals (especially of opposite sex).

---

*Most research that has addressed the issue of partner abuse has a primary emphasis on reduction of physical aggression but in such programs psychological aggression has been reduced significantly. It can be inferred that psychological aggression alone can be treated more easily than psychological aggression that does not occur simultaneously with physical aggression.

19. Discourages partner from obtaining further training or education that would enhance his/her self-esteem and opportunities for advancement.
20. Orders partner around in a dominating, controlling, and belittling manner.

___. _____

_____

___. _____

_____

___. _____

_____

LONG-TERM GOALS

1. Terminate verbal and/or psychological abuse and establish a relationship based in respect and a desire for mutual enhancement.
2. Replace hostile, threatening, and critical comments with respectful communication that builds self-esteem.
3. Eliminate threats to leave the relationship and/or to have sex with others.
4. Eliminate the use of controlling behaviors that attempt to keep the partner physically nearby and away from friends and family.
5. Eliminate the use of controlling behaviors that attempt to keep the partner from bettering herself/himself.
6. Evaluate alternatives to current relationship.

___. _____

_____

___. _____

_____

___. _____

_____

SHORT-TERM OBJECTIVES

▽ 1. Verbalize agreement to stop hostile comments and name-calling. (1, 2, 3)

THERAPEUTIC INTERVENTIONS

1. Obtain verbal commitment from the partners not to engage in name-calling or making hostile comments. ▽

2. Advise the partners of the need for individual therapy if anger cannot be controlled in the conjoint therapy sessions. ▽

3. Discuss with the partners the need for both to be psychologically ready before conjoint therapy is indicated, and to accept responsibility for minimizing any major negative events that might occur in therapy. ▽

▽ 2. Identify partner's comments that are especially damaging to self-esteem. (4, 5)

4. Have each partner describe comments by partner that hurt him/her the most. ▽

5. Have each partner describe the areas of his/her own life where he/she feels most vulnerable. ▽

▽ 3. Verbalize an understanding of the negative impact of abuse. (6, 7)

6. Using role-reversal technique, have the abusive partner assume abused partner's identity and then identify the emotional impact of the abusive behavior (or assign "Letter of Apology" in the *Adult Psychotherapy Homework Planner,* 2nd ed. by Jongsma). ▽

7. Confront any displays of or references to abusive behavior, and educate the partners regarding its destructive consequences (or assign "Alternatives to Destructive Anger" in the *Adult Psychotherapy Homework Planner,* 2nd ed. by Jongsma). ▽

▽ 4. Verbally agree not to use psychological coercion or threat of physical force to obtain sexual interaction. (8, 9)

8. Obtain commitment from the partners not to use physical force to coerce sexual interaction. ▽

9. Educate the partners that to have a positive sexual relationship, the sexual activity must be acceptable to both the partners. ▽

▽ 5. Identify the negative consequences of using coercion for sexual activity. (10, 11)

10. Educate the partners that pressure by one partner to engage in sexual activity usually leads to sexual aversions and/or avoidance and dislike by the other partner. ▽

11. Educate the partners that sexual behavior is one of the most sensitive of all human behaviors, and that aversive control by one partner can quickly lead to disinterest and sexual dysfunction in the other partner. ▽

▽ 6. Terminate threats to have sex with someone else. (12)

12. Obtain verbal commitment from the partners not to threaten to have sex with someone else. ▽

▽ 7. Terminate threats to leave partner. (13)

13. Obtain verbal commitment from the partners not to threaten to leave the relationship during the term of therapy; an agreement about the length of therapy should be developed at the beginning of treatment. ▽

▽ 8. Terminate all threats of physical aggression against the partner for any reason. (14)

14. Obtain a verbal commitment from the partners not to engage in any physical force against the other partner for any reason; be aware that when intense verbal intimidation exists, the risk for physical aggression also is high. ▽

▽ 9. Describe instances of coercion or threats of physical violence in the relationship. (15, 16)

15. Ask both partners to describe the extent to which psychological coercion and threats of violence are present in the relationship in general. ▽

16. Ask both partners to describe the perceived or experienced negative consequences of threatened violence. ▽

▽ 10. Abused, fearful partner accepts a referral to a safe environment. (17)

17. If the abused partner's fear of violence is intense, provide a referral to a safe environment

▽ 11. Verbalize an understanding of male control and misuse of power in our society. (18, 19, 20)

▽ 12. Both the partners agree to build each other's self-esteem through compliments, appreciation, and acts of kindness. (21)

13. Agree to accept and encourage contact by both the partners with friends and family as a means of improving the relationship. (22)

▽ 14. Agree to support each other in obtaining training or education. (23)

15. Abusive partner identifies feelings that motivate controlling behavior. (24)

(e.g., battered-women's shelter, abuse hot-line number). ▽

18. Review and discuss with the partners the role of patriarchy in American society. ▽

19. Review and discuss with the partners how the controlling partner misuses his/her power. ▽

20. Educate the partners regarding how controlling behaviors by one partner lead to dislike and avoidance by the other partner. ▽

21. Review with partners the evidence regarding the association between psychological aggression and poor self-esteem and/or depression; have the partners list specific ways for them to build self-esteem in each other (or assign "How Can We Meet Each Other's Needs and Desires?" in the *Adult Psychotherapy Homework Planner,* 2nd ed. by Jongsma). ▽

22. Educate the partners regarding the fact that external social support (e.g., contact with friends) and relationship satisfaction are positively related.

23. Educate the partners regarding the need for each partner to be able to venture out from the relationship with the sense that the other will be supportive of him/her (i.e., for bettering self through education or training or job enhancement). ▽

24. Have the abusive partner identify the feelings (e.g., jealousy, fears of inadequacy) that underlie the need for controlling behavior of either partner.

▽ 16. List the negative consequences of exerting control over the other partner. (25)

25. Assist the partners in listing the negative consequences of controlling behavior on the abused partner (e.g., resentment, avoidance, waning of caring feelings). ▽

▽ 17. Demonstrate respectful, accurate communication with their partner. (26, 27)

26. Have each partner listen to the other about a relationship matter without interrupting, and then paraphrase what the other said. ▽

27. Provide feedback and interpretation to the partners about their communication styles. ▽

▽ 18. Assess alternatives to the relationship and accept referrals regarding respite from the relationship. (28, 29)

28. In an individual session with the psychologically abused partner, have him/her evaluate the available alternatives to the current relationship. ▽

29. If necessary, refer psychologically abused partner to an agency for battered women and/or to a shelter. ▽

▽ 19. Abused partner read material on abusive relationships and building self-esteem. (30)

30. Suggest reading materials for the abused partner on abusive relationships and building self-esteem (e.g., *The Verbally Abusive Relationship* by Evans; *Surviving Domestic Violence* by Weiss; *The Dance of Anger* by Lerner; *Ten Days to Self-Esteem!* by Burns). ▽

▽ 20. Both partners agree to minimize negative relationship interactions in the presence of their children. (31, 32)

31. If the partners have children, review with the partners the evidence showing a significant link between open hostility between parents and psychopathology in children (i.e., increased incidence of conduct problems and anxiety problems). ▽

32. If the partners have children, have both partners commit to minimizing negative interactions in the presence of the children. ▽

—. _____   —. _____
   _____   _____
—. _____ , —. _____
   _____   _____
—. _____   —. _____
   _____   _____

DIAGNOSTIC SUGGESTIONS

ICD-9-CM	_ICD-10-CM_	_DSM-5_ Disorder, Condition, or Problem
309.0	F43.21	Adjustment Disorder, With Depressed Mood
309.24	F43.22	Adjustment Disorder, With Anxiety
309.28	F43.23	Adjustment Disorder, With Mixed Anxiety and Depressed Mood
305.00	F10.10	Alcohol Use Disorder, Mild
303.90	F10.20	Alcohol Use Disorder, Moderate or Severe
300.4	F34.1	Persistent Depressive Disorder
296.2x	F32.x	Major Depressive Disorder, Single Episode
296.3x	F33.x	Major Depressive Disorder, Recurrent Episode
V61.10	Z63.0	Relationship Distress with Spouse or Intimate Partner
995.82	T74.31XA	Spouse or Partner Psychological Abuse, Confirmed, Initial Encounter
995.82	T74.31XD	Spouse or Partner Psychological Abuse, Confirmed, Subsequent Encounter
995.82	T74.11XA	Spouse or Partner Violence, Physical, Confirmed, Initial Encounter
995.82	T74.11XD	Spouse or Partner Violence, Physical, Confirmed, Subsequent Encounter
V61.12	Z69.12	Encounter for Mental Health Services for Perpetrator of Spouse or Partner Psychological Abuse
995.81	Z69.11	Encounter for Mental Health Services for Victim of Spouse or Partner Psychological Abuse
301.7	F60.2	Antisocial Personality Disorder
301.83	F60.3	Borderline Personality Disorder
301.6	F60.7	Dependent Personality Disorder
301.81	F60.81	Narcissistic Personality Disorder

_____ _____ _____

_____ _____ _____

RECREATIONAL ACTIVITIES DISPUTE

BEHAVIORAL DEFINITIONS

1. Conflict over choice of leisure activities to be shared by partners.
2. Conflict over time spent by one partner in his/her individual recreational activities.
3. Uncomfortable feelings of disconnectedness due to one or both partners engaging extensively in separate, unshared recreational activities.
4. Disagreement over the manner in which vacation time is spent.
5. Erosion of quality or quantity of time spent in partner-pleasing activities.

__. _____
_____
_____

__. _____
_____
_____

__. _____
_____

LONG-TERM GOALS

1. Identify and plan regular positive activities, to be enjoyed both alone and together.
2. Discuss and respect each other's varying interests.
3. Find opportunities to enjoy elements of each other's hobbies or interests as a means of giving of self to the other partner.
4. Plan vacation opportunities in a manner that maximizes mutual enjoyment and minimizes conflict.

__. _____
_____

—. _____
 _____
—. _____
 _____

SHORT-TERM OBJECTIVES

1. Verbally define current level of satisfaction with recreational activities. (1, 2)

2. Generate lists of recreational activities that each partner would like to do alone, with partner, or with others. (3, 4)

▽ 3. Discuss and listen in a respectful manner to other partner's leisure-time likes and dislikes. (5, 6)

THERAPEUTIC INTERVENTIONS

1. Identify each partner's level of satisfaction with recreational activities that are done (a) individually and (b) as a couple.

2. Ask each partner to identify elements of recreational activities that he/she believes are in need of improvement (i.e., frequency, quality, particular activities).

3. Ask the partners to complete the *Inventory of Rewarding Activities* (Birchler & Weiss, 1977) to generate a list of desired activities in the following categories: (a) to do alone, (b) to do with partner, (c) to do with partner and other family members, (d) to do with partner and nonfamily members, and (e) to do with nonfamily members.

4. Ask the partners to discuss the similarities and differences of their Rewarding Activities lists; assist them in identifying interests that are shared with partner and those that are unique to each partner.

5. For important activities about which partners disagree, have partners discuss their points of view by taking turns as speakers (for example, "When I go

hunting, I feel alive and part of nature.").▽

6. After the speaker states his/her preferences, have the listener show respect for the other's point of view by paraphrasing it and by refraining from criticism. ▽

4. Identify and plan pleasurable activities of varying lengths. (7, 8, 9)

7. Assign each partner to independently list 5 to 10 activities or behaviors that he/she could do that the other partner would enjoy. ▽

8. Have each person classify the partner-enjoyable activities into those that can be done in 15–30 minutes, 1–2 hours, 4–6 hours, a full day, and a weekend. ▽

9. Have partners use their lists of rewarding activities to schedule one week's activities (e.g., work, responsibilities, chores, and leisure pursuits). ▽

5. Discuss the impact of planned pleasurable activities and contract for continued weekly planning. (10, 11)

10. Ask each partner to discuss the week's pleasurable activity assignment using "I" statements (for example, "When we went for a walk at the beach this weekend, I felt really peaceful and close to you. I'd like us to go for a walk at least once a weekend in the future."); have the listener respond using paraphrasing and reflecting skills. ▽

11. After reviewing and trouble-shooting the pleasurable activity assignment, have partners contract to schedule their activities weekly. ▽

6. Each partner construct a self-change plan regarding recreational pursuit differences. (12, 13)

12. Teach partners the five steps of a Self-Change Plan: (1) Describe the behavior to be changed; (2) Examine the pros and cons of

the current behavior; (3) Set a goal, describing as precisely as possible what is to happen; (4) Create Action Plan, pinpointing a specific plan for enacting the goal; and (5) Evaluate the enacting of a plan. Have the partners practice this in session on an aspect of recreational pursuit differences that each would like to change. ▽

13 Ask partners to make a global evaluation of how they did on the action plan before the next session. The rating scale is 0 = didn't think about it or do it; 1 = thought about it; 2 = gave it a weak try; 3 = tried, partially succeeded; and 4 = did a great job. Ask them to jot down short answers to the following: What did we actually do? What positives resulted? What negatives resulted? What do we need to do from here? ▽

▽ 7. Each partner identifies an activity that is primarily enjoyable to the other partner that he/she can occasionally show an interest in or participate in. (14, 15, 16)

14. Assign each partner to join in or arrange for, the other partner, at least three activities that are enjoyable for the other partner (scaled to fit their time demands) per week; have partners record the activity and rate the quality of satisfaction. ▽

15. Encourage each partner to commit to occasionally showing an interest or participating in an activity (e.g., attending a symphony concert) that is pleasurable to the other partner but not to self. ▽

16. Have partners contract to respect each other's interests and hobbies by not criticizing the

8. Each partner pursue an activity that is pleasurable to him/her while not allowing the activity to dominate the couple's available free time. (17, 18)

9. Use problem-solving skills to find agreement on how both partners can enjoy a vacation site. (19, 20)

10. Agree to spend equal time together at one partner's choice, followed by time together at other partner's choice. (21)

11. Plan and periodically implement a high-intensity day of positive activities that focus alternately on each partner's wishes. (22, 23)

other's hobby or other enjoyable activity.

17. Have partners contract to respect each other by not letting any one activity or hobby dominate own free time or the couple's available free time.

18. Have partners contract to respect each other's interests and hobbies by scheduling time each week for mutually enjoyable and individually enjoyable leisure activities.

19. If partners disagree on vacation sites (e.g., one likes the beach and the other does not), help them use problem-solving skills so each generates at least two ways in which they can still enjoy mutual destinations (e.g., one goes to the beach while the other shops in nearby town).

20. If partners disagree on vacation sites, help them each generate at least two ways to include others and thereby increase the attractiveness of the partner's preferred site (e.g., vacationing with another family to provide each partner with company to share favorite pursuits).

21. If partners disagree on vacation sites, help them each generate at least two ways to make destination choices equitable (e.g., one summer go to the beach, the next to the mountains).

22. Have partners plan a "love day" periodically, during which one partner receives from the other partner as many beneficial activities (especially benefits that

don't occur on typical days) as possible (for example, a husband might give his wife a backrub, take care of the children while she exercises, and then prepare a romantic, candlelight dinner). ▽

23. Ask partners to alternate who will be the recipient of "love day" and who will be the giver. ▽

__. _____   _____

     _____   __. _____

__. _____   _____

__. _____   _____

     _____   __. _____

__. _____   _____

DIAGNOSTIC SUGGESTIONS

ICD-9-CM	_ICD-10-CM_	_DSM-5_ Disorder, Condition, or Problem
309.0	F43.21	Adjustment Disorder, With Depressed Mood
309.24	F43.22	Adjustment Disorder, With Anxiety
309.28	F43.23	Adjustment Disorder, With Mixed Anxiety and Depressed Mood
300.4	F34.1	Persistent Depressive Disorder
300.02	F41.1	Generalized Anxiety Disorder
296.2x	F32.x	Major Depressive Disorder, Single Episode
296.3x	F33.x	Major Depressive Disorder, Recurrent Episode
V61.10	Z63.0	Relationship Distress with Spouse or Intimate Partner
_____	_____	_____
_____	_____	_____

RELIGIOUS/SPIRITUALITY DIFFERENCES

BEHAVIORAL DEFINITIONS

1. Upsetting verbal disagreements between the partners over religious faith (i.e., core beliefs about life and afterlife) and practices (e.g., communal worship, prayer).
2. Attempts by one partner to coerce other into accepting own religious and spiritual beliefs, values, or activities.
3. Reduced intimacy between the partners due to inability to constructively share deeply held core beliefs and values.
4. Conflicts between the partners about their children's religious training and expected attendance at worship services.
5. Arguments between the partners over proper child-discipline strategies, fueled at least in part by differing religious and spiritual beliefs about parenting.

—. _____
   _____
—. _____
   _____
—. _____
   _____

LONG-TERM GOALS

1. Recognize developmental changes in religious beliefs and/or changes in tolerance about the partner's religious and spiritual beliefs, values, or activities.

2. Commit selves to strengthening the relationship by: (a) identifying advantages of each other's beliefs, (b) respecting each other's views, and (c) accommodating each other's practices.
3. Increase intimacy of relationship by discussing core beliefs and existential meaning.
4. Agree to work together in parental roles of religious instruction and discipline.

—. _____
   _____

—. _____
   _____

—. _____
   _____

SHORT-TERM OBJECTIVES

THERAPEUTIC INTERVENTIONS

1. Each partner verbally traces the developmental history of religious and spiritual beliefs. (1, 2)

1. Ask each partner to identify the role that religion and spirituality played in his/her childhood home and family experience.

2. Have the partners trace changes that have taken place in their religious and spiritual beliefs, values, or activities as they have grown older (or assign "My History of Spirituality" in the *Adult Psychotherapy Homework Planner*, 2nd ed. by Jongsma).

2. Each partner identifies the impact of religious beliefs on the relationship. (3, 4)

3. Ask the partners to discuss the role that religious and spiritual beliefs played in their lives during the early stages of their relationship.

4. Ask the partners to discuss the meaning of marriage in their respective religious and spiritual belief systems.

3. Outline the history of, and reasons for, current conflict over

5. Identify ways that the partners' religious and spiritual beliefs,

religious and spiritual beliefs. (5, 6, 7)

4. Each partner identifies how his/her religious and spiritual beliefs strengthen the relationship. (8)

5. Each partner identifies how the couple's religious differences cause conflict in other areas of the relationship. (9)

6. Promise respect for other partner's religious and spiritual beliefs, values, or activities, and agree not to coerce other partner into belief conformity. (10, 11)

7. Share the meaning of commitment, respect, intimacy, forgiveness, and sexuality within each partner's religious and spiritual belief system. (12, 13)

values, or activities have changed since they met.

6. Identify when the partners' conflict over religious and spiritual beliefs, values, or activities began.

7. Ask the partners to describe when and how they argue or disagree about religious and spiritual beliefs, values, and activities.

8. Ask each client to describe ways in which his/her religious and spiritual beliefs, values, and activities strengthen the relationship.

9. Ask each client to describe the ways in which religious and spiritual differences accentuate conflict in other areas of the relationship (e.g., role strain, parenting).

10. Have the clients contract to respect each other's religious and spiritual beliefs by not criticizing the other's beliefs, values, or activities.

11. Have clients contract to respect each other's religious and spiritual beliefs by agreeing not to coerce the other into conforming to self's beliefs, values, or activities.

12. Ask each partner to discuss the values placed on (a) commitment, (b) respect, (c) intimacy, and (d) forgiveness within the framework of his/her religious and/or spiritual belief system.

13. Help the partners identify the impact that their differing religious and spiritual beliefs have on their sexual relationship.

8. Share how the meaning of commitment, respect, intimacy, forgiveness, and sexuality within each partner's religious and spiritual belief system is evidenced within the relationship. (14)

9. Each partner articulates own core beliefs, including the meaning of human existence. (15)

10. Each partner shares how own core beliefs have helped to provide meaning to his/her personal life. (16)

11. Verbalize how religious beliefs and practice are important for support of core beliefs. (17)

▽ 12. Demonstrate respect for the other partner's professed religious and spiritual beliefs by engaging in listener behaviors that facilitate the free exchange of views regarding the meaning of human existence. (18, 19, 20)

13. Verbalize reasons why it is important to self that the other partner agree in religious beliefs and practice; then offer constructive ways to respond to the ongoing disagreement. (21)

14. Have each partner discuss how the values placed on (a) commitment, (b) respect, (c) intimacy, and (d) forgiveness provide evidence of his/her religious and or spiritual belief.

15. Help each partner identify own core beliefs (e.g., the existence and nature of God, the nature of man, the meaning of human life, the existence and nature of an afterlife) and how he/she came to that belief system.

16. Have each partner consider and share the ways that religious and spiritual beliefs have added meaning to his/her personal life.

17. Have each partner consider and share the ways that religious and spiritual beliefs and practices reinforce his/her core beliefs.

18. Ask the listening partner to show respect for the speaker's beliefs by paraphrasing the speaker's beliefs, even if he/she does not agree with the speaker. ▽

19. Ask the listening partner to show respect for the speaker's beliefs by not responding with lecturing or preaching, even if he/she does not agree with the speaker. ▽

20 Ask the listening partner to show respect for the speaker's beliefs by not arguing against the speaker's beliefs. ▽

21. Allow each partner who so desires to describe (a) why it is important for him/her that the other partner accept and adopt his/her religious beliefs, and (b) how he/she will constructively

14. Identify the degree of flexibility available for accommodating divergent beliefs. (22, 23, 24)

▽ 15. Teach the partners how to construct a self-change plan and ask each to construct one regarding religious differences. (25, 26)

cope with a lack of agreement between them.

22. Help each partner identify what deviations from core beliefs he/she can accommodate or tolerate in the other partner.

23. Help each partner identify what deviations from core beliefs he/she cannot accommodate or tolerate in the other partner.

24. Have each partner identify his/her core belief regarding divorce.

25. Teach the partners the five steps of a Self-Change Plan: (1) Describe the behavior to be changed; (2) Examine the pros and cons of the current behavior; (3) Set a goal, describing as precisely as possible what is to happen; (4) Create an Action Plan, pinpointing a specific plan for enacting the goal; and (5) Evaluate enacting of the plan. Have the partners practice this in session on an aspect of religious differences that each would like to change. ▽

26. Ask the partners to make a global evaluation of how they did on the action plan before the next session. The rating scale is 0 = didn't think about it or do it; 1 = thought about it; 2 = gave it a weak try; 3 = tried, partially succeeded; and 4 = did a great job. Ask them to jot down short answers to the following: What did we actually do? What positives resulted? What negatives resulted? What do we need to do from here? ▽

▽ 16. Verbalize an understanding of the rationale for situational analysis. (27)

17. Complete situational analysis homework to increase efficacy at affecting positive outcomes in situations at home. (28, 29)

▽ 18. Identify whether self-talk thoughts or conclusions promote problem resolution, are directly relevant to the situation, and are based on reality. (30)

▽ 19. Verbalize self-talk conclusions that promote problem resolution, are directly relevant

27. Describe for the partners the goal of situational analysis in the following manner: "Accommodating to each other's religious beliefs happens one small situation at a time. To work toward the big goals, try to make changes in the way you think and behave in small, observable situations that have a beginning, middle, and end." Have client repeat rationale in his/her own words. ▽

28. Assign the partners situational analysis homework that asks each to identify (a) a problematic situation (e.g., a description of the beginning, middle, and end of an observable situation); (b) three cognitions that occurred during the situation; (c) the behavior during the situation; (d) the actual outcome; and (e) the desired outcome. ▽

29. Ask each partner to read aloud from the situational analysis homework sheet, and paraphrase his/her statements to make sure that the therapist understands the key elements of the situational analysis. ▽

30. Have each partner state whether each thought in his/her situational analysis was (a) helpful in getting the desired outcome; (b) anchored to the specific situation described (i.e., is situationally-specific, not global); and (c) accurate (i.e., overt evidence can be marshaled to support it). ▽

31. If any thought or conclusion fails to meet all three criteria (i.e., helpful, anchored to specific

to the situation, and are based on reality. (31)

situation, accurate), have the partner rework the thought or conclusion so that it does meet all three criteria. For example, "He doesn't care about me because he won't go to my church," can become "He has different beliefs and trying to *force* him to come with me is counterproductive." ▽

▽ 20. Choose desired outcomes that are achievable. (32)

32. Have the partner state whether the desired outcome was achievable (i.e., under his/her control). If not, help him/her rework the desired outcome so that it is achievable. For example, "I want him to come to church with me," can become "I will invite him to come to the Bible study on Wednesday night." ▽

▽ 21. Verbally generate a generalizable lesson to be learned from the specific situational analysis and apply it to other situations of conflict over religion. (33)

33. Ask the partner to summarize the situation by deriving a lesson to be learned from the situational analysis and whether the lesson can be applied to other situations. ▽

22. List the perceived advantages and disadvantages of belief-based community social activities. (34)

34. Have both partners address the advantages and disadvantages of the sense of community brought to the relationship by either partner's religious and spiritual activities.

▽ 23. Verbalize any explicit agreements that were made regarding the children's religious training before they were born and the current feelings about those agreements. (35, 36)

35. If the couple has children, identify whether an explicit agreement regarding their religious training was reached prior to their birth. ▽

36. If either partner has misgivings about the original agreement about the children's religious upbringing, have him/her verbalize that position using nonblaming "I" statements. ▽

24. Each partner states his/her current wishes for the religious training of the children. (37)

▽ 25. Reach an agreement on the children's religious training that each partner can accept and support. (38)

26. Identify the effects that the partners' religious and spiritual differences have on parenting. (39, 40)

37. Have each partner verbalize his/her current expectations for the children's religious instruction or practice.

38. Using communication and problem resolution skills (see chapter on Communication in this *Planner*), ask the partners to negotiate an agreement regarding their children's religious instruction and practice that both partners can abide by. ▽

39. If the couple has children, identify whether either's religious and/or spiritual beliefs guide his/her approach to discipline.

40. If religious and spiritual beliefs guide either partner's parenting practices, have both discuss the strengths and conflicts arising from that approach.

—. _____   —. _____
   _____   _____
—. _____   —. _____
   _____   _____
—. _____   —. _____
   _____   _____

DIAGNOSTIC SUGGESTIONS

ICD-9-CM	_ICD-10-CM_	_DSM-5_ Disorder, Condition, or Problem
V62.89	Z65.8	Religious or Spiritual Problem
V61.10	Z63.0	Relationship Distress with Spouse or Intimate Partner
_____	_____	_____
_____	_____	_____

RETIREMENT

BEHAVIORAL DEFINITIONS

1. Depression and anxiety symptoms related to retirement.
2. Inability to find meaningful activities to replace employment.
3. Increased time spent with partner is resulting in increased conflict and confusion regarding role assignments in the household.
4. Grieving the loss of structure and recognition that was associated with employment.
5. Frequent arguments or arguing in ways that cause significant upset.
6. Experiencing increased difficulty resolving interpersonal problems.
7. Frequent misunderstandings during discussions.
8. Consistently very low desire for—or no pleasurable anticipation of—sexual activity.
9. Recurrent lack of usual physiological response of sexual excitement and arousal (e.g., erection, vaginal lubrication).
10. Consistent lack of subjective sense of enjoyment and pleasure during sexual activity.
11. Avoidance of communication regarding sexual matters.

__. _____
  _____
__. _____
  _____
__. _____
  _____

LONG-TERM GOALS

1. Reduce symptoms of depression and anxiety related to ambiguity of direction and values in life.
2. Recognize advantages that usually come only with maturity and retirement.

3. Partners communicate about feelings and resolve problems without escalating hostility.
4. Become connected or reconnected to partner, family members, volunteer opportunities, and/or religious community.
5. Express increased satisfaction with sexual relationship.
6. Develop accepting attitudes toward changes in the intensity and frequency of sexual activity across a life span.

—. _____
   _____
—. _____
   _____
—. _____
   _____

SHORT-TERM OBJECTIVES

▽ 1. Express, verbally and in writing, overall level of relationship dissatisfaction and the specific areas of dissatisfaction. (1)

▽ 2. Identify the strengths and needs of the relationship. (2)

▽ 3. Describe the origin, development, satisfaction, and present state of the relationship. (3, 4)

THERAPEUTIC INTERVENTIONS

1. Assess current level of relationship satisfaction, using interview and/or self-report instruments (e.g., *Couples Satisfaction Inventory* by Funk & Rogge, *Relationship Satisfaction Questionnaire* by Burns & Sayers, or the *Marital Satisfaction Inventory-Revised* by Snyder); provide feedback regarding test results. ▽

2. Have partners identify the strengths and needs of the relationship via interviews and questionnaires (e.g., *Revised Conflict Tactics Scale* by Straus et al., *Conflicts and Problem-Solving Scales* by Kerig, or the *Sexual History Form* by LoPiccolo); provide feedback regarding test results. ▽

3. Assess the partners' history of, and satisfaction with, the relationship by interviewing the couple; appropriate questions might be: "How did the two of

you meet?" "What attracted you to each other?" "What qualities or characteristics did you find that you liked about your partner?" "How did the two of you decide to get married?" "What have been the highs and lows of your marriage?"▽

4. Assess the partners' current satisfaction with their adjustment to retirement by interviewing the couple; appropriate questions might be "How was the adjustment to retirement?" "How did the two of you plan for what your lives would be like?" "What do you like about the way your lives are now?" "What changes would you make in your retirement life?"▽

▽ 4. Report any steps taken to dissolve the relationship. (5, 6)

5. Assess the steps taken toward divorce by administering a questionnaire (e.g., *Marital Status Inventory* by Weiss & Cerreto) and/or by interviewing the client about his/her sense of hope and vision for the future. ▽

6. Have the client state his/her point of view on (a) the pros and cons of preserving the relationship, and (b) the pros and cons of separation or divorce. ▽

▽ 5. Identify current problem areas and changes that self and other partner could make to improve the relationship and/or retirement life. (7, 8)

7. Have the partners identify the current problem areas in the relationship or retirement life.▽

8. Assign each partner to list changes for self and the other partner that would improve the relationship and their life of retirement (e.g., modified instructions for the "Areas of Change" questionnaire by Weiss and Birchler, or assign "Positive and Negative Contributions to the Relationship: Mine and

▽ 6. Identify specific communication deficits. (9, 10)

▽ 7. Verbalize the thoughts that are associated with anxiety and worry over the future. (11, 12)

▽ 8. Organize a list of thoughts, behaviors, actual outcomes, and desired outcomes via situational analysis of retirement transition-problem experiences. (13, 14)

Yours" in the *Adult Psychotherapy Homework Planner*, 2nd ed. by Jongsma); review and discuss the lists in session. ▽

9. Have the couple attempt to solve a major problem while the therapist quietly watches and takes notes about communication skills and deficits. ▽

10. Praise the couple for things they do well (such as making eye contact or attempting to define the problem) and provide direct feedback regarding things that need improvement (such as maintaining a civil tone of voice or overcoming a tendency to interrupt). ▽

11. Probe for cognitive distortions that lead to anxiety and uneasiness around their retirement and future. ▽

12. Assign homework to track events/thoughts that precipitate anxious and depressed feelings for use in situational analyses (e.g., "Negative Thoughts Trigger Negative Feelings" in the *Adult Psychotherapy Homework Planner*, 2nd ed. by Jongsma). ▽

13. Demonstrate how to organize a situational analysis. Have each client choose from his/her homework specific retirement-related problem-eliciting situations and tell what his/her interpretations/ cognitions were, what his/her behavior was, and what the actual outcome of the situation was. ▽

14. As the concluding step in the situational analysis, have the client describe what his/her desired outcome was in the specified situation. ▽

▽ 9. Verbalize thoughts that were unhelpful, global, or inaccurate, and then state more beneficial self-talk. (15, 16)

15. Help the client determine whether each thought was (a) accurate, (b) anchored to the specific situation, and (c) helpful in getting the desired outcome. ▽

16. If any thoughts are not accurate, anchored, and helpful in achieving the desired outcome, have the client rework the thoughts so they meet criteria. (For example, "I don't have a purpose to my days without a job to go to" can become "I now have time to make contributions to my family and community that I never had while working.") ▽

▽ 10. Partners implement the two overarching communication skills of: "Be Clear" and "Be Considerate." (17, 18, 19)

17. Teach the partners communication skills that emphasize that interchanges should be (a) clear (i.e., be specific, share thoughts and feelings, pay attention, ask clarifying questions, summarize content and feelings); and (b) considerate (i.e., include positives, show consideration when expressing negatives, let partner know that one is listening even if one disagrees, reserve judgment). ▽

18. Ask the partners to discuss a low-conflict area of desired change and ask them to rate how well they did being clear. ▽

19. Ask the partners to discuss a low-conflict area of desired change and ask them to rate how well they did being considerate. ▽

▽ 11. Practice defining problems in specific, nonblaming terms. (20, 21, 22)

20. Have the partners take turns pinpointing problems (that is, making requests for changes that are specific, observable, and ask for increases rather than decreases in the other partner's behavior). ▽

21. Have the partners use the "speaker-listener" technique, with

the listener trying to convey understanding after the speaker makes an "I" statements in the following form: "When _____ happens, I feel _____. I would like _____." ▽

▽ 12. Practice sharing thoughts and feelings in a manner that promotes intimacy. (23)

22. If either partner is mind reading the other, have him/her rephrase statements so that he/she is speaking only for self and expressing their own perceptions. ▽

23. Have partners share their feelings regarding issues about which they'd like to be closer; provide a list of "emotion" words, if necessary, to cue partners to the subtleties of words expressing feelings. ▽

13. Articulate the values and goals for living a meaningful life using Covey's four human needs and the approach taken to fulfill those needs. (24, 25, 26, 27, 28)

24. Ask the partners to read *First Things First* (Covey, Merrill, & Merrill), which posits that cross-cultural wisdom literature contains four key human needs "to live, to love, to learn, to leave a legacy."

25. Ask the partners to consider their approach to fulfilling the need "to live" ("Our *physical* need for such things as food, clothing, economic well-being, health," Covey et al., p. 45) by having them write and discuss (a) their past and current goals for meeting financial needs, and (b) the pros and cons of their current approach.

26. Ask the partners to consider their approach to fulfilling the need "to love" ("Our *social* need to relate to other people, to belong, to love, to be loved," Covey et al., p. 45) by having them write and discuss (a) their past and current goals for having rich, satisfying

relationships with others, and (b) the pros and cons of their current approach.

27. Ask the partners to consider their approach to fulfilling the need "to learn" ("Our *mental* need to develop and to grow," Covey et al., p. 45) by having them write and discuss (a) their past and current goals for learning, growing, and being open to new experiences and skills, and (b) the pros and cons of their current approach.

28. Ask the partners to consider their approach to fulfilling the need "to leave a legacy" ("Our *spiritual* need to have a sense of meaning, purpose, personal congruence, and contribution," Covey et al., p. 45) by having them write and discuss (a) their past and current goals for having a sense of direction and purpose, and (b) the pros and cons of their current approach.

14. Verbally define current level of satisfaction with recreational activities. (29, 30)

29. Identify each partner's level of satisfaction with recreational activities that are done (a) individually and (b) as a couple.

30. Ask each partner to identify elements of recreational activities that he/she believes are in need of improvement (i.e., frequency, quality, particular activities).

15. Generate lists of recreational activities that each partner would like to do alone, with partner, or with others. (31, 32)

31. Ask partners to complete the *Inventory of Rewarding Activities* (Birchler & Weiss, 1977) to generate a list of desired activities in the following categories: (a) to do alone, (b) to do with partner, (c) to do with partner and other family members, (d) to do with partner and nonfamily members, and (e) to do with nonfamily members.

▽ 16. Describe the history of the sexual relationship and identify any problems. (33, 34)

▽ 17. Describe the positive aspects of the physical/sexual relationship. (35)

▽ 18. Identify sexual expectations in the relationship and how they have changed in retirement. (36, 37)

▽ 19. Identify and resolve, if possible, any physical disorder or medication that is inhibiting sexual desire. (38, 39)

▽ 20. Report an increase in sexual thoughts and/or fantasy when not engaged in sexual activity with partner. (40)

32. Ask partners to discuss the similarities and differences of their Rewarding Activities lists; assist them in identifying interests that are shared with partner and those that are unique to each partner.

33. Assess the frequency of sexual interactions across the history of the relationship. ▽

34. Assess the partners' enjoyment of sexual interactions across the history of the relationship. ▽

35. Ask the partners to describe the positive sexual aspects of their current relationship. ▽

36. Have each client describe how expectations about his/her sexual life have changed. ▽

37. Assist the clients in interpreting how the frequency and satisfaction of their sexual encounters correspond to that of others of their ages. ▽

38. Assess role of any known or possible existing physical condition (e.g., diabetes, substance abuse, depression, anxiety disorders) or medication (e.g., antihypertensive medication, antidepressant medication) that could interfere with sexual functioning. ▽

39. If clients report erectile dysfunction, ask male client to talk to a physician about receiving medication to help achieve satisfying erections (e.g., Viagra, Cialis, Levitra). ▽

40. Request that clients indulge in sexual fantasies that increase sexual desire toward partner. ▽

▼ 21. Read books and/or watch educational videos on sexual functioning and sexuality. (41, 42)

41. If religious views permit, encouraged clients to purchase educational videos for enjoyable sex in later years (e.g., "Great Sex Over 50" DVD Set, Sinclair Institute) (see references for videos in Bibliography). ▼

42. Suggest that the clients read books on sexual behavior and sexual functioning, such as *Sex for Dummies* (Westheimer, 1995) or *Coping with Erectile Dysfunction: How to Regain Confidence and Enjoy Great Sex* (Metz & McCarthy). ▼

▼ 22. Engage in sensate focus activity alone and with partner. (43)

43. Instruct the clients in use of sensate focus (i.e., at first, taking turns providing sensual touch without genital or breast contact; later, adding genital and breast stimulation). ▼

▼ 23. Discuss sensate focus activities with the partner in therapy sessions, and change sexual stimulation activities based on feedback from partner. (44)

44. Obtain feedback from the clients about the sensate focus exercises, and assist in minimizing any behaviors that affect either partner negatively. ▼

__. _____   __. _____
   _____   _____
__. _____   __. _____
   _____   _____
__. _____   __. _____
   _____   _____

DIAGNOSTIC SUGGESTIONS

ICD-9-CM	*ICD-10-CM*	*DSM-5* Disorder, Condition, or Problem
V62.89	Z60.0	Phase of Life Problem
309.0	F43.21	Adjustment Disorder, With Depressed Mood
309.24	F43.22	Adjustment Disorder, With Anxiety
309.28	F43.23	Adjustment Disorder, With Mixed Anxiety and Depressed Mood
_____	_____	_____
_____	_____	_____

SEPARATION AND DIVORCE

BEHAVIORAL DEFINITIONS

1. Thoughts about ending the marriage (or the relationship, if not married).
2. Moving out of the home to establish separate living arrangements due to dissatisfaction with the relationship.
3. Initiation of legal proceedings for separation, divorce, and/or child custody.
4. Confusion about how to best deal with the feelings and welfare of the children.
5. Anger, hurt, and fear regarding breaking the partnership and having to face life as a single person.
6. Spiritual conflict over the breaking of marriage vows.
7. Depression and withdrawal as a part of the grief process related to the loss of the relationship.

—. _____
   _____
—. _____
   _____
—. _____
   _____

LONG-TERM GOALS

1. Evaluate the possibility of resolving the differences and review the pros and cons of remaining married.
2. Consistently uphold "the best interests of the children" as paramount and act accordingly, regardless of the final fate of the marriage.
3. Learn healthy ways to manage and express anger.
4. Learn to cope with the confusion and varied losses that separation entails.
5. Cooperate in reaching a reasonable separation and fair divorce agreement.
6. Reduce conflict, hurt, and angry feelings.

250

7. Establish and maintain healthy co-parenting practices.

—. _____

 _____

—. _____

 _____

—. _____

 _____

SHORT-TERM OBJECTIVES

▽ 1. Express, verbally and in writing, overall level of relationship dissatisfaction and the specific areas of dissatisfaction. (1)

▽ 2. Identify the strengths and needs of the relationship. (2)

▽ 3. Describe the origination, development, and present state of the relationship. (3, 4)

THERAPEUTIC INTERVENTIONS

1. Assess current level of relationship satisfaction, using interview and/or self-report instruments (e.g., Couples Satisfaction Inventory by Funk and Rogge, Relationship Satisfaction Questionnaire by Burns & Sayers, or the Marital Satisfaction Inventory-Revised by Snyder); provide feedback regarding test results. ▽

2. Have partners identify the strengths and needs of relationship via interviews and questionnaires (e.g., Conflicts and Problem-Solving Scales by Kerig, or the Sexual History Form by LoPiccolo); provide feedback regarding test results. ▽

3. Assess the current developmental stage of relationship (e.g., early marriage, parents of young children, long-term marriage); ask partners to list changes they have noted in their relationship as they moved from one stage to the next. ▽

4. Assess the history of the relationship (appropriate questions might be: "How did the two of you meet?" "What attracted you to each other?" "What qualities or

▽ 4. State degree of dissatisfaction with the relationship and own thoughts or actions taken toward dissolving the relationship. (5)

5. Describe any suspicions regarding the other partner having had an affair. (6)

6. Describe the frequency, impact, and function of psychological and/or or physical intimate partner violence (IPV). (7, 8)

▽ 7. Process a decision regarding reasons for and against remaining in the relationship. (9, 10)

characteristics did you find that you liked about your partner?" "How did the two of you decide to get married?" "What have been the highs and lows during dating and your marriage?"). ▽

5. Assess the steps each partner has taken toward divorce, using the Marital Status Inventory (Weiss & Cerreto) and by interviews with each partner about his/her sense of hope and vision for the future of the relationship. ▽

6. Ask each partner to verbalize any suspicions held regarding the other partner having had an affair; assess the presence or suspicion of affairs in the relationship (see chapters on Infidelity and Jealousy in this *Planner*).

7. Have both couples privately and confidentially complete the Revised Conflict Tactics Scale (CTS2; Straus, Hamby, Boney-McCoy, & Sugarman).

8. Privately interview each partner about psychological abuse and intimate partner violence (IPV) including (a) antecedents, (b) impact, (c) function, (d) fear, (e) safety issues, (f) extent of psychological coercion or abuse, (g) openness to discuss issues dyadically, and (h) resistance to disclose or discuss violence (see chapters on Psychological Abuse and IPV in this *Planner*).

9. Ask partners to discuss the following questions: "Why did we choose to get together?" "How have we developed and matured as individuals and as a unit over the years?" "What are our strengths/accomplishments as a

couple?" "What struggles have we survived or surmounted over the years?" "What are the challenges?" "How do our current troubles fit into the entire tapestry of our relationship?" ▽

10. Provide partners with Baucom, Snyder, & Gordon's (2008, p. 304) handout detailing "Factors to Consider in Reaching a Decision about Your Relationship" and ask them to discuss each item within the session (i.e., domains of "Evaluating Your Partner," "Evaluating Your Relationship," "Evaluating Yourself," and "Evaluating Your Relationship with the Environment, Including Other People"). ▽

8. List the members of each partner's extended family who have ended committed relationships, and discuss the impact that this history may have on a decision to divorce. (11)

11. Review the extended family history in regard to divorce and have each partner verbalize how this history may be affecting the decision to divorce.

9. Identify any cultural, ethnic, or religious beliefs that may have a bearing on a decision to divorce and verbalize a resolution of such conflicts. (12)

12. Ask each partner to identify his/her subcultural identification and its influence on attitude about divorce (e.g., ethnicity, religious identification); facilitate a resolution of conflict between behavior and beliefs.

▽ 10. Verbally commit to: (a) relationship therapy, (b) ambivalence therapy, or (c) separation therapy. (13, 14, 15)

13. Establish the type of treatment that will be conducted by describing and agreeing on (a) relationship therapy (i.e., the affair will end and the goal will be to salvage the relationship); (b) ambivalence therapy (i.e., the goal will be to clarify the future of the relationship); or (c) separation therapy (i.e., either client is determined to end the relationship, and the goal is to separate under the best possible terms). ▽

14. Negotiate a "non-collusion contract" with both partners, stipulating that the therapist will not agree to secrecy with either partner, thus establishing the therapist's role as working for the mutual well-being of the couple. ▽

15. Clarify for the partners the role of the therapist: to (a) aid the family in making the separation or divorce transition, and (b) help both partners deal with the turbulent emotions experienced during this process. Emphasize that the therapist's role is to serve the best interests of all family members; however, he/she will not be a mediator or judge. ▽

11. Both partners agree to make no threats nor take any action to hurt themselves or others. (16, 17)

16. Ask partners to agree: (a) not to make threats regarding own safety; (b) not to make threats about the safety of others; and (c) to stop discussing difficult topics at home if either partner believes that the discussion is beginning to escalate out-of-control; ask them to avoid deep discussions at home about the future of the relationship during the first phase of treatment.

17. Assess for suicidality and homicidality by asking each client individually if they have any thoughts, intent, or means to hurt themselves or others.

▽ 12. Each partner constructs and implements a self-change plan regarding an anger evoking situation. (18, 19)

18. Self-Change Plan ([1] *Describe* the behavior to be changed; [2] *Examine* the pros and cons of the current behavior; [3] *Set a goal*, describing as precisely as possible what is to happen; [4] *Create an action plan*, pinpointing a specific plan for enacting the goal; [5] *Evaluate* enacting of plan. Have

the partners practice this in session on an area that has evoked anger that each would like to change. ▽

19. Have both partners agree to use self-change plans to improve their own anger responses instead of managing the other's behavior. ▽

▽ 13. Contract to discuss angry feelings respectfully by balancing concern for the other partner's feelings with the need to express self. (20)

20. Teach both partners the speaker skill of "editing" or "measured truthfulness" (i.e., each balances the need to comment about the other against a concern for the other's feelings); have them practice this skill on areas of conflict, and contract to use at home. ▽

▽ 14. Implement the use of "Pause, Calm, and Think" (i.e., time-out) technique to modulate anger. (21, 22)

21. Teach the partners the "Pause, Calm, and Think" technique: *Pause* the conversation (i.e., letting the other partner know that you want to pause the discussion); *Calm down* (e.g., focusing on diaphragmatic breathing, counting to 10, focusing on calming self down); *Think* (e.g., taking responsibility for ways in which you are making the conflict worse; planning ways to respond in a mindful, nonescalating manner instead of automatic, escalating manner; examining thinking by asking self "How true is this thought?" "Is it about just the situation?" "Will it help me get what I want?"). ▽

22. Practice using "Pause, Calm, and Think" within the session with situations from a real life experience of the couple and then assign at-home implementation. ▽

▽ 15. Partners implement the two overarching communication

23. Teach the partners the communication skill that emphasizes that

skills of: "Be Clear" and "Be Considerate." (23, 24, 25)

16. Each partner identifies how he/she behaved in ways that improved the relationship, and how he/she behaved in ways that harmed the relationship. (26)

▽ 17. Verbalize empathy for each other while each partner states how divorce will impact personal and social life, immediate and extended family relationship, and spirituality. (27)

▽ 18. Each partner verbalizes a dedication to being sensitive to their children's thoughts, needs, and feelings during this time of insecurity. (28, 29)

interchanges should be (a) clear (i.e., be specific; share thoughts and feelings; pay attention; ask clarifying questions; summarize content and feelings); and (b) considerate (i.e., include positives, show consideration when expressing negatives, let partner know that one is listening even if one disagrees; reserve judgment). ▽

24. Ask the partners to discuss a low-conflict area of desired change and ask them to rate how well they did being clear. ▽

25. Ask the partners to discuss a low-conflict area of desired change and ask them to rate how well they did being considerate. ▽

26. Ask each partner to turn to the other and express the ways self has (a) contributed to the downfall of the relationship, and (b) in what ways he/she has attempted to make the relationship work.

27. Ask each partner to verbalize the implications of divorce in the following areas: (a) personal, (b) family (including children), (c) religious, and (d) social; have the other partner paraphrase the first person's statements in each area to increase understanding and empathy between the two partners. ▽

28. Sensitize the partners to the upheaval that children face by having them discuss the anticipated effects on their children. ▽

29. Have partners verbally contract with each other and with the therapist that all decisions in the

divorce and separation process will be made with the "best interests of the children" as the paramount concern. ▽

19. Agree on how and what to tell the children regarding the impending divorce; practice the disclosure. (30)

30. Using role-playing techniques, have the partners rehearse telling the children together about the divorce; have them explain that (a) they both love the children very much, (b) they plan to divorce, (c) the divorce is not the children's fault, (d) there is nothing the children can do to get parents back together, and (e) they will both continue to love and see the children.

20. Report on the experience of telling the children regarding the divorce, and agree on what further explanation or support may be necessary. (31)

31. Review the experience of parents telling the children of the divorce or separation and probe the needs for further explanation or support; attempt to reach agreement on this issue.

▽ 21. Negotiate the terms and conditions of the separation, reaching agreement as to whether and when one partner will move out. (32)

32. Facilitate a discussion and decision-making, pending legal advice, regarding whether and when one partner will move out of the house. If an in-house separation is financially necessary, negotiate the terms and conditions. ▽

▽ 22. Clarify new boundaries by establishing the new goals of the altered relationship (e.g., to provide the children with healthy home environments), the new prescriptions (e.g., each person supporting the other's role in the children's lives), and proscriptions (e.g., no future sexual contact). (33)

33. Facilitate an agreement between the partners about new relationship goals (e.g., keeping the welfare of the children primary) and new relationship boundaries such as what forms of contact are acceptable (e.g., planning around children's activities) as well as what are prohibited (e.g., sexual intimacies). ▽

23. Each partner constructively express his/her emotional pain about the decline of the relationship and verbalize new

34. Using individual sessions as needed, allow each partner to express his/her anger, disappointment, and disapproval

short- and long-term goals for personal life. (34)

▽ 24. Verbalize an understanding of the differences between litigation, arbitration, and mediation as a means of dissolving the marriage. Agree to one choice. (35)

▽ 25. Develop a co-parenting agreement that is in the best interest of the children and deals with the child's residence, emotional support, financial support, and custody and visitation. (36)

26. Each partner outlines a plan for how to increase his/her social life and strengthen his/her social and spiritual support system. (37)

27. Cooperate with bringing children to sessions to listen to them express their emotional reactions and needs. (38)

over what has happened; balance these expressions of hurt with an elicitation of his/her goals for coping with short-term and long-term situations with the other partner and children.

35. Educate partners regarding the three choices available for dissolving the marriage: (a) litigation, which is an adversarial legal process; (b) arbitration, in which a third party, whom each partner typically helps choose, makes decisions regarding property and custody; and (c) mediation, in which the partners come to their own agreement, with the help of a trained mediator. ▽

36. Facilitate the development of a co-parenting agreement in which the partners pledge that (a) the children's primary residence will be established in their best interests; (b) neither parent will belittle the other and his/her family members in front of the children; (c) parents will avoid placing the children in loyalty conflicts; and (d) the parents agree regarding terms of financial support for the children. ▽

37. Using individual sessions, assist each partner in developing a varied social network (e.g., asking others to socialize; beginning or increasing involvement in club, community, volunteer, and/or church activities; dating).

38. Conduct parent-child sessions when necessary, to ensure that the children's emotional needs are being attended to.

28. Accept and follow through on referral to divorce and single-parent support groups. (39)

29. Verbalize the effect divorce has had on religious beliefs and practices. (40)

39. Encourage partners to attend local divorce therapy groups and/or self-help groups (e.g., Parents without Partners).

40. Assess whether the divorce has affected either partner's religious and spiritual connections, and assist in problem-solving if he/she has difficulty reestablishing connections (e.g., switching parishes, investigating churches that welcome divorced members).

__. _____   __. _____
   _____   _____

__. _____   __. _____
   _____   _____

__. _____   __. _____
   _____   _____

DIAGNOSTIC SUGGESTIONS

ICD-9-CM	ICD-10-CM	DSM-5 Disorder, Condition, or Problem
309.0	F43.21	Adjustment Disorder, With Depressed Mood
309.24	F43.22	Adjustment Disorder, With Anxiety
309.28	F43.23	Adjustment Disorder, With Mixed Anxiety and Depressed Mood
309.4	F43.25	Adjustment Disorder, With Mixed Disturbance of Emotions and Conduct
300.4	F34.1	Persistent Depressive Disorder
300.02	F41.1	Generalized Anxiety Disorder
296.xx	F32.x	Major Depressive Disorder, Single Episode
296.xx	F33.x	Major Depressive Disorder, Recurrent Episode
V61.12	Z69.12	Encounter for Mental Health Services for Perpetrator of Spouse or Partner Violence, Physical
V61.10	Z63.0	Relationship Distress with Spouse or Intimate Partner
301.6	F60.7	Dependent Personality Disorder
301.83	F60.3	Borderline Personality Disorder
301.81	F60.81	Narcissistic Personality Disorder
_____	_____	_____
_____	_____	_____

SEXUAL ABUSE[1]

BEHAVIORAL DEFINITIONS

1. Verbal demands for sexual interaction.
2. Physical pressure exerted to get the partner to fulfill sexual demands.
3. Threat of force used to get the partner to cooperate with demands for intercourse or other sexual activity.
4. Verbal demands for a type of sexual activity with which the partner is clearly uncomfortable.
5. Physical demands for a type of sexual activity with which the partner is clearly uncomfortable.
6. Criticism of partner for being "frigid" or "impotent."
7. Threats to withhold sex from partner in the future.
8. Threats to have sex with someone else.
9. Threats to leave the partner.
10. Very low desire for sexual activity due to resentment or fear related to coercion used by partner for sexual activity.
11. Avoidance of any sexual interaction due to resentment or fear related to coercion used by partner for sexual activity.

---

[1]Sexual abuse usually occurs in conjunction with psychological and physical abuse. In fact, sexual abuse with physical force is much less common than physical abuse. Thus, sexual abuse with physical force is a more unusual pattern in a relationship, and it is difficult to change. Psychological abuse, particularly in the form of threats and critical comments about the partner's sexual style, is much more common, and is an issue that all couples and family therapists should be prepared to address. The level of coercion and the abused partner's degree of fear of the abusive partner should be assessed individually (i.e., without the abusive partner present). If either coercion and/or fear are high, then individual therapy with the abusive partner, usually the male, is in order before conjoint therapy. Once conjoint therapy begins, clinicians should make diagnostic judgments about the need for combinations of individual and conjoint therapy.

There are few if any controlled outcome studies of a random control trial nature. However, in treatment programs for partner aggression, sexual aggression is addressed. The use of the label E in the current section is based on treatments for partner abuse of a physical nature as the intervention principles and objectives have such significant overlap. However, the use of the label E should not be interpreted to mean that there are random control trials that have shown how sexual aggression can be reduced in a couple context.

12. Complaints by one or both partners about lack of love and caring.
13. Avoidance of communication with partner regarding sexual matters.

—. _____

_____

—. _____

_____

—. _____

_____

LONG-TERM GOALS

1. Eliminate all types of coercion (physical or verbal) used by one partner to get the other partner to fulfill sexual demands.
2. Eliminate critical comments of partner's sexual style.
3. Eliminate threats to have sex with others.
4. Eliminate threats to leave the relationship.
5. Increase general relationship satisfaction.
6. Increase communication in general, and about sexual matters in particular.
7. Increase desire for, and enjoyment of, healthy, voluntary sexual activity.
8. Develop accepting attitude of variability in "normal" sexual activity.
9. Develop accepting attitude of changes in sexual activity across a life span.
10. Evaluate alternatives to current relationship.

—. _____

_____

—. _____

_____

—. _____

_____

SHORT-TERM OBJECTIVES	THERAPEUTIC INTERVENTIONS
▽ 1. Agree to a clear ground rule that no physical force will be employed for any sexual interaction. (1, 2)	1. Obtain verbal commitment from both partners not to employ physical force for any sexual interaction. ▽

2. Obtain written commitment from both partners not to employ physical force for any sexual interaction. ▽

▽ 2. Agree to a clear ground rule that sexual interactions will only be engaged in if both partners desire to engage in such activity. (3)

3. Educate the clients that to have a positive sexual relationship, the sexual activity must be acceptable to both partners. ▽

▽ 3. Verbalize an understanding of the fragility of sexual behavior and how it can become less functional with negative feedback or punishment. (4, 5)

4. Educate the clients that pressure to have sexual activity usually leads to sexual aversions and/or avoidance and dislike of the partner. ▽

5. Educate the clients that sexual behavior is one of the most susceptible of all human behaviors to aversive control, and that aversive control of sexual activity can quickly lead to a lack of interest and sexual dysfunction of the partner. ▽

▽ 4. Agree to a clear ground rule that there will be no threats to have sex with someone else. (6, 7)

6. Obtain a verbal commitment from partners not to threaten to have sex with someone else. ▽

7. Obtain a commitment from both partners not to have sex with someone else during the course of therapy. This commitment should be obtained individually (i.e., not in the presence of the other partner). ▽

▽ 5. Agree to a clear ground rule that there will be no threats to leave partner during the therapy process. (8)

8. Obtain a verbal commitment from partners not to threaten to leave the relationship during therapy (an agreement about a particular time span for the therapy should be developed at the beginning of treatment). ▽

▽ 6. Agree to a clear ground rule that there will be no physical aggression against the partner for any reason. (9, 10)

9. Obtain a verbal commitment from partners not to employ physical force against the other partner for any reason. ▽

7. Describe the nature and extent of any psychological coercion used within the relationship. (11)

8. Describe the nature and extent of any physical aggression within the relationship. (12)

9. State the degree of fear that has resulted from coercion within the relationship, and what effect the fear has had on loving feelings, sexual arousal, and sexual desire. (13)

10. Verbalize an understanding of the effects on a relationship of control and misuse of power in American society. (14, 15, 16)

11. Describe the history of the sexual relationship and identify where conflicts about sexual matters began to occur. (17, 18)

12. Verbalize an understanding of the norms of sexual activity and how patterns within the relationship relate to those norms. (19)

10. Obtain a written commitment from partners not to employ physical force against the other partner for any reason. ▽

11. Ask both partners to describe the extent to which psychological coercion is used in the relationship in general. ▽

12. Ask both partners to describe the extent to which physical aggression is used in the relationship in general. ▽

13. Ask both partners to describe any fears they have of their partner and how this fear affects the intimate aspects of the relationship. ▽

14. Discuss the role of patriarchy in American society. ▽

15. Discuss how the controlling partner misuses his/her power. ▽

16. Educate the clients regarding how controlling behaviors lead to dislike and avoidance of their partner. ▽

17. Have the clients describe their initial expectations about their sexual life. ▽

18. Have the clients describe how their expectations about their sexual life changed with the beginning of conflict over intimacy. ▽

19. Assist clients in interpreting how the frequency, nature, and satisfaction of their sexual encounters corresponds to that of others of their age in our culture. ▽

▽ 13. Describe the positive aspects of the nonsexual portion of the relationship. (20)

▽ 14. Describe the positive aspects of the sexual portion of the relationship. (21)

▽ 15. Communicate openly and without criticism, especially about sexual matters. (22, 23, 24)

▽ 16. Describe the causes for the decline in frequency and enjoyment of sexual encounters. (25)

▽ 17. Abusive partner describes any physical abuse of self or others in childhood and how these experiences could affect current abuse of his/her partner. (26)

▽ 18. Abused partner describes any physical abuse of self or others in childhood and how these experiences could affect his/her toleration of the current sexual abuse. (27)

▽ 19. Abusive partner describes developmental history of hostile feelings toward the opposite sex that affect current disrespectful treatment of partner. (28)

20. Ask both partners to describe the positive, nonsexual aspects of their current relationship.▽

21. Ask both partners to describe the positive, sexual aspects of their current relationship.▽

22. Have each partner listen without interrupting while the other partner speaks about a nonsexual matter, and then have him/her validate without interpretation what the other said.▽

23. Have each partner communicate about a sexual matter without interruption, and then obtain validation from the other partner.▽

24. Provide feedback and interpretation to the partners about their communication styles.▽

25. Ask the partners to describe the perceived causes for the decline in frequency and enjoyment of sexual activity.▽

26. Explore with the abusive or critical partner whether there has been a history of physical abuse of self or others in childhood family experience.▽

27. Explore with the abused partner whether there is a history of physical abuse of self or others in a childhood family experience that could be a basis for expecting or tolerating abuse now.▽

28. Explore with the abusive partner whether there is a history of anger toward the opposite sex that has roots in unresolved childhood experiences.▽

▽ 20. Abusive partner verbalizes feelings of low self-esteem and lack of trust in others that feeds the abusive behavior toward his/her partner. (29)

▽ 21. Verbalize understanding that sexual coercion or degrading criticism changes sexual behaviors into acts of domination and/or submission. (30)

▽ 22. Describe any traumatic sexual experiences experienced outside of the relationship. (31)

▽ 23. Agree to terminate any sexual activity that triggers negative emotions related to earlier sexual trauma. (32)

▽ 24. Engage in sensate focus with the partners. (33)

▽ 25. Discuss sensate focus activities with the partners in therapy sessions, and change sexual stimulation activities based on feedback from the other partner. (34)

▽ 26. Assess alternatives to relationship, and receive referrals for safely escaping from abuse. (35, 36, 37)

29. Probe the degree to which the abuser trusts that sexual activity would be freely and happily engaged in by the other partner if coercion was not present (that is, does he/she feel lovable and able to trust anyone?).

30. Confront sexual coercion or belittling criticism as a means of domination that degrades the other partner from a role as lover to that of a victim. ▽

31. Have each client identify any traumatic sexual experiences that he/she encountered with anyone. ▽

32. Advise the partners to cease any sexual activity that triggers memories of traumatic events. ▽

33. Instruct each client in use of sensate focus technique to teach their partner how to touch self. ▽

34. Obtain feedback from the clients about the sensate focus exercises, and assist in minimizing any behaviors that affect either partner negatively. ▽

35. In an individual session, discuss with the sexually abused client the alternatives to the current relationship. ▽

36. In a confidential individual session, help the sexually abused client evaluate the alternatives to the current relationship. ▽

37. If necessary, refer the sexually abused client to an agency for battered women and/or to a shelter. ▽

—. _____   —. _____

     _____   _____

—. _____   —. _____

     _____   _____

—. _____   —. _____

     _____   _____

DIAGNOSTIC SUGGESTIONS

ICD-9-CM	_ICD-10-CM_	_DSM-5_ Disorder, Condition, or Problem
302.72	F52.22	Female Sexual Interest/Arousal Disorder
302.73	F52.31	Female Orgasmic Disorder
302.71	F52.0	Male Hypoactive Sexual Desire Disorder
312.34	F63.81	Intermittent Explosive Disorder
302.74	F52.21	Erectile Disorder
302.70	F52.9	Unspecified Sexual Dysfunction
V61.12	Z69.12	Encounter for Mental Health Services for Perpetrator of Spouse or Partner Violence, Physical
995.83	T74.21XA	Spouse or Partner Violence, Sexual, Confirmed, Initial Encounter
302.79	F52.0	Male Hypoactive Sexual Desire Disorder
V61.12	Z69.12	Encounter for Mental Health Services for Perpetrator of Spouse or Partner Violence, Physical
995.81	Z69.11	Encounter for Mental Health Services for Victim of Spouse or Partner Violence, Physical
301.7	F60.2	Antisocial Personality Disorder
_____	_____	_____
_____	_____	_____

SEXUAL DYSFUNCTION

BEHAVIORAL DEFINITIONS

1. Consistently very low desire for, or no pleasurable anticipation of, sexual activity.
2. Strong avoidance of, and/or repulsion to, any and all sexual contact in spite of a relationship of mutual caring and respect.
3. Recurrent lack of usual physiological response of sexual excitement and arousal (e.g., erection, vaginal lubrication).
4. Consistent lack of subjective sense of enjoyment and pleasure during sexual activity.
5. Persistent delay in, or absence of, reaching orgasm after achieving arousal, in spite of sensitive sexual pleasuring by a caring partner.
6. Genital pain before, during, or after sexual intercourse.
7. Consistent or recurring involuntary spasm of the vagina (i.e., vaginismus) that prohibits penetration for sexual intercourse.
8. Expressions of general relationship dissatisfaction.
9. Verbalizations of a lack of love and/or caring by one or both partners.
10. Avoidance of communication regarding sexual matters.
11. Critical comments regarding the partner's lack of sexual responsiveness.
12. Statements of low self-esteem by the partner with sexual dysfunction.
13. Statements of low self-esteem by the partner who perceives the sexual dysfunction of the other partner to be his/her fault.
14. Depressed mood in one or both partners.

—. _____
   _____

—. _____
   _____

—. _____
   _____

LONG-TERM GOALS

1. Increase desire for, and enjoyment of, sexual activity.
2. Increase and maintain physiological arousal during sexual interactions.
3. Reach orgasm on a regular basis.
4. Eliminate pain associated with any aspect of the sexual interaction; eliminate spasms that prevent intromission.
5. Increase communication and general relationship satisfaction.
6. Increase both partners' self-esteem.
7. Develop accepting attitude toward variability in "normal" sexual activity.
8. Develop accepting attitudes toward changes in the intensity and frequency of sexual activity across a life span.

__. _____
   _____
__. _____
   _____
__. _____
   _____

SHORT-TERM OBJECTIVES

▽ 1. Describe the history of the sexual relationship and identify when conflicts about sexual matters began to occur. (1, 2, 3)

THERAPEUTIC INTERVENTIONS

1. Assess the frequency of sexual interactions across the history of the partners' relationship. ▽

2. Assess the partners' enjoyment of sexual interactions across the history of their relationship. ▽

3. Ask the partners to describe the perceived causes of decline in sexual activity and enjoyment thereof (e.g., sexual coercion, sexual aggression, infidelity, relationship decline, childhood experiences, etc.); or assign "Factors Influencing Negative Sexual Attitudes" in the *Adult Psychotherapy Homework Planner*, 2nd ed. by Jongsma). ▽

▽ 2. Identify the positive aspects of the nonsexual portion of the relationship. (4, 5)

▽ 3. Describe the positive aspects of the sexual relationship. (6, 7)

▽ 4. Communicate openly and without criticism, especially about sexual matters. (8, 9, 10)

▽ 5. Identify sexual expectations in the relationship and how they have changed across time. (11, 12, 13)

4. Ask the partners to describe the positive nonsexual aspects of the beginning of their relationship. ▽

5. Ask the partners to describe the positive nonsexual aspects of their current relationship. ▽

6. Ask the partners to describe the positive sexual aspects of the beginning of their relationship. ▽

7. Ask the partners to describe the positive sexual aspects of their current relationship. ▽

8. Ask the partners to communicate with each other about a nonsexual matter; listener should allow partner to speak without interruption and, to demonstrate understanding, should para-phrase the speaker's intent. ▽

9. Ask the partners to communicate with each other about a sexual matter; listener should allow partner to speak without interruption and, to demonstrate understanding, should para-phrase the speaker's intent. ▽

10. Provide feedback and inter-pretation to the partners about their communication styles. ▽

11. Ask each partner to describe initial expectations about his/her sexual life. ▽

12. Have each partner describe how expectations about his/her sexual life have changed. ▽

13. Assist the partners in interpreting how the frequency and satisfaction of their sexual encounters correspond to that of other people their age. ▽

▽ 6. Describe any past traumatic experience that now may be impacting sexual interactions. (14, 15)

▽ 7. Identify any religious beliefs or training that may be interfering with experiencing pleasure from sexual activity. (16)

▽ 8. Cease any activity that triggers memories of past traumatic experiences until the feelings related to that activity can be resolved. (17)

▽ 9. Discuss the development of sexual attitudes in the family-of-origin. (18)

▽ 10. Identify and resolve, if possible, any physical disorder or medication that is inhibiting sexual desire. (19, 20)

14. Have each partner discuss any past traumatic sexual experiences. ▽

15. Probe about thoughts during sexual activities and ascertain whether the traumatic sexual encounter triggers negative emotions during sexual overtures or activity; if found, resolve past traumas that impact current sexual pleasure. ▽

16. Examine whether religious beliefs or training interferes with engaging in sexual activity desired by either partner; if interferences exist, attempt to neutralize current impact, or define acceptable sexual practices. ▽

17. Recommend that the partners temporarily cease any sexual activity that triggers memories of traumatic events until traumatic memories are properly resolved (for treatment ideas for sexual abuse see *The Sexual Abuse Victim and Sexual Offender Treatment Planner* by Budrionis and Jongsma). ▽

18. Assist the partners in identifying family-of-origin experiences that enhance and those that deter one or both partners from currently experiencing sexual pleasure. ▽

19. Assess the role of any known or possible existing physical condition that could interfere with sexual functioning (e.g., diabetes, substance abuse, depression, anxiety disorders). ▽

20. Assess the role of any medication that could interfere with sexual functioning (e.g., antihypertensive medication, antidepressant

medication); after obtaining a release, discuss this issue with the partner's prescribing physician to consider alternative medications. ▽

11. Verbalize feelings regarding body image and how it relates to sexual functioning. (21)

21. Explore whether the decrease in the frequency and range of sexual activities is related to a decline in body image (e.g., increased body weight, lack of muscle tone, or the residual effects of surgery).

12. Verbalize an improved body image due to increased exercise, improved dress, and/or a more healthy diet. (22, 23)

22. Encourage a positive change in attitude regarding the partner's body image (or assign "Study Your Body: Clothed and Unclothed" in the *Adult Psychotherapy Homework Planner*, 2nd ed. by Jongsma).

23. Assign a change in exercise, dress, and/or diet to enhance partner's body image.

13. Identify causes and remedies for low self-esteem within the relationship. (24)

24. Assess the role of self-esteem in sexual functioning, and identify the factors in the relationship that lead to positive and negative feelings.

▽ 14. Identify whether a perceived or real emotionally intimate or sexual relationship with another partner creates continuing resentment and/or jealousy. (25)

25. Probe hurt or angry feelings that relate to perceived or actual extramarital affairs by one of the partners, and make certain that such relationships have stopped. ▽

▽ 15. Verbalize whether any same-sex activity and/or fantasy impedes sexual functioning with the partner, openly acknowledging plans for future direction of sexual interest. (26, 27)

26. Assess (in individual sessions) whether there are any same-sex desires, attractions, or behaviors on the part of either partner that interfere with heterosexual functioning. ▽

27. If there are same-sex activities or fantasies that interfere with the couple's sexual relationship, explore the sexual identity issue and its implication for the future of heterosexual relationships. ▽

▽ 16. Report an increase in sexual thoughts and/or fantasy when not engaged in sexual activity with the partner. (28)

▽ 17. Read books and/or watch educational videos on sexual functioning and sexuality. (29, 30, 31)

28. Request that the partners indulge in sexual fantasies while not engaged with the partner sexually that increase sexual desire toward their partner. ▽

29. Request that the partners read material on sexual fantasies (e.g., *My Secret Garden* by Friday, *Women on Top* by Friday, *Becoming Orgasmic: A Sexual Growth Program for Women* by Heiman & LoPiccolo). ▽

30. If religious views permit, the partners, especially females, can be encouraged to purchase educational videos of sexual activities to teach enhancement of fantasy, masturbation, and a variety of heterosexual sexual behaviors (e.g., *Self-Loving* by Dodson, and the *Better Sex Video Series: Vols. 1–3* by the Sinclair Institute). ▽

31. Suggest that the partners read books on sexual behavior and sexual functioning (e.g., *Sex for Dummies* by Westheimer, *The New Male Sexuality* by Zilbergeld, *The New Joy of Sex* by Comfort, *The Gift of Sex* by Penner & Penner, and *When a Woman's Body Says No to Sex* by Valins). ▽

▽ 18. Engage in sensate focus activity alone and with partner. (32)

▽ 19. Discuss sensate focus activities with the partners in therapy sessions, and change sexual stimulation activities based on feedback from the other partner. (33)

32. Instruct both partners in the use of sensate focus to learn how to touch each other. ▽

33. Obtain feedback from the partners about the sensate focus exercises, and assist in minimizing any behaviors that affect either partner negatively (or assign "Journaling the Response to Nondemand Sexual Pleasuring [Sensate Focus]" in the *Adult Psychotherapy Homework Planner*, 2nd ed. by Jongsma). ▽

▽ 20. Report progress on graduated self-controlled vaginal penetration with the partner. (34, 35, 36)

34. Assign the partner body exploration and awareness exercises that reduce inhibition and desensitize him/her to sexual aversion. ▽

35. Direct the partner's use of masturbation and/or vaginal dilator devices to reinforce relaxation and success surrounding vaginal penetration. ▽

36. Direct the partners in sexual exercises that allow for partner-controlled level of genital stimulation and gradually increased vaginal penetration. ▽

__. _____

_____

__. _____

_____

__. _____

_____

__. _____

_____

__. _____

_____

DIAGNOSTIC SUGGESTIONS

ICD-9-CM	_ICD-10-CM_	_DSM-5_ Disorder, Condition, or Problem
302.73	F52.31	Female Orgasmic Disorder
302.72	F52.21	Erectile Disorder
294.89	F06.8	Other Specified Mental Disorder Due to Another Medical Condition, Sexual Desire Disorder
302.72	F52.22	Female Sexual Interest/Arousal Disorder
302.71	F52.0	Male Hypoactive Sexual Desire Disorder
302.74	F52.32	Delayed Ejaculation
302.75	F52.4	Premature Ejaculation
V61.21	Z69.011	Encounter for Mental Health Services for Perpetrator of Parental Child Neglect
995.53	T74.22XA	Child Sexual Abuse, Confirmed, Initial Encounter
302.70	F52.9	Unspecified Sexual Dysfunction
_____	_____	_____
_____	_____	_____

TRANSITION TO PARENTHOOD STRAINS

BEHAVIORAL DEFINITIONS

1. Lack of agreement between the parents regarding caring for the infant (e.g., sleeping, feeding, responding when crying, playing).
2. Frequent arguments or disagreements between the partners.
3. Negative cognitions that interfere with appropriate child care or that exacerbate couple conflicts.
4. Inability of partners to support each other (e.g., day-to-day instrumental support, affection, and caring).
5. Conflict over balancing work, household, relationship, family, and community responsibilities.
6. Parents having difficulty reestablishing sexual relationship since the birth of their baby.

—. _____
   _____
—. _____
   _____
—. _____
   _____

LONG-TERM GOALS

1. Both partners form attachment bond with the infant.
2. Partners agree on and participate in infant care.
3. Each partner notices and verbalizes appreciation for infant care and support.
4. Partners manage stress without taking it out on the infant or partner.
5. Partners discuss and agree on strategy for balancing work, household, relationship, family, and community responsibilities.

6. Partners discuss feelings about sex/rejection and eventually reestablish sexual relationship.

—. _____
_____

—. _____
_____

—. _____
_____

SHORT-TERM OBJECTIVES

▽ 1. Play with the baby and support the other parent doing so. (1, 2, 3)

▽ 2. Each partner develops competence in managing the infant's sleeping, feeding, and crying and supports other parent doing so. (4, 5, 6)

THERAPEUTIC INTERVENTIONS

1. Ask each parent to generate times for (a) fun activities to do with the baby (e.g., time of day when he/she is available and the baby is quiet and alert); and (b) bonding interaction (e.g., showing affection, carrying and holding the baby, making eye contact and talking to the baby). ▽

2. Ask parents to share plans with each other. ▽

3. Ask each partner to generate ways in which he/she could support the other's plans for activity with the baby. ▽

4. Have both parents list (a) how they've been successfully managing the infant's sleeping, feeding, and crying; (b) areas in which they've been challenged or are having difficulty; and (c) how they're supporting the other's efforts. ▽

5. Ask parents to describe conflicts over how they're responding to infant's sleeping, feeding, and crying. ▽

▽ 3. Each partner constructs and implements a self-change plan that would help in the transition to parenthood. (7, 8)

▽ 4. Partners implement the two overarching communication skills of: "Be Clear" and "Be Considerate." (9, 10, 11)

6. Ask both parents to read material on a baby's first year of development (e.g., *Your Baby's First Year* by the American Academy of Pediatrics, or *What to Expect the First Year* by Murkoff, Mazel, Eisenberg, & Hathaway). ▽

7. Teach the partners the five steps of a Self-Change Plan: (1) Describe the behavior to be changed; (2) Examine the pros and cons of the current behavior; (3) Set a goal, describing as precisely as possible what is to happen; (4) Create an Action Plan, pinpointing a specific plan for enacting the goal; and (5) Evaluate enacting of the plan. Have the partners practice this in session on an area which has evoked anger that each would like to change. ▽

8. Ask both partners to agree to use self-change plans to improve their own transition behaviors instead of managing the other's behavior. ▽

9. Teach the partners the communication skill that emphasizes that interchanges should be: (a) clear (i.e., be specific, share thoughts and feelings, pay attention, ask clarifying questions, summarize content and feelings); and (b) considerate (i.e., include positives, show consideration when expressing negatives, let the partner know that one is listening even if one disagrees, reserve judgment). ▽

10. Ask the partners to discuss a low-conflict area of desired

change and ask them to rate how well they did being clear. ▽

11. Ask the partners to discuss a low-conflict area of desired change and ask them to rate how well they did being considerate. ▽

▽ 5. Practice defining problems in specific, nonblaming terms. (12, 13, 14)

12. Have the partners take turns pinpointing problems (that is, making requests for change that are specific, observable, and ask for increases rather than decreases in the other partner's behavior). ▽

13. Have the partners use the "speaker-listener" technique, with the listener trying to convey understanding after the speaker makes an "I" statement in the following form: "When _____ happens, I feel _____. I would like _____." ▽

14. If either partner is mind-reading the other, have him/her rephrase statements so that he/she is speaking only for self and expressing his/her own perceptions.

▽ 6. Practice listening in a manner that promotes empathy and understanding through the use of paraphrasing, reflecting, and validating skills. (15, 16, 17)

15. While one partner is serving as the speaker, have the listening partner *paraphrase* (i.e., summarize content) by repeating back in his/her own words, the speaker's overt point (e.g., "You would like me to balance the checkbook with you each month."). ▽

16. While one partner is serving as the speaker, have the listening partner *reflect* (i.e., summarize feelings) by repeating back, in his/her own words, the speaker's underlying emotion (e.g., "You're frustrated about our inability to save money."). ▽

▽ 7. Verbalize an understanding of communication that is either focused on problem-solving or on venting. (18, 19)

▽ 8. Organize a list of thoughts, behaviors, actual outcomes, and desired outcomes via situational analysis. (20, 21)

▽ 9. Verbalize thoughts that were inaccurate, global, or unhelpful, and then state more beneficial self-talk. (22, 23)

17. Have the listening partner practice *validation* skills (i.e., the listener conveys that he/she understands and can empathize with the speaker's feelings, even if not agreeing with them). ▽

18. Teach the partners that communication tends to serve one of two purposes—venting (i.e., sharing feelings) or problem-solving; have partners identify how they feel when one person is pursuing venting and the other reacts as if problem-solving is the goal. ▽

19. Role-play the couple discussing a current problem involving the baby while having the listener ask the speaker which he/she wants out of the discussion — venting or problem-solving. ▽

20. In session, ask a partner to think of a recent stressful situation (with the partner or with the baby) and tell what his/her desired outcome was, what his self-talk (e.g., interpretations/ cognitions) was, what his/her behavior was, and what the actual outcome of the situation was. ▽

21. As the concluding step in the situational analysis, have the partner describe what his/her desired outcome was in the specified conflict situation. ▽

22. Help the partners determine whether each thought in their situational analysis was: (a) accurate, (b) anchored to the specific situation, and (c) helpful in getting the desired outcome. ▽

23. If any thoughts do not meet all three criteria (increase likelihood

of achieving desired outcome, situationally-specific, and accurate) help the client rework the thought so that it does meet all three criteria (for example, "The baby has been crying forever—I can't take this!" "It hasn't been forever—a couple of hours of crying every day can be normal."). ▽

▽ 10. Track stressful child-related situations at home and identify thoughts or behaviors that could be modified to achieve better outcomes. (24)

24. Assign situational analysis homework to each partner that asks them to identify a stressful situation associated with the baby and then to describe the desired outcomes, thoughts/ interpretations, behaviors, and actual outcomes. ▽

▽ 11. Implement the use of the "Pause, Calm, and Think" (i.e., time-out) technique to modulate stress/anger. (25, 26)

25. Teach the partners the "Pause, Calm, and Think" technique: *Pause* the conversation (i.e., letting the other partner know that you want to pause the discussion or need a break from taking care of the infant); *Calm* down (e.g., focusing on diaphragmatic breathing, counting to 10, focusing on calming self down); *Think* (e.g., taking responsibility for ways in which you are making the conflict worse; planning ways to respond in a mindful, nonescalating manner instead of automatic, escalating manner; examining thinking by asking self "How TRUE is this thought?" "Is it about JUST THIS SITUATION?" "Will it HELP me get what I want?"). ▽

26. Role-play using "Pause, Calm, and Think" within the session with situations from a real life experience of the couple and then assign at-home implementation. ▽

▽ 12. Attend to and compliment other partner for helpful or caring behaviors. (27, 28, 29, 30)

27. Ask each partner to discuss the day-to-day things (i.e., instrumental) that he/she does to be supportive of the other. ▽

28. Ask each partner to discuss the things that he/she does to be affectionate. ▽

29. Ask each partner what pluses and minuses parenting has had on the level of caring in the relationship. ▽

30. Ask each partner to discuss ways in which he/she shows appreciation for the helpful or caring behaviors the other is doing and ways he/she could increase the level of appreciation shown. ▽

▽ 13. Ask partners to find time to show that they care for each other. (31, 32, 33, 34)

31. Have each partner generate ideas for what he/she can do to show caring and ideas for what he/she would like from the partner that would be quick (i.e., take less than five minutes). ▽

32. Have each partner generate ideas for what he/she can do to show caring and ideas for what he/she would like from the partner that would take 10 to 15 minutes. ▽

33. Have each partner generate ideas for what he/she can do to show caring and ideas for what he/she would like from the partner that would take more than 30 minutes. ▽

34. Ask partners to share their lists and plan to implement at least one caring behavior from each list. ▽

▽ 14. Verbalize how a problem may be opened for discussion. (35)

35. Use role-playing and modeling to teach the partners how to effectively approach the other to discuss a problem (despite the

▽ 15. Define the exact nature of one problem before trying to resolve it. (36, 37)

▽ 16. Use problem-solving skills to resolve a problem associated with caring for the baby. (38, 39, 40, 41)

perceived lack of time when caring for an infant).▽

36. Teach the partners to first agree to their mutual satisfaction that a problem has been correctly pinpointed before actually trying to solve the problem; have them practice this in session on areas of conflict.▽

37. Have both partners agree to discuss only one problem during problem-solving sessions.▽

38. Choose a moderate area of conflict associated with caring for the baby (e.g., conflict over division of responsibility) that has been pinpointed and have the partners practice brainstorming, whereby each partner generates at least two solutions to a problem before trying to solve that problem.▽

39. Teach the partners to evaluate the pros and cons of the brainstormed solutions and have them practice this in session on the area of conflict.▽

40. Teach the partners how to select specific, operationalized plan for attaining a solution based on the pros and cons of that solution; ask the partners to implement the selected action solution before the next session.▽

41. Ask the partners to give an evaluation of how they did on the action plan before the next session. The rating scale is 0 = didn't think about it or do it; 1 = thought about it; 2 = gave it a weak try; 3 = tried, partially succeeded; and 4 = did a great job. Ask them to jot down short

answers to the following: What did we actually do? What positives resulted? What negatives resulted? What do we need to do from here?▽

▽ 17. Communicate desires regarding the affectionate/sexual relationship. (42, 43, 44)

42. Ask the partners to discuss their thoughts about how the birth of the baby has changed their affectionate/sexual relationship.▽

43. Have the partners discuss their expectations for resumption of their affectionate/sexual relationship.▽

44. Focusing on the skills of being clear and being considerate; have the partners problem-solve ways they could slowly increase affection without unduly pressuring either partner.▽

___. _____   ___. _____
     _____   _____
___. _____   ___. _____
     _____   _____
___. _____   ___. _____
     _____   _____

DIAGNOSTIC SUGGESTIONS

ICD-9-CM	_ICD-10-CM_	_DSM-5_ Disorder, Condition, or Problem
300.4	F34.1	Persistent Depressive Disorder
296.xx	F32.x	Major Depressive Disorder, Single Episode
296.xx	F33.x	Major Depressive Disorder, Recurrent Episode
309.24	F43.22	Adjustment Disorder, With Anxiety
309.0	F43.21	Adjustment Disorder, With Depressed Mood
309.28	F43.23	Adjustment Disorder, With Mixed Anxiety and Depressed Mood
V61.10	Z63.0	Relationship Distress with Spouse or Intimate Partner
_____	_____	_____
_____	_____	_____

WORK/HOME ROLE STRAIN

BEHAVIORAL DEFINITIONS

1. Perception by one partner that self or family is not placed as a high enough priority in the other partner's life because of too great an emphasis on employment interests.
2. Contention by one or both partners that the other partner is not meeting his/her fair share of responsibilities in relationship, family, home maintenance, or work.
3. Partner conflict over current allocation of time to work, home, and chore roles.
4. Arguments between partners over role imbalances.
5. Perceived difficulty in meeting role expectations.
6. Perceived disorganization or time inefficiencies in attempts to meet key role responsibilities.

__. _____
   _____
__. _____
   _____
__. _____
   _____

LONG-TERM GOALS

1. Meet the basic responsibilities of work, relationship, and family in a mutually agreeable manner.
2. Satisfactorily balance the competing demands of work and family.
3. Clarify the values that guide life choices and time allocation.
4. Bring time allocation into harmony with espoused values.
5. Develop tolerance and empathy for the other partner's attempts to meet conflicting role demands.

6. Change thinking and behavioral patterns that create conflict or interfere with sincere attempts to meet conflicting role demands.

—. _____
   _____

—. _____
   _____

—. _____
   _____

SHORT-TERM OBJECTIVES

1. Verbally define current level of satisfaction and stress in work and family roles. (1, 2)

2. Verbally identify how current work, relationship, and home roles are met. (3, 4, 5, 6)

THERAPEUTIC INTERVENTIONS

1. Assess each partner's satisfaction with, and stress due to, work and family roles.

2. Query both partners about their work schedules (e.g., How many hours do they typically work? What shift does each work? Do they bring work home?).

3. Ask the couple to describe a typical workday and a typical weekend day (e.g., What time do they get up? What is their morning routine? How does the workday go? What is their evening routine? Do they have set patterns, or is there a lot of variability each day?).

4. Assess how chores at home are divided among family members (e.g., Is there an explicit plan?).

5. If the couple has children, assess each partner's satisfaction with the other's involvement in caring for the children.

6. Have the couple describe how the current role arrangement came about. Did they discuss their current family/work time and responsibility allocations

3. Identify how the demands of employment interfere with the responsibilities of home and family, and identify how the demands of family or relationship interfere with work responsibilities. (7, 8)

4. Identify how work stress leads to relationship conflicts. (9)

5. Have partner(s) articulate their values and goals for living a meaningful life using Covey's four human needs.
(10, 11, 12, 13, 14)

explicitly, or did the current arrangement evolve implicitly?

7. Ask the couple to describe the ways that family demands interfere with the employment role.

8. Ask the couple to describe the ways that employment demands interfere with the family role.

9. Ask the couple to describe the ways in which work stress may precipitate relationship conflicts.

10. Ask the partners to read First Things First (Covey, Merrill, & Merill), which posits that cross-cultural wisdom literature contains four key human needs "to live, to love, to learn, to leave a legacy."

11. Ask partners to consider their approach to fulfilling the need "to live" ("Our physical need for such things as food, clothing, economic well-being, health," Covey et al., p. 45) by having them write and discuss (a) their past and current goals for meeting financial needs, and (b) the pros and cons of their current approach.

12. Ask partners to consider their approach to fulfilling the need "to love" ("Our social need to relate to other people, to belong, to love, to be loved," Covey et al., p. 45) by having them write and discuss (a) their past and current goals for having rich, satisfying relationships with others, and (b) the pros and cons of their current approach.

13. Ask partners to consider their approach to fulfilling the need "to learn" ("Our mental need to

develop and to grow," Covey et al., p. 45) by having them write and discuss (a) their past and current goals for learning, growing, and being open to new experiences and skills, and (b) the pros and cons of their current approach.

14. Ask partners to consider their approach to fulfilling the need "to leave a legacy" ("Our spiritual need to have a sense of meaning, purpose, personal congruence, and contribution," Covey et al., p. 45) by having them write and discuss (a) their past and current goals for having a sense of direction and purpose, and (b) the pros and cons of their current approach.

6. Identify the impact of various influences on expectations regarding own and partner's roles in the relationship. (15)

15. Have both partners describe what expectations they perceive parents, friends, religious beliefs, subcultural groups, and society have for them in their work and home roles.

▽ 7. Verbalize an understanding of the other partner's dilemma in meeting competing role demands. (16, 17)

16. Ask partners to define for each other the dilemmas each faces in trying to meet their varied and sometimes competing role demands. ▽

17. While one partner serves as the speaker, have the other use positive listener skills (i.e., paraphrasing and reflecting) to demonstrate that he/she is trying to understand and empathize with the speaker's dilemmas in role demands. ▽

▽ 8. Verbalize an understanding of the other partner's feelings generated by the current role arrangement. (18, 19)

18. Ask each partner to describe how both the positive and negative aspects of the current role arrangement affect him/her emotionally (e.g., "I feel proud

and successful about my work accomplishments lately, but I feel that I'm missing a lot of what's going on with the kids."). ▽

19. While one partner serves as the speaker, have the listener validate and empathize with his/her perspective regarding the positive and negative aspects of the current role arrangement. ▽

▽ 9. Each partner constructs a self-change plan regarding a work/home role strain situation. (20, 21)

20. Teach partners the five steps of a Self-Change Plan: (1) Describe the behavior to be changed; (2) Examine the pros and cons of the current behavior; (3) Set a goal, describing as precisely as possible what is to happen; (4) Create an Action Plan, pinpointing a specific plan for enacting the goal, and (5) Evaluate enacting of the plan. Have the partners practice this in session on a work/home role strain situation that each would like to change. ▽

21. Ask partners to make a global evaluation of how they did on the action plan before the next session. The rating scale is 0 = didn't think about it or do it; 1 = thought about it; 2 = gave it a weak try; 3 = tried, partially succeeded; and 4 = did a great job. Ask them to jot down short answers to the following: What did we actually do? What positives resulted? What negatives resulted? What do we need to do from here? ▽

▽ 10. Verbalize an understanding of the rationale for situational analysis. (22)

22. Describe for the partners the goal of situational analysis (McCullough) in the following manner: "Achieving a balance between work and home happens one small situation at a time. To

▽ 11. Complete situational analysis homework to increase efficacy at effecting positive outcomes in situations at home. (23, 24)

work toward the big goals, try to make changes in the way you think and behave in small, observable situations that have a beginning, middle, and end." Have client repeat rationale in his/her own words. ▽

23. Assign the partners situational analysis homework that asks each to identify (a) a problematic situation (e.g., a description of the beginning, middle, and end of an observable situation); (b) three cognitions that occurred during the situation; (c) the behavior during the situation; (d) the actual outcome; and (e) the desired outcome. ▽

24. Ask client to read aloud from the situational analysis homework sheet, and paraphrase his/her statements to make sure that the therapist understands the key elements of the situational analysis. ▽

▽ 12. Identify whether one's thoughts or conclusions promote problem resolution, are directly relevant to the situation, and are based on reality. (25)

25. Have each partner state whether each thought in his/her situational analysis was (a) helpful in getting the desired outcome; (b) anchored to the specific situation described (i.e., is situationally-specific, not global); and (c) accurate (i.e., overt evidence can be marshaled to support it). ▽

▽ 13. Verbalize self-talk conclusions that promote problem resolution, are directly relevant to the situation, and are based on reality. (26)

26. If any thought or conclusion fails to meet all three criteria (i.e., helpful, anchored to specific situation, accurate), have partner rework the thought or conclusion so that it does meet all three criteria. For example, "He doesn't care about his children," can become "He seems to be having a hard time finding time for both work and home lately.

After the kids are in bed, I'll ask him if he feels up to discussing the strain." ▽

▽ 14. Each partner states the conclusion desired regarding the other partner's role behavior and how it can be achieved. (27, 28)

27. For each thought or conclusion identified, have each partner state what he/she would like the other partner to do instead of stating what the other partner is doing. ▽

28. Have each partner identify what he/she can do to increase the probability of attaining desired behavior from the other partner, versus complaining about the other's behavioral faults. For example, "She doesn't spend enough time at home," can become "I want to be supportive so that our home is one she would want to come home to." ▽

▽ 15. Choose desired outcomes that are achievable. (29)

29. Have the partner state whether the desired outcome is achievable (i.e., under his/her control). If not, help him/her rework the desired outcome so that it is achievable. For example, "I want him to listen to me when I tell him what needs to be done around the house" can become "I want to ask him to schedule a time for us to talk about what needs to be done around the house." ▽

▽ 16. Verbalize a generalizable lesson to be learned from the specific situational analysis and apply it to other situations of conflict. (30)

30. Ask the partner to summarize the situation by deriving a lesson to be learned from the situational analysis and whether the lesson can be applied to other conflict situations; apply this lesson to the next situation. ▽

▽ 17. Identify areas of disagreement regarding time allocation, and attempt to reach mutually agreeable solutions using problem-solving skills. (31, 32, 33, 34)

31. If either partner is upset with the proposed allocation of time, have him/her use problem-solving skills to pinpoint the problem (e.g., "It upsets me when I see that your time allocation places most of the

daily burden for child care on me. I'd like to have more help."); have the other partner use paraphrasing and/or reflection to indicate understanding (or assign "Applying Problem-Solving to Interpersonal Conflict" in the *Adult Psychotherapy Homework Planner*, 2nd ed. by Jongsma).▽

32. Ask each partner to generate at least two possible sources of assistance to ease home and work role demands (e.g., family members, child care, household help, project delegation).▽

33. Ask each partner to generate at least two ways of reallocating their time to provide mutual support and benefits.▽

34. Assist the partners in evaluating the pros and cons of the brainstormed solutions and help them choose a mutually preferred solution.▽

▽ 18. Enact and evaluate solutions to time allocation problems. (35, 36)

35. Have the partners (a) agree exactly how the solution to the time allocation conflict would be carried out, (b) contract with each other to enact it, and (c) write down their perceptions of the results (for discussion in a future session).▽

36. Discuss the partners' perceptions of the results and help them determine whether the solution could be improved in any way.▽

▽ 19. Contract with the partner regarding both partners' ongoing role expectations, and how recurrent problematic situations will be resolved. (37, 38)

37. Ask the partners to write and sign a work/home contract that details explicit expectations, requirements, and rewards for each partner in carrying out his/her responsibilities.▽

38. Have the partners discuss and develop explicit written

agreements regarding difficult daily work/home strains (e.g., Bill will watch the baby for 15 minutes while Beth changes out of her work clothes). ▽

20. Cope with limited time resources by identifying and contracting to meet basic family or relationship needs. (39, 40)

39. If the partners' time resources are insufficient to meet current standards, help them identify whether standards can be explicitly modified to meet resources (e.g., partners will clean for company and to maintain adequate levels of hygiene, but otherwise will clean the house no more than once per month).

40. If work schedules make family time difficult to schedule, help the partners establish brief routines that maintain some family contact and closeness (e.g., a short phone ritual during a work break).

__. _____

_____

__. _____

_____

__. _____

_____

__. _____

_____

__. _____

_____

__. _____

_____

DIAGNOSTIC SUGGESTIONS

ICD-9-CM	_ICD-10-CM_	_DSM-5_ Disorder, Condition, or Problem
309.24	F43.22	Adjustment Disorder, With Anxiety
309.0	F43.21	Adjustment Disorder, With Depressed Mood
309.28	F43.23	Adjustment Disorder, With Mixed Anxiety and Depressed Mood
300.4	F34.1	Persistent Depressive Disorder
300.02	F41.1	Generalized Anxiety Disorder
296.xx	F32.x	Major Depressive Disorder, Single Episode
296.xx	F33.x	Major Depressive Disorder, Recurrent Episode
_____	_____	_____
_____	_____	_____

Appendix A

BIBLIOTHERAPY SUGGESTIONS

Alcohol Abuse

Stromberg, G., & Merrill, J. (2009). *Second chances: Top executives share their stories of addiction & recovery*. New York, NY: McGraw-Hill.

Frederiksen, L. (2008). *If you loved me, you'd stop! What you really need to know when your loved one drinks too much*. Menlo Park, CA: KLJ Publishing.

Anger

Christensen, A., & Jacobson, N. S. (2000). *Reconcilable differences*. New York, NY: Guilford Press.

Cordova, J. V. (2009). *The marriage checkup: A scientific program for sustaining and strengthening marital health*. New York, NY: Jason Aronson.

Deffenbacher, J. L., & McKay, M. (2008). *Overcoming situational and general anger: Client manual*. Oakland, CA: New Harbinger Publications.

Notarius, C., & Markman, H. (1994). *We can work it out: Making sense of marital conflict*. New York, NY: Putnam.

Anxiety

Barlow, D. H., & Craske, M. (2007). *Mastering your anxiety and panic—Workbook* (4th ed.). New York, NY: Oxford University Press.

Craske, M., & Barlow, D. (2006). *Mastering your anxiety and worry—Workbook* (2nd ed.). New York, NY: Oxford University Press.

Blame

Knaus, W. J. (2000). *Take charge now!: Powerful techniques for breaking the blame habit*. New York, NY: John Wiley & Sons.

Miller, J. G. (2005). *QBQ! The question behind the question: What to really ask yourself to eliminate blame, complaining, and procrastination*. New York, NY: Penguin.

Tannen, D. (1990). *You just don't understand: Women and men in conversation*. New York, NY: Ballantine Books.

Wetzler, S., & Cole, D. (1998). *Is it you or is it me?: How we turn our emotions inside out and blame each other*. New York, NY: HarperCollins.

Blended Family Problems

Kaufman, T. S. (1993). *The combined family: A guide to creating successful step-relationships*. New York, NY: Plenum.

Wisdom, S., & Green, J. (2002). *Stepcoupling: Creating and sustaining a strong marriage in today's blended family*. New York, NY: Three Rivers Press.

Communication

Christensen, A., & Jacobson, N. S. (2000). *Reconcilable differences*. New York, NY: Guilford Press.

Cordova, J. V. (2009). *The marriage checkup: A scientific program for sustaining and strengthening marital health*. New York, NY: Jason Aronson.

Fincham, F. D., Fernandes, L. O. L., & Humphreys, L. (1993). *Communicating in relationships: A guide for couples and professionals*. Champaign, IL: Research Press.

Fruzzetti, A. (2006). *The high conflict couple*. Oakland, CA: New Harbinger Publications.

Gottman, J. M., Gottman, J. S., & Declaire, J. (2006). *Ten lessons to transform your marriage*. New York, NY: Crown Publishing.

Johnson. S. (2008). *Hold me tight: Seven conversations for a lifetime of love*. New York, NY: Little, Brown and Company.

Markman, H. J., Stanley, S. M., & Blumberg, S. L. (2010). *Fighting for your marriage*. San Francisco, CA: Jossey-Bass.

Markman, H. J., Stanley, S. M., Blumberg, S. L., Jenkins, N. H., & Whiteley, C. (2003). *12 hours to a great marriage: A step-by-step guide for making love last*. San Francisco, CA: Jossey-Bass.

Notarius, C., & Markman, H. (1994). *We can work it out: Making sense of marital conflict*. New York, NY: Putnam.

Wile, D. B. (1993). *After the fight: Using your disagreements to build a stronger relationship*. New York, NY: Guilford Press.

Wile, D. B. (2008). *After the honeymoon: How conflict can improve your relationship* (rev. ed.). Oakland, CA: Collaborative Couple Therapy Books.

Dependency

Beattie, M. (2009). *The new codependency: Help and guidance for today's generation.* New York, NY: Simon & Schuster.

Norwood. R. (1985). *Women who love too much: When you keep wishing and hoping he'll change.* New York, NY: Pocket Books.

Depression Due to Relationship Problems

Wiffen, V. E. (2009). *A secret sadness: The hidden relationship patterns that make women depressed.* Oakland, CA: New Harbinger Publications.

Depression Independent of Relationship Problems

Fittern, F., & Gulas, B. (2002). *Working in the dark: Keeping your job while dealing with depression.* Center City, MN: Hazelden.

Strauss, C. J., & Manning, M. (2004). *Talking to depression: Simple ways to connect when someone in your life is depressed.* New York, NY: New American Library.

Styron, W. (1990). *Darkness visible: A memoir of madness.* New York, NY: Vintage Books.

Williams, M., Teasdale, J., Segal, Z., & Kabat-Zinn, J. (2007). *The mindful way through depression: Freeing yourself from chronic unhappiness.* New York, NY: Guilford Press.

Disillusionment With Relationship

Covey, S. (1997). *The seven habits of highly effective families.* New York, NY: Golden Books.

Fincham, F. D., Fernandes, L. O. L., & Humphreys, L. (1993). *Communicating in relationships: A guide for couples and professionals.* Champaign, IL: Research Press.

Gottman, J. M., Gottman, J. S., & Declaire, J. (2006). *Ten lessons to transform your marriage.* New York, NY: Crown Publishing.

Johnson. S. (2008). *Hold me tight: Seven conversations for a lifetime of love.* New York, NY: Little, Brown and Company.

Kramer, P. D. (1999). *Should you leave?* New York, NY: Penguin.

Markman, H. J., Stanley, S. M., & Blumberg, S. L. (2010). *Fighting for your marriage.* San Francisco, CA: Jossey-Bass.

Markman, H. J., Stanley, S. M., Blumberg, S. L., Jenkins, N. H., & Whiteley, C. (2003). *12 hours to a great marriage: A step-by-step guide for making love last.* San Francisco, CA: Jossey-Bass.

Eating Disorders

Bays, J. C. (2009). *Mindful eating: A guide to rediscovering a healthy and joyful relationship with food.* Boston, MA: Shambhala.
Roth, G. (2003). *Breaking free from emotional eating.* New York, NY: Plume.
Schaefer, J., & Rutledge, T. (2004). *Life without Ed: How one woman declared independence from her eating disorder and how you can too.* New York, NY: McGraw-Hill.
Schaefer, J. (2009). *Goodbye Ed, hello me: Recover from your eating disorder and fall in love with life.* New York, NY: McGraw-Hill.

Financial Conflict

Rich, J. (2003). *The couple's guide to love & money.* Oakland, CA: New Harbinger Publications.
Thakor, M., & Kedar, S. (2009). *Get financially naked: How to talk money with your honey.* Avon, MA: Adams Media.
Bach, D. (2001). *Smart couples finish rich: 9 steps to creating a rich future for you and your partner.* New York, NY: Broadway Books.

Infidelity

Glass, S. P. (2003). *Not "just friends": Protect your relationship from infidelity and heal the trauma of betrayal.* New York, NY: Free Press.
Snyder, D. K., Baucom, D. H., & Gordon, K. C. (2007). *Getting past the affair: How to cope, heal, and move on—Together or apart.* New York, NY: Guilford Press.
Spring, J. A. (1996). *After the affair: Healing the pain and rebuilding trust when a partner has been unfaithful.* New York, NY: HarperCollins.
Spring. J. A. (2005). *How can I forgive you?: The courage to forgive, the freedom not to.* New York, NY: HarperCollins.

Internet Sexual Use

Weiss, R. & Schneider, J. P. (2006). *Untangling the web: Sex: porn, and fantasy obsession in the internet age.* New York, NY: Alyson Books.

Leahy, M. (2008). *Porn nation: Conquering America's #1 addiction*. Chicago, IL: Northfield Publishing.

US Census Bureau. (2007). "Computer and internet use in the United States: October 2007." Retrieved August 30, 2010 from, http://www.census.gov/population/www/socdemo/computer/2007.html

Intimate Partner Violence—Intimate Terrorism

Bancroft, L. (2002). *Why does he do that?: Inside the minds of angry and controlling men*. New York, NY: Berkley Books.

Betancourt, M., & McAfee, R. E. (2009). *What to do when love turns violent: A practical resource for women in abusive relationships*. Bloomington, IN: iUniverse.

DeBecker, G. (1999). *The gift of fear*. New York, NY: Dell.

Fruzzetti, A. (2006). *The high conflict couple*. Oakland, CA: New Harbinger Publications.

Jacobson, N. S., & Gottman, J. M. (2007). *When men batter women: New insights into ending abusive relationships*. New York, NY: Simon & Schuster.

Murphy-Milano, S. (2010). *Time's up: How to escape abusive and stalking relationships guide*. Indianapolis, IN: Dog Ear Publishing.

Intimate Partner Violence—Situational (Bi-Directional) Couple Violence

Christensen, A., & Jacobson, N. S. (2000). *Reconcilable differences*. New York, NY: Guilford Press.

Fruzzetti, A. (2006). *The high conflict couple*. Oakland, CA: New Harbinger Publications.

Markman, H. J., Stanley, S. M., & Blumberg, S. L. (2010). *Fighting for your marriage*. San Francisco, CA: Jossey-Bass.

Intolerance

Christensen, A. & Jacobson, N. S. (2000). *Reconcilable differences*. New York, NY: Guilford Press.

Cordova, J. V. (2009). *The marriage checkup: A scientific program for sustaining and strengthening marital health*. New York, NY: Jason Aronson.

Hayes, S. C. & Smith, S. (2005). *Get out of your mind and into your life: The new Acceptance and Commitment Therapy*. Oakland, CA: New Harbinger.

Walser, R. D., & Westrup, D. (2009). *The mindful couple: How acceptance and mindfulness can lead you to the love you want*. Oakland, CA: New Harbinger.

Jealousy

Craske, M., & Barlow, D. (2006). *Mastering your anxiety and worry—Workbook* (2nd ed.). New York, NY: Oxford University Press.

Snyder, D. K., Baucom, D. H., & Gordon, K. C. (2007). *Getting past the affair: How to cope, heal, and move on—Together or apart.* New York, NY: Guilford Press.

Job Stress

Fittern, F., & Gulas, B. (2002). *Working in the dark: Keeping your job while dealing with depression.* Center City, MN: Hazelden.

Hellman, P. (2002). *Naked at work (and other fears): How to stay sane when your job drives you crazy.* New York, NY: New American Library.

Oher, J., Conti, D. J., & Jongsma, A. E. Jr. (1998). *The employee assistance treatment planner.* New York, NY: John Wiley & Sons.

Wiley, A. R., Branscomb, K., & Wang, Y. Z. (2007). Intentional harmony in the lives of working parents: Program development and evaluation. *Family Relations, 56*(3), 318–328.

Life-Changing Events

Christensen, A., & Jacobson, N. S. (2002). *Reconcilable differences.* New York, NY: Guilford Press.

Cordova, J. V. (2009). *The marriage checkup: A scientific program for sustaining and strengthening marital health.* New York, NY: Jason Aronson.

Covey, S. (1997). *The seven habits of highly effective families.* New York, NY: Golden Books.

Dishion, T. J., & Patterson, S. G. (2005). *Parenting young children with love, encouragement and limits.* Champaign, IL: Research Press.

Petch, J., Halford, W. K., & Creedy, D. K. (2010). Promoting a positive transition to parenthood: A randomized clinical trial of couple relationship education. *Prevention Science, 11,* 89–100.

Loss of Love/Affection

Brander, B. (2004). *Love that works: The art and science of giving.* Radnor, PA: Templeton Foundation Press.

Goldstein, A., & Brandon, M. (2004). *Reclaiming desire: 4 keys to finding your lost libido.* New York, NY: Rodale.

Hendrickson, G., & Hendrickson, K. (2004). *Lasting love: The 5 secrets of growing a vital, conscious relationship.* New York, NY: Rodale.

Kramer, P. D. (1997). *Should you leave? A psychiatrist explores intimacy and autonomy—and the nature of advice.* New York, NY: Scribner.

McCarthy, B., & McCarthy, E. (2002). *Sexual awareness: Couple sexuality for the twenty-first century*. Cambridge, MA: Da Capo Press.

McWilliams, P., Bloomfield, H. H., & Colgrove, M. (1993). *How to survive the loss of a love*. Los Angeles, CA: Prelude Press.

Midlife Transition Problems

Covey, S. R., Merrill, R. R., & Merrill, A. R. (1996). *First things first*. New York, NY: Free Press.

Only One Partner Willing to Attend Therapy

Beck, A. T. (1988). *Love is never enough*. New York, NY: Harper & Row.

Covey, S. (1997). *The seven habits of highly effective families*. New York, NY: Golden Books.

Kramer, P. D. (1999). *Should you leave*? New York, NY: Penguin.

Markman, H. J., Stanley, S. M., & Blumberg, S. L. (2010). *Fighting for your marriage*. San Francisco, CA: Jossey-Bass.

Young, J. E., & Klosko, J. S. (1994). *Reinventing your life: The breakthough program to end negative behavior ... and feel great again*. New York, NY: Plume.

Parenting Conflicts—Adolescents

Forgatch, M., & Patterson, G. R. (1987). *Parents and adolescents. Vol. II: Family problem solving*. Eugene, OR: Castalia.

Patterson, G. R., & Forgatch, M. (1987). *Parents and adolescents: Living together. Vol. I: The basics*. Eugene, OR: Castalia.

Parenting Conflicts—Children

Cordova, J. V. (2009). *The marriage checkup: A scientific program for sustaining and strengthening marital health*. New York, NY: Jason Aronson.

Dishion, T. J., & Patterson, S. G. (2005). *Parenting young children with love, encouragement and limits*. Champaign, IL: Research Press.

Markie-Dadds, C., Sanders, M. R., & Turner, K. M. T. (1999). *Every parent's self-help workbook*. Brisbane, QLD, Australia: Families International Publishing. Available from http://www.triplep-america.com/pages/parents/selfhelp.html

Patterson, G. R. (1975). *Families: Applications of social learning to family life*. Champaign, IL: Research Press.

Sanders, M. R. (2004). *Every parent: A positive approach to children's behavior*. Sydney: Penguin Books. Available from http://www.triplep-america.com/pages/parents/selfhelp.html

Personality Differences

Bittlingmaier, B. (2000). *Shape up your personality—shape up your marriage*. New York, NY: Writer's Showcase.

Shackelford, R. (2002). *Married to an opposite: Making personality differences work for you (psychology, religion, and spirituality)*. Westport, CT: Praeger.

Tannen, D. (1990). *You just don't understand: Women and men in conversation*. New York, NY: Ballantine Books.

Psychological Abuse

Dugan, M. K., & Hock, R. R. (2000). *It's my life now: Starting over after an abusive relationship or domestic violence*. New York, NY: Routledge.

Evans, P. (1992). *The verbally abusive relationship: How to recognize it and how to respond*. Avon, MA: Adams Media Corporation.

Forward, S. (1997). *Emotional blackmail: When the people in your life use fear, obligation, and guilt to manipulate you*. New York, NY: Harper Collins.

Kramer, P. D. (1997). *Should you leave? A psychiatrist explores intimacy and autonomy—and the nature of advice*. New York, NY: Scribner.

Recreational Activities Dispute

Christensen, A., & Jacobson, N. S. (2000). *Reconcilable differences*. New York, NY: Guilford Press.

Godek, G. J. P. (2007). *1001 ways to be romantic* (2nd ed.). Naperville, IL: Sourcebooks.

Notarius, C., & Markman, H. (1994). *We can work it out: Making sense of marital conflict*. New York, NY: Putnam.

Phillippe, C., McMurry, S., Bordon, R., & Currington, R. (2008). *Fun & creative dates for married couples: 52 ways to enjoy life together*. New York, NY: Howard Books.

Rietzsch, L. K. (2008). *How to date your spouse*. Brigham City, UT: Brigham Distributing.

Religious/Spirituality Differences

Christensen, A., & Jacobson, N. S. (2000). *Reconcilable differences*. New York, NY: Guilford Press.

Cordova, J. V. (2009). *The marriage checkup: A scientific program for sustaining and strengthening marital health*. New York, NY: Jason Aronson.

Gottman, J. M., Gottman, J. S., & Declaire, J. (2006). *Ten lessons to transform your marriage*. New York, NY: Crown Publishing.

Markman, H. J., Stanley, S. M., & Blumberg, S. L. (2010). *Fighting for your marriage*. San Francisco, CA: Jossey-Bass.

Retirement

Battaglia, B. (2008). *Changing lanes: Couples redefining retirement*. Seattle, WA: Booksurge.

Covey, S. R., Merrill, R. R., & Merrill, A. R. (1996). *First things first*. New York, NY: Free Press.

Yogev, S. (2001). *For better or for worse . . . but not for lunch*. Chicago, IL: Contemporary Books.

Separation and Divorce

Ahrons, C. R. (2004). *The good divorce: Keeping your family together when your marriage comes apart*. New York, NY: HarperCollins.

Emery, R. E. (2006). *The truth about children and divorce: Dealing with the emotions so you and your children can thrive*. New York, NY: Plume.

Hetherington, E. M., & Kelly, J. (2003). *For better or for worse: Divorce reconsidered*. New York, NY: Norton.

Wallerstein, J., Lewis, J. M., & Blakeslee, S. (2000). *The unexpected legacy of divorce: A 25 year landmark study*. New York, NY: Hyperion.

Sexual Abuse

Dugan, M. K., & Hock, R. R. (2000). *It's my life now: Starting over after an abusive relationship or domestic violence*. New York, NY: Routledge.

Kramer, P. D. (1997). *Should you leave? A psychiatrist explores intimacy and autonomy—and the nature of advice*. New York, NY: Scribner.

Sexual Dysfunction

Goldstein, A., & Brandon, M. (2004). *Reclaiming desire: 4 keys to finding your lost libido*. New York, NY: Rodale.

Comfort, A. (2009). The joy of sex: *The timeless guide to love making, ultimate revised edition*. New York, NY: Crown.

Kerner, I. (2004). She comes first: *The thinking man's guide to pleasuring a woman*. New York, NY: HarperCollins.

Kerner, I. (2008). Passionista: *The empowered woman's guide to pleasuring a man*. New York, NY: HarperCollins.
(*Note*: This book has also been published under the title *He Comes Next*.)

McCarthy, B., & McCarthy, E. (2002). *Sexual awareness: Couple sexuality for the twenty-first century*. Cambridge, MA: Da Capo Press.

Transition to Parenthood Strains

American Academy of Pediatrics. (2010). *Your baby's first year* (3rd ed.). New York, NY: Bantam.

Cowan, C. P., & Cowan, P. A. (1999). *When partners become parents*. New York, NY: Routledge.

Gottman, J. M., & Gottman, J. S. (2008). *And baby makes three: The six-step plan for preserving marital intimacy and rekindling romance after baby arrives*. New York, NY: Three Rivers Press.

Halford, W. K., Heyman, R. E., Slep, A. M. S., Petch, J., & Creedy, D. K. (2009). *Couple CARE for parents of newborns* (DVD and Workbook). Available by emailing Richard.Heyman@Stonybrook.edu

Murkoff, H. E., Eisenberg, A., & Hathaway, S. (1996). *What to expect the first year*. New York, NY: Workman.

Work/Home Role Strain

Covey, S. (1997). *The seven habits of highly effective families: Building a beautiful family culture in a turbulent world*. New York, NY: Golden Books.

Appendix B

PROFESSIONAL REFERENCES FOR EVIDENCE-BASED CHAPTERS

Alcohol Abuse

Fals-Stewart, W. (2004, April). *Substance abuse and domestic violence: Many issues, some answers.* Invited address presented at the conference Substance Abuse and Antisocial Behavior across the Lifespan: Research Findings and Clinical Implications, Toronto, Canada.

Fals-Stewart, W., Klosterman, K., & Clinton-Sherrod, M. (2009). Substance abuse and intimate partner violence. In K. D. O'Leary & E. M. Woodin (Eds.), *Psychological and Physical Aggression in Couples: Causes and Interventions.* Washington, DC: American Psychological Association.

McCrady, B., Epstein, E. E., Cook, S., & Jensen, N. (2009). A randomized trial of individual and couple behavioral alcohol treatment for women. *Journal of Consulting and Clinical Psychology, 77*, 243–256.

O'Leary, K. D. (2008). Couple therapy and physical aggression. In A. S. Gurman (Ed.), *Clinical handbook of couple therapy* (pp. 478–498). New York, NY: Guilford Press.

O'Leary, K. D., & Cohen, S. (2007). Treatment of psychological and physical aggression in a couple context. In J. Hammel & A. Nicholls (Eds.), *Family interventions in domestic violence: A handbook of gender inclusive theory and treatment* (pp. 363–380). New York, NY: Springer.

Saha, T.D., Chou, P., & Grant, B. F. (2006). Toward an alcohol use disorder continuum, using item response theory: Results from the National Epidemiological Survey on Alcohol and Related Conditions. *Psychological Medicine, 36*, 931–941.

Saunders, J. B., Aaslan, O. G., Barbor, T. F., LaFuente, J. R., & Grant, M. (2006). Development of the Alcohol Use Disorders Identification Test (AUDIT): WHO Collaborative Project on Early Detection of Persons with Harmful Alcohol Consumption–II. *Addiction, 88*, 791–804.

Anger

DiGuiseppe, R., & Tafrate, R. C. (2003). Anger treatment for adults: A meta-analytic review. *Clinical Psychology: Science and Practice, 10*, 70–84.

Donohue, B., & Cavenagh, N. (2003). Anger (negative impulse) management. In W. O'Donohue, J. Fisher, & S. Hayes (Eds.), *Cognitive behavior therapy: Applying empirically supported techniques in your practice* (pp. 115–123). Hoboken, NJ: John Wiley & Sons.

Fruzzetti, A. E. (2006). *The high conflict couple: A dialectical behavior therapy guide to finding peace, intimacy, and validation.* Oakland, CA: New Harbinger Publications.

Halford, W. K. (2001). *Brief therapy for couples: Helping partners help themselves.* New York, NY: Guilford Press.

Halford, W. K., Moore, E. M., Wilson, K. L., Dyer, C., & Farrugia, C. (2004). Benefits of a flexible delivery relationship education: An evaluation of the Couple CARE program. *Family Relations, 53*, 469–476.

Heyman, R. E., & Slep, A. M. S. (2007). Therapeutic treatments for violence. In D. J. Flannery, A. T. Vazsonyi, & I. Waldman (Eds.), *The Cambridge handbook of violent behavior* (pp. 602–617). New York, NY: Cambridge University Press.

Jacobson, N. S., & Christensen, A. (1996). *Acceptance and change in couple therapy: A therapist's guide to transforming relationships.* New York, NY: Norton.

Jacobson, N. S., Christensen, A., Prince, S. E., Cordova, J., & Eldridge, K. (2000). Integrative Behavioral Couple Therapy: An acceptance-based, promising new treatment for couple discord. *Journal of Consulting and Clinical Psychology, 68*, 351–355.

McCullough, J. P. (2000). *Treatment for chronic depression: Cognitive behavioral analysis system of psychotherapy (CBASP).* New York, NY: Guilford Press.

Novaco, R. W. (1975). *Anger control: The development and evaluation of an experimental treatment.* Lexington, MA: D. C. Heath.

Shadish, W. R., & Baldwin, S. A. (2005). Effects of behavioral marital therapy: A meta-analysis of randomized controlled trials. *Journal of Consulting and Clinical Psychology, 73*, 6–14.

Wilson, K. L., & Halford, W. K. (2008). Processes of change in self-directed couple relationship education. *Family Relations, 57*, 625–635.

Anxiety

Byrne, M., Carr, A., & Clark, M. (2004). The efficacy of couples-based interventions for panic disorder with agoraphobia. *Journal of Family Therapy, 26*, 105–125.

Craske, M. G., & Barlow, D. H. (2006). *Mastery of your anxiety and panic: Therapist guide* (4th ed.). New York, NY: Oxford University Press.

Emmelkamp, P. M. G., & Gerlsma, C. (1994). Marital functioning and the anxiety disorders. *Behavior Therapy, 25*, 407–429.

Shadish, W. R., & Baldwin, S.A. (2005). Effects of behavioral marital therapy: A meta-analysis of randomized controlled trials. *Journal of Consulting and Clinical Psychology, 73*, 6–14.

Zinbarg, R. E., Craske, M. G., & Barlow, D. H. (2006). *Mastery of your anxiety and worry: Therapist guide* (2nd ed.). New York, NY: Oxford University Press.

Blame

Fincham, F. D., Hall, J., & Beach, S. R. (2006). Forgiveness in marriage: Current status and future directions. *Family Relations, 55*(4), 415–427.

Halford, W. K. (2001). *Brief therapy for couples: Helping partners help themselves.* New York, NY: Guilford Press.

Jacobson, N. S., & Margolin, G. (1979) *Marital therapy: Strategies based on social learning and behavior exchange principles.* New York, NY: Brunner/Mazel.

Makinen, J. A., & Johnson, J. A. (2006). Resolving attachment injuries in couples using emotionally focused therapy: Steps toward forgiveness and reconciliation. *Journal of Consulting and Clinical Psychology, 74*(6), 1055–1064.

Mamalakis, P. M. (2001). Painting a bigger picture: Forgiveness therapy with pre-marital infidelity: A case study. *Journal of Family Psychotherapy, 12*(1), 2001, 39–54.

O'Leary, K. D., Heyman, R. E., & Neidig, E. H. (1999). Treatment of wife abuse: A comparison of gender-specific and conjoint approaches. *Behavior Therapy, 30*, 475–505.

Blended Family Problems

Bengston, V. L. (2001). Beyond the nuclear family: The increasing import of multi-generational bonds. *Journal of Marriage and the Family, 63*, 1–16.

Bray, J. H., & Easling, I. (2005). Remarriage and stepfamilies. In W. Pinsoff & J. L. Lebow (Eds.), *Family psychology: The art of the science* (pp. 267–294). New York, NY: Oxford University Press.

Laidlaw, K., & Pachana, N. A. (2009). Aging, mental health, and demographic change: Challenges for psychotherapists. *Professional Psychology: Research and Practice, 40*(6), 601–608.

Communication

Christensen, A., Atkins, D. C., Berns, S., Wheeler, J., Baucom, D. H., & Simpson, L. E. (2004). Traditional versus Integrative Behavioral Couple Therapy for significantly and chronically distressed married couples. *Journal of Consulting and Clinical Psychology, 72*, 176–191.

Epstein, N., & Baucom, D. H. (2002). *Enhanced cognitive-behavioral therapy for couples: A contextual approach*. Washington, DC: American Psychological Association.

Gottman, J. M. (1999). *The marriage clinic*. New York, NY: Norton.

Greenberg, L. S., & Johnson, S. M. (1988). *Emotionally focused therapy for couples*. New York, NY: Guilford Press.

Halford, W. K., Moore, E. M., Wilson, K. L., Dyer, C., & Farrugia, C. (2004). Benefits of a flexible delivery relationship education: An evaluation of the Couple CARE program. *Family Relations, 53*, 469–476.

Halford, W. K. (2001). *Brief therapy for couples: Helping partners help themselves*. New York, NY: Guilford Press.

Heyman, R. E. (2001). Observation of couple conflicts: Clinical assessment applications, stubborn truths, and shaky foundations. *Psychological Assessment, 13*, 5–35.

Jacobson, N. S., & Christensen, A. (1996). *Acceptance and change in couple therapy: A therapist's guide to transforming relationships*. New York, NY: Norton.

Jacobson, N. S., Christensen, A., Prince, S. E., Cordova, J., & Eldridge, K. (2000). Integrative Behavioral Couple Therapy: An acceptance-based, promising new treatment for couple discord. *Journal of Consulting and Clinical Psychology, 68*, 351–355.

Johnson, S. M. (2004). *The practice of emotionally focused marital therapy: Creating connection* (2nd ed.). New York, NY: Brunner/Routledge.

Markman, H., Stanley, S., & Blumberg, S. L. (2001) *Fighting for your marriage*. San Francisco, CA: Jossey-Bass.

Shadish, W. R., & Baldwin, S. A. (2005). Effects of behavioral marital therapy: A meta-analysis of randomized controlled trials. *Journal of Consulting and Clinical Psychology, 73*, 6–14.

Snyder, D. K., Heyman, R. E., & Haynes, S. N. (2005). Evidence-based approaches to assessing couple distress. *Psychological Assessment, 17*, 288–307.

Dependency

Beattie, M. (1992). *Codependent no more: Beyond codependency*. New York, NY: MJF Books.

Cohen, S., O'Leary, K. D., & Foran, H. (2010). A randomized clinical trial of a brief, problem-focused couple therapy for depression. *Behavior Therapy, 41*(4), 433–446.

Jongsma, A. E., & Peterson, M. (2006). *The complete adult psychotherapy treatment planner* (4th ed.). Hoboken, NJ: John Wiley & Sons.

Rathus, J., & O'Leary, K. D. (1998). Spouse-specific dependency scale: Scale development. *Journal of Family Violence, 12*, 159–168.

Depression Due to Relationship Problems

Beach, S. R. H., & O'Leary, K. D. (1986). The treatment of depression occurring in the context of marital discord. *Behavior Therapy, 17*, 43–49.

Bodenmann, G., Plancherel, B., Beach, S. R. H., Widmer, K., Gabriel, B., Meuwly, N., Charvoz, L., Hautzinger, M., & Schramm, E. (2008). Effects of a coping-oriented couples therapy on depression: A randomized clinical trial. *Journal of Consulting and Clinical Psychology, 76,* 944–954.

Cohen, S., O'Leary, K. D., & Foran, H. (2010). A randomized clinical trial of a brief, problem-focused couple therapy for depression. *Behavior Therapy, 41*(4), 433–446.

Dessaulles, A., Johnson, S. M., & Denton, W. H. (2003). Emotion-focused therapy for couples in the treatment of depression: A pilot study. *American Journal of Family Therapy, 31,* 345–353.

Emanuels-Zuurveen, L., & Emmelkamp, P. M. (1996). Individual behavioural-cognitive therapy v. marital therapy for depression in martially distressed couples. *British Journal of Psychiatry, 169,* 181–188.

Jacobson, N. S., Dobson, K., Fruzzetti, A. E., Schmaling, K. B., & Salusky, S. (1991). Marital therapy as a treatment for depression. *Journal of Consulting and Clinical Psychology, 59,* 547–557.

Depression Independent of Relationship Problems

Cohen, S., O'Leary, K. D., & Foran, H. (2010). A randomized clinical trial of a brief, problem-focused couple therapy for depression. *Behavior Therapy, 41*(4), 433–446.

Dessaulles, A., Johnson, S. M., & Denton, W. H. (2003). Emotion-focused therapy for couples in the treatment of depression: A pilot study. *American Journal of Family Therapy, 31,* 345–353.

Jacobson, N. S., Dobson, K., Fruzzetti, A. E., Schmaling, K. B., & Salusky, S. (1991). Marital therapy as a treatment for depression. *Journal of Consulting and Clinical Psychology, 59,* 547–557.

Disillusionment With Relationship

Baucom, D. H., Sayers, S. L., & Sher, T. G (1990). Supplementing behavioral *marital therapy* with cognitive restructuring and emotional expressiveness training: An outcome investigation. *Journal of Consulting and Clinical Psychology, 58*(5), 636–645.

Christensen, A., Atkins, D. C., Berns, S., Wheeler, J., Baucom, D. H., & Simpson, L. E. (2004). Traditional versus Integrative Behavioral Couple Therapy for significantly and chronically distressed married couples. *Journal of Consulting and Clinical Psychology, 72,* 176–191.

Epstein, N., & Baucom, D. H. (2002). *Enhanced cognitive-behavioral therapy for couples: A contextual approach.* Washington, DC: American Psychological Association.

Greenberg, L. S., & Johnson, S. M. (1988). *Emotionally focused therapy for couples.* New York, NY: Guilford Press.

Greenberg, L., Ford, C. L., Alden, L. S., & Johnson, S. M. (1993). In-session change in emotionally focused therapy. *Journal of Consulting and Clinical Psychology, 61*(1), 78–84.

Halford, W. K., Moore, E. M., Wilson, K. L., Dyer, C., & Farrugia, C. (2004). Benefits of a flexible delivery relationship education: An evaluation of the Couple CARE program. *Family Relations, 53,* 469–476.

Halford, W. K. (2001). *Brief therapy for couples: Helping partners help themselves.* New York, NY: Guilford Press.

Makinen, J. A., & Johnson, J. A. (2006). Resolving attachment injuries in couples using emotionally focused therapy: Steps toward forgiveness and reconciliation. *Journal of Consulting and Clinical Psychology, 74*(6), 1055–1064.

O'Leary, K. D., & Arias, I. (1983). The influence of marital therapy on sexual satisfaction. *Journal of Sex and Marital Therapy, 9,* 171–181.

Eating Disorders

Le Grange, D., Crosby, R. D., Rathouz, P. J., & Leventhal, B. L. (2007). A randomized controlled comparison of family-based treatment and supportive psychotherapy for adolescent bulimia nervosa. *Archives of General Psychiatry, 64,* 1049–1056.

Russell, G. F. M., Szmukler, G. I., Dare, C., & Eisler, I. (1987). An evaluation of family therapy in anorexia nervosa and bulimia nervosa. *Archives of General Psychiatry, 44,* 1047–1056.

Wilson, G. T., Grilo, C. M., & Vitousek, K. M. (2007). Psychological treatment of eating disorders. *American Psychologist, 62*(3), 199–216.

Financial Conflict

Aniol, J. C., & Snyder, D. N. (1997 Differential assessment of financial and relationship distress: Implications for couples therapy. *Journal of Marital & Family Therapy, 23*(3), 347–352.

Baucom, D. H., Shoham, V., Mueser, K. T., Daiuto, A. D., & Stickle, T. R. (1998). Empirically supported couple and family interventions for marital distress and adult mental health problems. *Journal of Consulting and Clinical Psychology, 66*(1), 53–88.

Benjamin, M., & Irving, H. (2001). Money and mediation: Patterns of conflict in family mediation of financial matters. *Mediation Quarterly, 18*(4), 349–361.

Christensen, A., Atkins, D. C., Yi, J., Baucom, D. H., & George, W. H. (2006). Couple and individual adjustment for two years following a randomized clinical trial comparing traditional versus integrative behavioral couple therapy. *Journal of Consulting and Clinical Psychology, 74*(6), 1180–1191.

Shadish, W. R., & Baldwin, S. A. (2005). Effects of behavioral marital therapy: A meta-analysis of randomized controlled trials. *Journal of Consulting and Clinical Psychology, 73*(1), 6–14.

Infidelity

Atkins, D. C., Marin, R. A., Lo, T. T. Y., Klann, N., & Halweg, K. (2010). Outcomes of couples with infidelity in a community-based sample of couple therapy. *Journal of Family Psychology, 24,* 212–216.

Baucom, D. H., Gordon, K. C., Snyder, D. K., Atkins, D. C., & Christensen, A. (2006). Treating affair couples: Clinical considerations and initial findings. *Journal of Cognitive Psychotherapy, 20,* 375–392.

Baucom, D. H., Snyder, D. K., & Gordon, K. C. (2009). *Helping couples get past the affair.* New York, NY: Guilford Press.

Cano, A., & O'Leary, K. D. (1997). Romantic jealousy and affairs: Research and implications for couple therapy. *Journal of Sex and Marital Therapy, 23,* 249–275.

Funk, J. L., & Rogge, R. D. (2007). Testing the ruler with item response theory: Increasing precision of measurement for relationship satisfaction with the Couples Satisfaction Index. *Journal of Family Psychology, 21,* 572–583.

Glass, S. P., & Wright, T. L. (1997). Reconstructing marriages after the trauma of infidelity. In W. K. Halford & H. J. Markman (Eds.), *Clinical handbook of marriage and couples intervention* (pp. 471–507). New York, NY: John Wiley & Sons.

Halford, W. K. (2001). *Brief therapy for couples: Helping partners help themselves.* New York, NY: Guilford Press.

Halford, W. K., Moore, E. M., Wilson, K. L., Dyer, C., & Farrugia, C. (2004). Benefits of a flexible delivery relationship education: An evaluation of the Couple CARE program. *Family Relations, 53,* 469–476.

Kerig, P. K. (1996). Assessing the links between marital conflict and child development: The Conflicts and Problem-Solving Scales. *Journal of Family Psychology, 10,* 454–473.

McCullough, J. P. (2000). *Treatment for chronic depression: Cognitive behavioral analysis system of psychotherapy (CBASP).* New York, NY: Guilford Press.

Shadish, W. R., & Baldwin, S. A. (2005). Effects of behavioral marital therapy: A meta-analysis of randomized controlled trials. *Journal of Consulting and Clinical Psychology, 73,* 6–14.

Snyder, D. K. (1997). *Marital Satisfaction Inventory, revised.* Los Angeles, CA: Western Psychological Services.

Straus, M. A., Hamby, S. L., Boney-McCoy, S., & Sugarman, D. B. (1996). The revised Conflict Tactics Scales (CTS2): Development and preliminary psychometric data. *Journal of Family Issues, 17,* 283–316.

Weiss, R. L., & Birchler, G. R. (1975). *Areas of Change Questionnaire.* Unpublished manuscript, University of Oregon, Eugene. Available by emailing Richard. Heyman@Stonybrook.edu.

Weiss, R. L. (1982). *Cost-benefit Exchange Questionnaire.* Unpublished manuscript, University of Oregon, Eugene. Available by emailing Richard.Heyman@Stony brook.edu.

Wilson, K. L., & Halford, W. K. (2008). Processes of change in self-directed couple relationship education. *Family Relations, 57,* 625–635.

Internet Sexual Use

Buzzell, T. (2005). Demographic characteristics of persons using pornography in three technological contexts. *Sexuality & Culture, 9*(1), 28–48.

Dworkin, A. (1981). *Pornography: Men possessing women.* London, England: Women's Press.

Firestone, R. W., Firestone, L. A., & Catlett, J. (2008). *Sex and love in intimate relationships.* Washington, DC: American Psychological Association.

Leitenberg, H., & Henning, K. (1995). Sexual fantasy. *Psychological Bulletin, 117,* 469–496.

Salwen, J., O'Leary, K. D., Foran, H., Jose, A., & Kar, H. L. (2010). Pornography use among college students. Unpublished manuscript. Stony Brook University. Stony Brook, NY.

Seto, M. C., Maric, A., & Barbaree, H. (2001). The role of pornography in the etiology of sexual aggression. *Aggression and Violent Behavior, 6,* 35–53.

Stern, S. E., & Handel, A. D. (2001). Sexuality and mass media: The historical context of psychology's reaction to sexuality on the Internet [Electronic version]. *Journal of Sex Research, 38,* 283–291.

Intimate Partner Violence—Intimate Terrorism

Baucom, D. H., Snyder, D. K., & Gordon, K.C. (2009). *Helping couples get past the affair.* New York, NY: Guilford Press.

Family Violence Prevention Fund. (2002). National Consensus Guidelines on identifying and responding to domestic violence victimization in health care settings. Downloaded on March 1, 2010 from http://www.endabuse.org/userfiles/file/Consensus.pdf.

Fruzzetti, A. E. (2006). *The high conflict couple: A dialectical behavior therapy guide to finding peace, intimacy, and validation.* Oakland, CA: New Harbinger Publications.

Halford, W. K. (2001). *Brief therapy for couples: Helping partners help themselves.* New York, NY: Guilford Press.

Johnson, M. P. (2008). *A typology of domestic violence: Intimate terrorism, violent resistance, and situational couple violence.* Boston, MA: Northeastern University Press.

McCollum, E. E., & Stith, S. M. (2009). Couples treatment for interpersonal violence: A review of outcome research literature and current clinical practices. *Violence and Victims, 23,* 187–201.

McCullough, J. P. (2000). *Treatment for chronic depression: Cognitive behavioral analysis system of psychotherapy (CBASP)*. New York, NY: Guilford Press.

McMahon, M., & Pence, E. (1996). Physical aggression in intimate relationships can be treated within a marital context under certain circumstances: Comment. *Journal of Interpersonal Violence, 11*, 452–455.

Neidig, P. H., & Friedman, D. (1984). *Spouse abuse: A treatment program for couples*. Champaign, IL: Research Press.

O'Leary, K. D. (1996). Physical aggression in intimate relationships can be treated within a marital context under certain circumstances. *Journal of Interpersonal Violence, 11*, 450–452.

Stith, S. M., Rosen, K. H., McCollum, E. E., & Thomsen, C. J. (2004). Treating intimate partner violence within intact couple relationships: Outcomes of multi-couple versus individual couple therapy. *Journal of Marital and Family Therapy, 30*, 305–318.

Stosny, S. (1995). *Treating attachment abuse: A compassionate approach*. New York, NY: Springer.

Straus, M. A., Hamby, S. L., Boney-McCoy, S., & Sugarman, D. B. (1996). The revised Conflict Tactics Scales (CTS2): Development and preliminary psychometric data. *Journal of Family Issues, 17*, 283–316.

Wilson, K. L., & Halford, W. K. (2008). Processes of change in self-directed couple relationship education. *Family Relations, 57*, 625–635.

Intimate Partner Violence—Situational (Bi-Directional) Couple Violence

DiGuiseppe, R., & Tafrate, R. C. (2003). Anger treatment for adults: A meta-analytic review. *Clinical Psychology: Science and Practice, 10*, 70–84.

Family Violence Prevention Fund. (2002). National Consensus Guidelines on identifying and responding to domestic violence victimization in health care settings. Downloaded on March 1, 2010 from http://www.endabuse.org/userfiles/file/Consensus.pdf.

Fruzzetti, A. E. (2006). *The high conflict couple: A dialectical behavior therapy guide to finding peace, intimacy, and validation*. Oakland, CA: New Harbinger Publications.

Halford, W. K. (2001). *Brief therapy for couples: Helping partners help themselves*. New York, NY: Guilford Press.

Jacobson, N. S., & Christensen, A. (1996). *Acceptance and change in couple therapy: A therapist's guide to transforming relationships*. New York, NY: Norton.

Johnson, M. P. (2008). *A typology of domestic violence: Intimate terrorism, violent resistance, and situational couple violence*. Boston, MA: Northeastern University Press.

LaTaillade, J. J., Epstein, N. B., & Werlinich, C. A. (2006). A conjoint treatment of intimate partner violence: A cognitive behavioral approach. *Journal of Cognitive Psychotherapy, 20*, 393–410.

McCullough, J. P. (2000). *Treatment for chronic depression: Cognitive behavioral analysis system of psychotherapy (CBASP)*. New York, NY: Guilford Press.

McMahon, M., & Pence, E. (1996). Physical aggression in intimate relationships can be treated within a marital context under certain circumstances: Comment. *Journal of Interpersonal Violence, 11*, 452–455.

Novaco, R. W. (1975). *Anger control: The development and evaluation of an experimental treatment*. Lexington, MA: D. C. Heath.

O'Leary, K. D. (1996). Physical aggression in intimate relationships can be treated within a marital context under certain circumstances. *Journal of Interpersonal Violence, 11*, 450–452.

Shadish, W. R., & Baldwin, S.A. (2005). Effects of behavioral marital therapy: A meta-analysis of randomized controlled trials. *Journal of Consulting and Clinical Psychology, 73*, 6–14.

Stith, S. M., Rosen, K. H., McCollum, E. E., & Thomsen (2004). Treating intimate partner violence within intact couple relationships: Outcomes of multi-couple versus individual couple therapy. *Journal of Marital and Family Therapy, 30*, 305–318.

Stosny, S. (1995). *Treating attachment abuse: A compassionate approach*. New York, NY: Springer.

Straus, M. A., Hamby, S. L., Boney-McCoy, S., & Sugarman, D. B. (1996). The revised Conflict Tactics Scales (CTS2): Development and preliminary psychometric data. *Journal of Family Issues, 17*, 283-316.

Wilson, K. L., & Halford, W. K. (2008). Processes of change in self-directed couple relationship education. *Family Relations, 57,* 625–635.

Intolerance

Burns D. D., & Sayers, S. L. (1988). *Development and validation of a brief relationship satisfaction scale: Cognitive and affective components of marital satisfaction.* Unpublished manuscript. Available by emailing Steven.Sayers@VA.gov.

Epstein, N., & Baucom, D. H. (2002). *Enhanced cognitive-behavioral therapy for couples: A contextual approach*. Washington, DC: American Psychological Association.

Fruzzetti, A. E. (2006). *The high conflict couple: A dialectical behavior therapy guide to finding peace, intimacy, and validation*. Oakland, CA: New Harbinger Publications.

Funk, J. L., & Rogge, R. D. (2007). Testing the ruler with item response theory: Increasing precision of measurement for relationship satisfaction with the Couples Satisfaction Index. *Journal of Family Psychology, 21*, 572–583.

Haley, J. (1987). *Problem-solving therapy* (2nd ed.). San Francisco, CA: Jossey-Bass.

Halford, W. K. (2001). *Brief therapy for couples: Helping partners help themselves*. New York, NY: Guilford Press.

Jacobson, N. S., & Christensen, A. (1996). *Acceptance and change in couple therapy: A therapist's guide to transforming relationships*. New York, NY: Norton.

Johnson, S. M. (2004). *The practice of emotionally focused marital therapy: Creating connection* (2nd ed.). New York, NY: Brunner/Routledge.

Kerig, P. K. (1996). Assessing the links between marital conflict and child development: The conflicts and problem-solving scales. *Journal of Family Psychology, 10,* 454–473.

LoPiccolo, J. (1987). Sexual History Form. In K. D. O'Leary (Ed.), *Assessment of marital discord.* Hillsdale, NJ: Erlbaum.

Shadish, W. R., & Baldwin, S. A. (2005). Effects of behavioral marital therapy: A meta-analysis of randomized controlled trials. *Journal of Consulting and Clinical Psychology, 73,* 6–14.

Snyder, D. K. (1997). *Marital Satisfaction Inventory, revised.* Los Angeles, CA: Western Psychological Services.

Straus, M. A., Hamby, S. L., Boney-McCoy, S., & Sugarman, D. B. (1996). The revised Conflict Tactics Scales (CTS2): Development and preliminary psychometric data. *Journal of Family Issues, 17,* 283–316.

Watzlawick, P., Weakland, J. H., & Fisch, R. (1974). *Change: Principles of problem formation and problem resolution.* New York, NY: Norton.

Weiss, R. L. (1982). *Cost-benefit Exchange Questionnaire.* Unpublished manuscript, University of Oregon, Eugene. Available by emailing Richard.Heyman@ Stonybrook.edu.

Weiss, R. L., & Birchler, G. R. (1975). *Areas of Change Questionnaire.* Unpublished manuscript, University of Oregon, Eugene. Available by emailing Richard. Heyman@Stonybrook.edu.

Weiss, R. L., & Cerreto, M. C. (1980). The Marital Status Inventory: Development of a measure of dissolution potential. *The American Journal of Family Therapy, 8,* 80–86.

Wilson, K. L., & Halford, W. K. (2008). Processes of change in self-directed couple relationship education. *Family Relations, 57,* 625–635.

Jealousy

Baucom, D. H., Gordon, K. C., Snyder, D. K., Atkins, D. C., & Christensen, A. (2006). Treating affair couples: Clinical considerations and initial findings. *Journal of Cognitive Psychotherapy, 20,* 375–392.

Baucom, D. H., Snyder, D. K., & Gordon, K. C. (2009). *Helping couples get past the affair.* New York, NY: Guilford Press.

Cano, A., & O'Leary, K. D. (1997). Romantic jealousy and affairs: Research and implications for couple therapy. *Journal of Sex and Marital Therapy, 23,* 249–275.

Epstein, N., & Baucom, D. H. (2002). *Enhanced cognitive-behavioral therapy for couples: A contextual approach.* Washington, DC: American Psychological Association.

Funk, J. L., & Rogge, R. D. (2007). Testing the ruler with item response theory: Increasing precision of measurement for relationship satisfaction with the Couples Satisfaction Index. *Journal of Family Psychology, 21,* 572–583.

Halford, W. K. (2001). *Brief therapy for couples: Helping partners help themselves.* New York, NY: Guilford Press.

Kerig, P. K. (1996). Assessing the links between marital conflict and child development: The conflicts and problem-solving scales. *Journal of Family Psychology, 10*, 454–473.

LoPiccolo, J. (1987). Sexual History Form. In K. D. O'Leary (Ed.), *Assessment of marital discord*. Hillsdale, NJ: Erlbaum.

Markman, H., Stanley, S., & Blumberg, S. L. (2001) *Fighting for your marriage*. San Francisco, CA: Jossey-Bass.

Shadish, W. R., & Baldwin, S. A. (2005). Effects of behavioral marital therapy: A meta-analysis of randomized controlled trials. *Journal of Consulting and Clinical Psychology, 73*, 6–14.

Snyder, D. K. (1997). *Marital Satisfaction Inventory, revised*. Los Angeles, CA: Western Psychological Services.

Straus, M. A., Hamby, S. L., Boney-McCoy, S., & Sugarman, D. B. (1996). The revised Conflict Tactics Scales (CTS2): Development and preliminary psychometric data. *Journal of Family Issues, 17*, 283–316.

Weiss, R. L. (1982). *Cost-benefit Exchange Questionnaire*. Unpublished manuscript, University of Oregon, Eugene. Available by emailing Richard.Heyman@ Stonybrook.edu.

Weiss, R. L., & Birchler, G. R. (1975). *Areas of Change Questionnaire*. Unpublished manuscript, University of Oregon, Eugene. Available by emailing Richard.Heyman@Stonybrook.edu.

Wilson, K. L., & Halford, W. K. (2008). Processes of change in self-directed couple relationship education. *Family Relations, 57,* 625–635.

Zinbarg, R. E., Craske, M. G., & Barlow, D. H. (2006). *Mastery of your anxiety and worry: Therapist guide* (2nd ed.). New York, NY: Oxford University Press.

Job Stress

Bodenmann, G., Plancherel, B., Beach, S. R. H., Widmer, K., Gabriel, B., Meuwly, N., Charvoz, L., Hautzinger, M., & Schramm, E. (2008). Effects of a coping-oriented couples therapy on depression: A randomized clinical trial. *Journal of Consulting and Clinical Psychology, 76*, 944–954.

Cohen, S., O'Leary, K. D., & Foran, H. (2010). A randomized clinical trial of a brief, problem-focused couple therapy for depression. *Behavior Therapy,41* (4), 433–446.

Del Vecchio, T. D., & O'Leary, K. D. (2004). Effectiveness of anger treatments for specific anger problems: A meta-analytic review. *Clinical Psychology Review, 24*, 15–34.

Oher, J., Conti, D. J., & Jongsma, A. E. (1998). *The employee assistance treatment planner*. New York, NY: John Wiley & Sons.

Wiley, A. R., Branscomb, K., & Wang, Y. Z. (2007). Intentional harmony in the lives of working parents: Program development and evaluation. *Avail Family Relations, 56*(3), 318–328.

Life-Changing Events

Achenbach, T., & Edelbrock, C. (1981). Behavior problems and competencies reported by parents of normal and disturbed children aged four through sixteen. *Monographs of the Society for Research in Child Development, 46,* 188.

Hartley, S. L., Barker, E. T., Seltzer, M. M., Floyd, F., Greenberg, J., Orsmond, G., & Bolt, D. (2010). The relative risk and timing of divorce in families of children with an autism spectrum disorder. *Journal of Family Psychology,* 24(4), 449–457.

Jacobson, N. S., & Christensen, A. (1996). *Acceptance and change in couple therapy: A therapist's guide to transforming relationships.* New York, NY: Norton.

Sanders, M. R., & Dadds, M. R. (1993). *Behavioral family intervention.* Needham Heights, MA: Allyn & Bacon.

Shadish, W. R., & Baldwin, S. A. (2005). Effects of behavioral marital therapy: A meta-analysis of randomized controlled trials. *Journal of Consulting and Clinical Psychology, 73,* 6–14.

Wilson, K. L., & Halford, W. K. (2008). Processes of change in self-directed couple relationship education. *Family Relations, 57,* 625–635.

Loss of Love/Affection

Bauco, D. H., Sayers, S. L., & Sher, T. G (1990). Supplementing behavioral marital therapy with cognitive restructuring and emotional expressiveness training: An outcome investigation. *Journal of Consulting and Clinical Psychology, 58*(5), 636–645.

Greenberg, L., Ford, C. L., Alden, L. S., & Johnson, S. M. (1993). In-session change in emotionally focused therapy. *Journal of Consulting and Clinical Psychology, 61*(1), 78–84.

O'Leary, K. D., & Arias, I. (1983). The influence of marital therapy on sexual satisfaction. *Journal of Sex and Marital Therapy, 9,* 171–181.

Shadish, W. R., & Baldwin, S. A. (2005). Effects of behavioral marital therapy: A meta-analysis of randomly controlled trials. *Journal of Consulting and Clinical Psychology, 73,* 6–14.

Tsoi-Hoshman, L. (2007). Marital therapy: An integrative behavioral learning model. *Journal of Marital and Family Therapy, 2,* 179–191.

Midlife Transition Problems

Covey, S., Merrill, A. R., & Merrill, R. R. (1994). *First things first: To live, to love, to learn, to leave a legacy.* New York, NY: Simon & Schuster.

Halford, W. K. (2001). *Brief therapy for couples: Helping partners help themselves.* New York, NY: Guilford Press.

Halford, W. K., Moore, E. M., Wilson, K. L., Dyer, C., & Farrugia, C. (2004). Benefits of a flexible delivery relationship education: An evaluation of the Couple CARE program. *Family Relations, 53,* 469–476.

Henry, R. G., & Miller, R. B. (2004). Marital problems occurring in midlife: Implications for couples therapists. *The American Journal of Family Therapy, 32*, 405–417.

Hermans, H. J. M., & Oles, P. K. (1999). Midlife crisis in men: Affective organization of personal meanings. *Human Relations, 52,* 1403–1426.

McCullough, J. P. (2000). *Treatment for chronic depression: Cognitive behavioral analysis system of psychotherapy (CBASP).* New York, NY: Guilford Press.

Oles, P. K. (1999). *Midlife Crisis Scale.* Unpublished questionnaire, Catholic University of Lublin, Poland. Available by emailing Richard.Heyman@Stonybrook.edu.

Shadish, W. R., & Baldwin, S. A. (2005). Effects of behavioral marital therapy: A meta-analysis of randomized controlled trials. *Journal of Consulting and Clinical Psychology, 73*, 6–14.

Wilson, K. L., & Halford, W. K. (2008). Processes of change in self-directed couple relationship education. *Family Relations, 57,* 625–635.

Only One Partner Willing to Attend Therapy

Birchler, G. R., & Weiss, R. L. (1977). *Inventory of Rewarding Activities.* Unpublished questionnaire, University of Oregon, Eugene. Available by emailing Richard.Heyman@Stonybrook.edu.

Burns, D. D., & Sayers, S. L. (1988). *Development and validation of a brief relationship satisfaction scale: Cognitive and affective components of marital satisfaction.* Unpublished manuscript. Available by emailing Steven.Sayers@VA.gov.

Epstein, N., & Baucom, D. H. (2002). *Enhanced cognitive-behavioral therapy for couples: A contextual approach.* Washington, DC: American Psychological Association.

Funk, J. L., & Rogge, R. D. (2007). Testing the ruler with item response theory: Increasing precision of measurement for relationship satisfaction with the Couples Satisfaction Index. *Journal of Family Psychology, 21*, 572–583.

Greenberg, L. S., & Johnson, S. M. (1988). *Emotionally focused therapy for couples.* New York, NY: Guilford Press.

Halford, W. K. (2001). *Brief therapy for couples: Helping partners help themselves.* New York, NY: Guilford Press.

Halford, W. K., Moore, E. M., Wilson, K. L., Dyer, C., & Farrugia, C. (2004). Benefits of a flexible delivery relationship education: An evaluation of the Couple CARE program. *Family Relations, 53*, 469–476.

Halford, W. K., Sanders, M. R., & Behrens, B. C. (1994). Self-regulation in behavioral couples' therapy. *Behavior Therapy, 25*, 431–452.

Jacobson, N. S., & Christensen, A. (1996). *Acceptance and change in couple therapy: A therapist's guide to transforming relationships.* New York, NY: Norton.

Johnson, S. M. (2004). *The practice of emotionally focused marital therapy: Creating connection (2nd ed.).* New York, NY: Brunner/Routledge.

McCullough, J. P. (2000). *Treatment for chronic depression: Cognitive behavioral analysis system of psychotherapy (CBASP)*. New York, NY: Guilford Press.

Straus, M. A., Hamby, S. L., Boney-McCoy, S., & Sugarman, D. B. (1996). The revised Conflict Tactics Scales (CTS2): Development and preliminary psychometric data. *Journal of Family Issues, 17*, 283–316.

Weiss, R. L., & Cerreto, M. C. (1980). The Marital Status Inventory: Development of a measure of dissolution potential. *The American Journal of Family Therapy, 8*, 80–86.

Weiss, R. L. (1982). *Cost-benefit Exchange Questionnaire*. Unpublished questionnaire, University of Oregon, Eugene. Available by emailing Richard.Heyman@ Stonybrook.edu.

Wilson, K. L., & Halford, W. K. (2008). Processes of change in self-directed couple relationship education. *Family Relations, 57*, 625–635.

Parenting Conflicts—Adolescents

Epstein, N., & Baucom, D. H. (2002). *Enhanced cognitive-behavioral therapy for couples: A contextual approach*. Washington, DC: American Psychological Association.

Forgatch, M., & Patterson, G. R. (1987). *Parents and adolescents. Vol II: Family problem solving*. Eugene, OR: Castalia.

Gattis, K. S., Simpson, L. E., & Christensen, A. (2008). What about the kids? Parenting and child adjustment in the context of couple therapy. *Journal of Family Psychology, 22*, 833–842.

Halford, W. K. (2001). *Brief therapy for couples: Helping partners help themselves*. New York, NY: Guilford Press.

Markman, H., Stanley, S., & Blumberg, S. L. (2001). *Fighting for your marriage*. San Francisco, CA: Jossey-Bass.

McCullough, J. P. (2000). *Treatment for chronic depression: Cognitive behavioral analysis system of psychotherapy (CBASP)*. New York, NY: Guilford Press.

Patterson, G. R., & Forgatch, M. (1987). *Parents and adolescents: Living together. Vol I: The basics*. Eugene, OR: Castalia.

Prinz, R. J., Foster, S. L., Kent, R. N., & O'Leary, K. D. (1979). Multivariate assessment of conflict in distressed and nondistressed mother-adolescent dyads. *Journal of Applied Behavior Analysis, 12*, 691–700.

Robin, A. L., & Foster, S. L. (1989). *Negotiating parent-adolescent conflict*. New York, NY: Guilford Press.

Robin, A. L., Koepke, T., & Moye, A. (1990). Multidimensional assessment of parent-adolescent relations. *Psychological Assessment, 2*, 451–459.

Roehling, P. V., & Robin, A. L. (1986). Development and validation of the family beliefs inventory: A measure of unrealistic beliefs among parents and adolescents. *Journal of Consulting and Clinical Psychology, 54*, 693–697.

Shadish, W. R., & Baldwin, S. A. (2005). Effects of behavioral marital therapy: A meta-analysis of randomized controlled trials. *Journal of Consulting and Clinical Psychology, 73*, 6–14.

Parenting Conflicts—Children

Achenbach, T. (2001). *Child Behavior Checklist*. Available from http://www.aseba.org/

Achenbach, T., & Edelbrock, C. (1981). Behavior problems and competencies reported by parents of normal and disturbed children aged four through sixteen. *Monographs of the Society for Research in Child Development, 46,* 188.

Arnold, D. S., O'Leary, S. G., Wolff, L. S., & Acker, M. M. (1993). The parenting scale: A measure of dysfunctional parenting in discipline situations. *Psychological Assessment, 5,* 137–144.

Briesmeister, J. M., & Schaefer, C. E. (Eds.). (2007). *Handbook of parent training* (2nd ed.). Hoboken, NJ: John Wiley & Sons.

Cummings, E. M., & Davies, P. T. (2010). *Marital conflict and children: An emotional security perspective.* New York, NY: Guilford Press.

Epstein, N., & Baucom, D. H. (2002). *Enhanced cognitive-behavioral therapy for couples: A contextual approach.* Washington, DC: American Psychological Association.

Halford, W. K. (2001). *Brief therapy for couples: Helping partners help themselves.* New York, NY: Guilford Press.

Markman, H., Stanley, S., & Blumberg, S. L. (2001). *Fighting for your marriage.* San Francisco, CA: Jossey-Bass.

Sanders, M. R. (1992). *Every parent: A positive approach to children's behavior.* Sydney, Australia: Addison-Wesley.

Sanders, M. R., & Dadds, M. R. (1993). *Behavioral family intervention.* Needham Heights, MA: Allyn & Bacon.

Sanders, M. R., Lynch, M. E., & Markie-Dadds, C. (1994). *Every parent's workbook: A positive guide to positive parenting.* Brisbane, Australia: Australian Academic Press.

Sanders, M. R., Markie-Dadds, C., & Nicholson, J. M. (1997). Concurrent interventions for marital and children's problems. In W. K. Halford & H. J. Markman (Eds.), *Clinical handbook of marriage and couples interventions* (pp. 509–536). New York, NY: John Wiley & Sons.

Shadish, W. R., & Baldwin, S. A. (2005). Effects of behavioral marital therapy: A meta-analysis of randomized controlled trials. *Journal of Consulting and Clinical Psychology, 73,* 6–14.

Personality Differences

Karney, B. R., & Bradbury, T. N. (1995). The longitudinal course of marital quality and stability: A review of theory, method, and research. *Psychological Bulletin, 118,* 3–34.

Kelly, E. L., & Conley, J. J. (1987). Personality and compatibility: A prospective analysis of marital stability and marital satisfaction. *Journal of Personality and Social Psychology, 52,* 27–40.

Kim, A., Martin, D., & Martin, M. (1989). Effects of personality on marital satisfaction: Identification of source traits and their role in marital stability. *Family Therapy, 16*(3), 243–248.

Mendonca, J. D., & Hunt, A. (1982). Brief marital therapy outcome: Personality correlates. *The Canadian Journal of Psychiatry, 27*(4), 291–295.

Shiota, M. N., & Levenson, R. W. (2007). Birds of a feather don't always fly farthest: Similarity in big five personality predicts more negative marital satisfaction trajectories in long-term marriages. *Psychology and Aging, 22*(4), 666–675.

Psychological Abuse

Babcock, J., Green, C. E., & Robie, C. (2004). Does batterers' treatment work? A meta-analytic review of domestic violence treatment. *Clinical Psychology Review, 23*, 1023–1053.

Brannen, S. J., & Rubin, A. (1996). Comparing the effectiveness of gender-specific and couples groups in a court-mandated-spouse-abuse treatment program. *Research on Social Work Practice, 6,* 405–424.

Deschner, J., & McNeil, J. (1986). Results of anger control training for battering couples. *Journal of Family Violence, 1,* 111–120.

Geller, J. (2007). Conjoint therapy for the treatment of partner abuse: Indications and contraindications. In A. R. Roberts (Ed.), *Battered women and their families: Intervention strategies and treatment programs* (3rd ed.). New York, NY: Springer.

Neidig, E. H., & Friedman, D. (1984). *Spouse abuse: A treatment program for couples.* Champaign, IL: Research Press.

O'Leary, K. D. (2008). Couple therapy and physical aggression. In A. S. German (Ed.), *Clinical handbook of couple therapy* (pp. 478–498). New York, NY: Guilford Press.

O'Leary, K. D., & Cohen, S. (2006). Treatment of psychological and physical aggression in a couple context. In J. Hamel & T. L. Nicholls (Eds.), *Family interventions in domestic violence* (pp. 363–380). New York, NY: Springer.

O'Leary, K. D., Heyman, R. E., & Neidig, E. H. (1999). Treatment of wife abuse: A comparison of gender-specific and conjoint approaches. *Behavior Therapy, 30,* 475–505.

Stitch, S. M., Rosen, K. H., & McCollum, E. E. (2003). Effectiveness of couple treatment for spouse abuse. *Journal of Marital & Family Therapy, 29,* 407–426.

Recreational Activities Dispute

Birchler, G. R., & Weiss, R. L. (1977). *Inventory of rewarding activities.* Unpublished questionnaire, University of Oregon, Eugene. Available by emailing Richard .Heyman@Stonybrook.edu.

Epstein, N., & Baucom, D. H. (2002). *Enhanced cognitive-behavioral therapy for couples: A contextual approach*. Washington, DC: American Psychological Association.

Halford, W. K. (2001). *Brief therapy for couples: Helping partners help themselves*. New York, NY: Guilford Press.

Jacobson, N. S., & Margolin, G. (1979). *Marital therapy*. New York, NY: Brunner/Mazel.

Markman, H., Stanley, S., & Blumberg, S. L. (2001). *Fighting for your marriage*. San Francisco, CA: Jossey-Bass.

Shadish, W. R., & Baldwin, S. A. (2005). Effects of behavioral marital therapy: A meta-analysis of randomized controlled trials. *Journal of Consulting and Clinical Psychology, 73*, 6–14.

Weiss, R. L., Hops, H., & Patterson, G. R. (1973). A framework for conceptualizing marital conflict: A technology for altering it, some data for evaluating it. In L. D. Handy & E. L. Mash (Eds.), *Behavior change: Methodology concepts and practice* (pp. 309–342). Champaign, IL: Research Press.

Wilson, K. L., & Halford, W. K. (2008). Processes of change in self-directed couple relationship education. *Family Relations, 57*, 625–635.

Religious/Spirituality Differences

Halford, W. K. (2001). *Brief therapy for couples: Helping partners help themselves*. New York, NY: Guilford Press.

Halford, W. K., Moore, E. M., Wilson, K. L., Dyer, C., & Farrugia, C. (2004). Benefits of a flexible delivery relationship education: An evaluation of the Couple CARE program. *Family Relations, 53*, 469–476.

Markman, H., Stanley, S., & Blumberg, S. L. (2001). *Fighting for your marriage*. San Francisco, CA: Jossey-Bass.

McCullough, J. P. (2000). *Treatment for chronic depression: Cognitive behavioral analysis system of psychotherapy (CBASP)*. New York, NY: Guilford Press.

Shadish, W. R., & Baldwin, S. A. (2005). Effects of behavioral marital therapy: A meta-analysis of randomized controlled trials. *Journal of Consulting and Clinical Psychology, 73*, 6–14.

Wilson, K. L., & Halford, W. K. (2008). Processes of change in self-directed couple relationship education. *Family Relations, 57*, 625–635.

Retirement

Birchler, G. R., & Weiss, R. L. (1977). *Inventory of rewarding activities*. Unpublished questionnaire, University of Oregon, Eugene. Available by emailing Richard .Heyman@Stonybrook.edu.

Burns, D. D., & Sayers S. L. (1988). *Development and validation of a brief relationship satisfaction scale: Cognitive and affective components of marital satisfaction.* Unpublished manuscript. Available by emailing Steven.Sayers@VA.gov.

Covey, S., Merrill, A. R., & Merrill, R. R. (1994). *First things first: To live, to love, to learn, to leave a legacy.* New York, NY: Simon & Schuster.

Epstein, N., & Baucom, D. H. (2002). *Enhanced cognitive-behavioral therapy for couples: A contextual approach.* Washington, DC: American Psychological Association.

Funk, J. L., & Rogge, R. D. (2007). Testing the ruler with item response theory: Increasing precision of measurement for relationship satisfaction with the Couples Satisfaction Index. *Journal of Family Psychology, 21,* 572–583.

Halford, W. K. (2001). *Brief therapy for couples: Helping partners help themselves.* New York, NY: Guilford Press.

Heyman, R. E. (2001). Observation of couple conflicts: Clinical assessment applications, stubborn truths, and shaky foundations. *Psychological Assessment, 13,* 5–35.

Jacobson, N. S., & Margolin, G. (1979). *Marital therapy.* New York, NY: Brunner/Mazel.

Jones, J., Doss, B. D., & Christensen, A. (2001). Integrative behavioral couple therapy. In J. Harvey & A. Wenzel (Eds.), *Close romantic relationships: Maintenance and enhancement* (pp. 321–344). Mahwah, NJ: Erlbaum.

Kerig, P. K. (1996). Assessing the links between marital conflict and child development: The Conflicts and Problem-Solving Scales. *Journal of Family Psychology, 10,* 454–473.

LoPiccolo, J. (1987). Sexual History Form. In K. D. O'Leary (Ed.), *Assessment of marital discord* (pp. 338–355). Hillsdale, NJ: Erlbaum.

Markman, H., Stanley, S., & Blumberg, S. L. (2001). *Fighting for your marriage.* San Francisco, CA: Jossey-Bass.

Masters, W. H., & Johnson, V. E. (1970). *Human sexual inadequacy.* Boston, MA: Little, Brown and Company.

McCarthy, B. W. (1984). Strategies and techniques for the treatment of inhibited sexual desire. *Journal of Sex and Marital Therapy, 10,* 97–104.

McCullough, J. P. (2000). *Treatment for chronic depression: Cognitive behavioral analysis system of psychotherapy (CBASP).* New York, NY: Guilford Press.

Shadish, W. R., & Baldwin, S. A. (2005). Effects of behavioral marital therapy: A meta-analysis of randomized controlled trials. *Journal of Consulting and Clinical Psychology, 73,* 6–14.

Snyder, D. K. (1997). *Marital Satisfaction Inventory, revised.* Los Angeles, CA: Western Psychological Services.

Straus, M. A., Hamby, S. L., Boney-McCoy, S., & Sugarman, D. B. (1996). The revised conflict tactics scales (CTS2): Development and preliminary psychometric data. *Journal of Family Issues, 17,* 283–316.

Trudel, G., Boyer, R., Villeneuve, V., Anderson, A., Pilon, G. & Bounader, J. (2008). The Marital Life and Aging Well Program: Effects of a group preventive intervention on the marital and sexual functioning of retired couples. *Sexual and Relationship Therapy, 23,* 5–23.

Trudel, G., Villeneuve, V., Anderson, A., & Pilon, G. (2008). Sexual and marital aspects of old age: An update. *Sexual and Relationship Therapy, 23,* 161–169.

Weiss, R. L., & Birchler, G. R. (1975). *Areas of Change Questionnaire*. Unpublished manuscript, University of Oregon, Eugene. Available by emailing Richard. Heyman@Stonybrook.edu.

Weiss, R. L., & Cerreto, M. C. (1980). The Marital Status Inventory: Development of a measure of dissolution potential. *The American Journal of Family Therapy, 8*, 80–86.

Separation and Divorce

Baucom, D. H., Snyder, D. K., & Gordon, K. C. (2009). *Helping couples get past the affair*. New York, NY: Guilford Press.

Burns D. D., & Sayers, S. L. (1988). *Development and validation of a brief relationship satisfaction scale: Cognitive and affective components of marital satisfaction.* Unpublished manuscript. Available from Steven.Sayers@VA.gov.

Emery, R. E., Sbarra, D., & Grover, T. (2005). Divorce mediation: Research and reflections. *Family Court Review, 43*, 22–37.

Epstein, N., & Baucom, D. H. (2002). *Enhanced cognitive-behavioral therapy for couples: A contextual approach*. Washington, DC: American Psychological Association.

Funk, J. L., & Rogge, R. D. (2007). Testing the ruler with item response theory: Increasing precision of measurement for relationship satisfaction with the Couples Satisfaction Index. *Journal of Family Psychology, 21*, 572–583.

Halford, W. K. (2001). *Brief therapy for couples: Helping partners help themselves*. New York, NY: Guilford Press.

Halford, W. K., Moore, E. M., Wilson, K. L., Dyer, C., & Farrugia, C. (2004). Benefits of a flexible delivery relationship education: An evaluation of the Couple CARE program. *Family Relations, 53*, 469–476.

Jacobson, N. S., & Margolin, G. (1979). *Marital therapy*. New York, NY: Brunner/Mazel.

Kerig, P. K. (1996). Assessing the links between marital conflict and child development: The conflicts and problem-solving scales. *Journal of Family Psychology, 10*, 454–473.

Lebow, J. (2008). Separation and divorce issues in couple therapy. In A. S. Gurman (Ed.), *Clinical handbook of couple therapy* (4th ed.; 459–477). New York, NY: Guilford Press.

LoPiccolo, J. (1987). Sexual History Form. In K. D. O'Leary (Ed.), *Assessment of marital discord*. Hillsdale, NJ: Erlbaum.

Markman, H., Stanley, S., & Blumberg, S. L. (2001) *Fighting for your marriage*. San Francisco, CA: Jossey-Bass.

Pedro-Carroll, J. L. (2005). Fostering resilience in the aftermath of divorce: The role of evidence-based programs for children. *Family Court Review, 43*, 52–64.

Snyder, D. K. (1997). The revised Conflict Tactics Scales (CTS2): Development and preliminary psychometric data. *Journal of Family Issues, 17*, 283–316.

Weiss, R. L., & Cerreto, M. C. (1980). The Marital Status Inventory: Development of a measure of dissolution potential. *The American Journal of Family Therapy, 8*, 80–86.

Zhou, Q., Sandler, I. N., Millsap, R. E., Wolchik, S. A., & Dawson-McClure, S. R. (2008). Mother-child relationship quality and effective discipline as mediators of the six-year effects of the New Beginnings Program for children from divorced families. *Journal of Consulting and Clinical Psychology, 76*, 579–594.

Sexual Abuse

Kar, H. L., & O'Leary, K. D. (2010). Gender symmetry or asymmetry in intimate partner victimization? Not an either/or answer. *Partner Abuse, 1*(2), 152–168.

Macy, R. J., Giattina, M., Sangster, T. H., Crosby, C., & Montijo, N. J. (2009). Domestic violence and sexual assault services: Inside the black box. *Aggression and Violent Behavior, 14*(5), 359–373.

Monson, C. M., Langhinrichsen-Rohling, J., & Taft, C. T. (2009). Sexual aggression in intimate relationships. In K. D. O'Leary & E. M. Woodin (Eds.), *Psychological and physical aggression in couples: Causes and interventions* (pp. 37–57).Washington, DC: American Psychological Association.

O'Leary, K. D. (2008). Couple therapy and physical aggression. In A. S. Gurman (Ed.), *Clinical handbook of couple therapy* (pp. 478–498). New York, NY: Guilford Press.

Sexual Dysfunction

Baucom, D. H., Shoham, V., Mueser, K. T., Daiuto, A. D., & Stickle, T. R. (1998). Empirically supported couple and family interventions for marital distress and adult mental health problems. *Journal of Consulting and Clinical Psychology, 66*(1), 53–88.

Duterte, E., Segraves, E., & Althof, S. (2007). Psychotherapy and pharmacotherapy for sexual dysfunctions. In P. E. Nathan & J. M. Gorman (Eds.), *Treatments that work* (3rd ed.; pp. 531–560). New York, NY: Oxford University Press.

McCabe, M. (2005). The role of performance anxiety in the development and maintenance of sexual dysfunction in men and women. *International Journal of Stress Management, 12*(4), 379–388.

McCarthy, B., & Thestrup, W. (2008). Couple therapy and the treatment of sexual dysfunction. In A. Gurman, *Clinical handbook of couple therapy* (4th ed.; pp. 591–617). New York, NY: Guilford Press.

Rathus, J. H., & Sanderson, W. C. (1999). *Cognitive behavioral interventions for couples.* New York, NY: Jason Aronson.

Transition to Parenthood Strains

de Wolff, M. S., & van Ijzendoorn, M. H. (1997). Sensitivity and attachment: A meta-analysis on parental antecedents of infant attachment. *Child Development, 68*, 571–591.

Halford, W. K. (2001). *Brief therapy for couples: Helping partners help themselves.* New York, NY: Guilford Press.

Petch, J., & Halford, W. K. (2008). Psycho-education to enhance couples' transition to parenthood. *Clinical Psychology Review, 28,* 1125–1137.

Petch, J., Halford, W. K., & Creedy, D. K. (2010). Promoting a positive transition to parenthood: A randomized clinical trial of couple relationship education. *Prevention Science, 11,* 89–100.

Jacobson, N. S., & Margolin, G. (1979). *Marital therapy.* New York, NY: Brunner/Mazel.

Markman, H., Stanley, S., & Blumberg, S. L. (2001). *Fighting for your marriage.* San Francisco, CA: Jossey-Bass.

McCullough, J. P. (2000). *Treatment for chronic depression: Cognitive behavioral analysis system of psychotherapy (CBASP).* New York, NY: Guilford Press.

Shadish, W. R., & Baldwin, S. A. (2005). Effects of behavioral marital therapy: A meta-analysis of randomized controlled trials. *Journal of Consulting and Clinical Psychology, 73,* 6–14.

Wilson, K. L., & Halford, W. K. (2008). Processes of change in self-directed couple relationship education. *Family Relations, 57,* 625–635.

Work-Home Role Strain

Covey, S., Merrill, A. R., & Merrill, R. R. (1994). *First things first: To live, to love, to learn, to leave a legacy.* New York, NY: Simon & Schuster.

Epstein, N., & Baucom, D. H. (2002). *Enhanced cognitive-behavioral therapy for couples: A contextual approach.* Washington, DC: American Psychological Association.

Gottman, J. M. (1999). *The marriage clinic.* New York, NY: Norton.

Halford, W. K. (2001). *Brief therapy for couples: Helping partners help themselves.* New York, NY: Guilford Press.

Jacobson, N. S., & Christensen, A. (1996). *Acceptance and change in couple therapy: A therapist's guide to transforming relationships.* New York, NY: Norton.

Jacobson, N. S., & Margolin, G. (1979). *Marital therapy.* New York, NY: Brunner/Mazel.

Markman, H., Stanley, S., & Blumberg, S. L. (2001). *Fighting for your marriage.* San Francisco, CA: Jossey-Bass.

McCullough, J. P. (2000). *Treatment for chronic depression: Cognitive behavioral analysis system of psychotherapy (CBASP).* New York, NY: Guilford Press.

Shadish, W. R., & Baldwin, S. A. (2005). Effects of behavioral marital therapy: A meta-analysis of randomized controlled trials. *Journal of Consulting and Clinical Psychology, 73,* 6–14.

Wilson, K. L., & Halford, W. K. (2008). Processes of change in self-directed couple relationship education. *Family Relations, 57,* 625–635.

Appendix C

RECOVERY MODEL OBJECTIVES AND INTERVENTIONS

The Objectives and Interventions that follow are created around the 10 core principles developed by a multidisciplinary panel at the 2004 National Consensus Conference on Mental Health Recovery and Mental Health Systems Transformation, convened by the Substance Abuse and Mental Health Services Administration (SAMHSA, 2004):

1. **Self-direction:** Consumers lead, control, exercise choice over, and determine their own path of recovery by optimizing autonomy, independence, and control of resources to achieve a self-determined life. By definition, the recovery process must be self-directed by the individual, who defines his or her own life goals and designs a unique path toward those goals.

2. **Individualized and person-centered:** There are multiple pathways to recovery based on an individual's unique strengths and resiliencies as well as his or her needs, preferences, experiences (including past trauma), and cultural background in all of its diverse representations. Individuals also identify recovery as being an ongoing journey and an end result as well as an overall paradigm for achieving wellness and optimal mental health.

3. **Empowerment:** Consumers have the authority to choose from a range of options and to participate in all decisions—including the allocation of resources—that will affect their lives, and are educated and supported in so doing. They have the ability to join with other consumers to collectively and effectively speak for themselves about their needs, wants, desires, and aspirations. Through empowerment, an individual gains control of his or her own destiny and influences the organizational and societal structures in his or her life.

4. **Holistic:** Recovery encompasses an individual's whole life, including mind, body, spirit, and community. Recovery embraces all aspects of life, including housing, employment, education, mental health and healthcare treatment and services, complementary and naturalistic services, addictions treatment, spirituality, creativity, social networks, community participation, and family supports as determined by the person. Families, providers, organizations, systems, communities, and society play crucial roles in creating and maintaining meaningful opportunities for consumer access to these supports.

5. **Nonlinear:** Recovery is not a step-by-step process but one based on continual growth, occasional setbacks, and learning from experience. Recovery begins with an initial stage of awareness in which a person recognizes that positive change is possible. This awareness enables the consumer to move on to fully engage in the work of recovery.

6. **Strengths-based:** Recovery focuses on valuing and building on the multiple capacities, resiliencies, talents, coping abilities, and inherent worth of individuals. By building on these strengths, consumers leave stymied life roles behind and engage in new life roles (e.g., partner, caregiver, friend, student, employee). The process of recovery moves forward through interaction with others in supportive, trust-based relationships.

7. **Peer support:** Mutual support—including the sharing of experiential knowledge and skills and social learning—plays an invaluable role in recovery. Consumers encourage and engage other consumers in recovery and provide each other with a sense of belonging, supportive relationships, valued roles, and community.

8. **Respect:** Community, systems, and societal acceptance and appreciation of consumers—including protecting their rights and eliminating discrimination and stigma—are crucial in achieving recovery. Self-acceptance and regaining belief in one's self are particularly vital. Respect ensures the inclusion and full participation of consumers in all aspects of their lives.

9. **Responsibility:** Consumers have a personal responsibility for their own self-care and journeys of recovery. Taking steps toward their goals may require great courage. Consumers must strive to understand and give meaning to their experiences and identify coping strategies and healing processes to promote their own wellness.

10. **Hope:** Recovery provides the essential and motivating message of a better future—that people can overcome the barriers and obstacles that confront them. Hope is internalized, but can be fostered by peers, families, friends,

providers, and others. Hope is the catalyst of the recovery process. Mental health recovery not only benefits individuals with mental health disabilities by focusing on their abilities to live, work, learn, and fully participate in our society, but also enriches the texture of American community life. America reaps the benefits of the contributions individuals with mental disabilities can make, ultimately becoming a stronger and healthier Nation.[1]

The numbers used for Objectives in the treatment plan that follows correspond to the numbers for the 10 core principles. Each of the 10 Objectives was written to capture the essential theme of the like-numbered core principle. The numbers in parentheses after the Objectives denote the Interventions designed to assist the client in attaining each respective Objective. The clinician may select any or all of the Objectives and Intervention statements to include in the client's treatment plan.

One generic Long-Term Goal statement is offered should the clinician desire to emphasize a recovery model orientation in the client's treatment plan.

LONG-TERM GOAL

1. To live a meaningful life in a self-selected community while striving to achieve full potential during the journey of healing and transformation.

SHORT-TERM OBJECTIVES

1. Make it clear to therapist, family, and friends what path to recovery is preferred. (1, 2, 3, 4)

THERAPEUTIC INTERVENTIONS

1. Explore the client's thoughts, needs, and preferences regarding his/her desired pathway to recovery (from depression, bipolar disorder, posttraumatic stress disorder [PTSD], etc.).

2. Discuss with the client the alternative treatment interventions and community support resources that might facilitate his/her recovery.

---

[1]From: Substance Abuse and Mental Health Services Administration's (SAMHSA) National Mental Health Information Center: Center for Mental Health Services (2004). *National consensus statement on mental health recovery.* Washington, DC: Author. Available from http://mental health.samhsa.gov/publications/allpubs/sma05-4129/

2. Specify any unique needs and cultural preferences that must be taken under consideration during the treatment process. (5, 6)

3. Verbalize an understanding that decision making throughout the treatment process is self-controlled. (7, 8)

4. Express mental, physical, spiritual, and community needs and desires that should be integrated into the treatment process. (9, 10)

3. Solicit from the client his/her preferences regarding the direction treatment will take; allow for these preferences to be communicated to family and significant others.

4. Discuss and process with the client the possible outcomes that may result from his/her decisions.

5. Explore with the client any cultural considerations, experiences, or other needs that must be considered in formulating a mutually agreed-upon treatment plan.

6. Modify treatment planning to accommodate the client's cultural and experiential background and preferences.

7. Clarify with the client that he/she has the right to choose and select among options and participate in all decisions that affect him/her during treatment.

8. Continuously offer and explain options to the client as treatment progresses in support of his/her sense of empowerment, encouraging and reinforcing the client's participation in treatment decision making.

9. Assess the client's personal, interpersonal, medical, spiritual, and community strengths and weaknesses.

10. Maintain a holistic approach to treatment planning by integrating the client's unique mental, physical, spiritual, and community needs and assets into the plan; arrive at an

5. Verbalize an understanding that during the treatment process there will be successes and failures, progress and setbacks. (11, 12)

6. Cooperate with an assessment of personal strengths and assets brought to the treatment process. (13, 14, 15)

7. Verbalize an understanding of the benefits of peer support during the recovery process. (16, 17, 18)

agreement with the client as to how these integrations will be made.

11. Facilitate realistic expectations and hope in the client that positive change is possible, but does not occur in a linear process of straight-line successes; emphasize a recovery process involving growth, learning from advances as well as setbacks, and staying this course toward recovery.

12. Convey to the client that you will stay the course with him/her through the difficult times of lapses and setbacks.

13. Administer to the client the *Behavioral and Emotional Rating Scale (BERS): A Strength-Based Approach to Assessment* (Epstein).

14. Identify the client's strengths through a thorough assessment involving social, cognitive, relational, and spiritual aspects of the client's life; assist the client in identifying what coping skills have worked well in the past to overcome problems and what talents and abilities characterize his/her daily life.

15. Provide feedback to the client of his/her identified strengths and how these strengths can be integrated into short-term and long-term recovery planning.

16. Discuss with the client the benefits of peer support (e.g., sharing common problems, receiving advice regarding successful coping skills, getting encouragement, learning

of helpful community resources, etc.) toward the client's agreement to engage in peer activity.

17. Refer the client to peer support groups of his/her choice in the community and process his/her experience with follow-through.

18. Build and reinforce the client's sense of belonging, supportive relationship building, social value, and community integration by processing the gains and problem-solving the obstacles encountered through the client's social activities.

8. Agree to reveal when any occasion arises that respect is not felt from the treatment staff, family, self, or the community. (19, 20, 21)

19. Discuss with the client the crucial role that respect plays in recovery, reviewing subtle and obvious ways in which disrespect may be shown to or experienced by the client.

20. Review ways in which the client has felt disrespected in the past, identifying sources of that disrespect.

21. Encourage and reinforce the client's self-concept as a person deserving of respect; advocate for the client to increase incidents of respectful treatment within the community and/or family system.

9. Verbalize acceptance of responsibility for self-care and participation in decisions during the treatment process. (22)

22. Develop, encourage, support, and reinforce the client's role as the person in control of his/her treatment and responsible for its application to his/her daily life; adopt a supportive role as a resource person to assist in the recovery process.

10. Express hope that better functioning in the future can be attained. (23, 24)

23. Discuss with the client potential role models who have achieved a more satisfying life by using their personal strengths, skills, and social support to live, work, learn, and fully participate in society toward building hope and incentive motivation.

24. Discuss and enhance internalization of the client's self-concept as a person capable of overcoming obstacles and achieving satisfaction in living; continuously build and reinforce this self-concept using past and present examples supporting it.

Appendix D

SITUATIONAL ANALYSIS FORM

1. Describe situation here, as if you were describing a video. (Situations have a beginning, middle, and end.)
2. My desired outcome was:
3. My thinking in this situation was (include your "read" on the meaning of the situation): 1) 2) 3)
4. My behavior was (summarize what you *did* in the situation):
5. Did the actual outcome = your desired outcome? ❑ Yes ❑ No Why or why not? (your theory)
6. Lesson learned/"Moral" of the situation: